SUCCESS
WHILE OTHERS
FAIL

SUCCESS WHILE OTHERS FAIL

FAIL

Social Movement Unionism and the Public Workplace

PAUL JOHNSTON

ILR PRESS
Ithaca, New York

Copyright©1994 by Cornell University

Library of Congress Cataloging-in-Publication Data
Johnston, Paul, 1951 –
    Success while others fail : social movement unionism and the public workplace /
Paul Johnston.
        p.   cm.
    Includes bibliographical references and index.
    ISBN 0-87546-334-7   ISBN 0-87546-335-5 (pbk.)
    1. Trade-unions—Government employees—United States—Political activity.
2. Social movements—United States.   I. Title.
HD8005.2.U5J64   1994
322'.2—dc20
                                                        94-32761

Copies of this book may be ordered through bookstores or directly from

ILR Press
School of Industrial and Labor Relations
Cornell University
Ithaca, NY 14853-3901
607/255-2264

Printed on acid-free paper in the United States of America

5   4   3   2   1

To Naomi Bowden, Nancy Elliott, and
Maxine Jenkins—three women of uncommon
insight, valor, and commitment

It is a movement which has penetrated every section of the civil service. . . . Certain it is that no-one who is at all interested in the development of political processes dare neglect the richness of its possibilities.
—Harold Laski, *Authority in the Modern State*

Contents

Illustrations

Preface

Recent years have seen the emergence of new kinds of social movement unionism in the United States: in the public workplace, mainly in the 1960s and 1970s; in the private sector, mainly in the 1980s. The first represents a radically new kind of labor movement, deeply involved in our perennial contest over the public agenda and in the continuing turmoil of urban life and politics. The second points toward a resurgence of social movement unionism in parts of the private sector, which is one of several responses in that sector to the new labor relations environment since 1980.

In both sectors, these new union movements may converge with other new social movements. They often involve the women and nonwhite groups concentrated in the most crisis-ridden parts of the public sector, and concentrated as well at the core of the expanding lower-wage workforce. They are also often allied with grassroots environmental movements and with neighborhood-based social movements in American cities.

This book compares and analyzes the experiences of several different public and private sector workforces, each of which engaged in new social movement unionism in recent decades. This comparative strategy discloses some neglected history and surprising trends among private sector workers in the 1980s. The main aim of this comparison, however, is to examine the consequences of employment in political bureaucracy for the demands and the resources of public workers' movements.

The histories studied here are affected not only by drastic structural differences between the two sectors but also by the learning processes of participants: transplanting assumptions and strategies from other settings, discovering new pitfalls through painful experience, uncovering new strategic possibilities in conditions that vary between sectors and change over time. Explanations of these histories also depend, then, on attention to these learning processes and especially to the effects of institutional processes that shape and sometimes constrain them. This book reflects—and continues—my own participation in those ongoing learning processes.

Issues raised by public workers' movements and conditions faced by their unions take us beyond the terrain defined by working class movements facing capitalist employers, and beyond the horizon of much of today's industrial relations research. Some of the most dynamic streams of social research are today mapping these new territories, including organizational sociology and state theory, urban studies, research on social movements, and feminist studies of gender, work, and urban life. Here too, learning processes are unfinished and distorted by institutional processes. Among these fields, work is disjointed. And almost universally, these traditions neglect public workers' movements and unions, despite their recent prominence. I draw upon these different visions here, then, in a critical and synthetic manner, focusing them together on recent episodes of social movement unionism in and around the public workplace.

Acknowledgments

I am indebted to many friends, relations, co-workers, and colleagues for their toleration and support while I struggled with this project, first in my past life as a union organizer and now in my life as a sociologist. I thank all the union members, activists, and officials with whom, in both lives, I confronted the issues addressed here, and also the supervisors, public officials, and private employers who shared their knowledge and experience and otherwise cooperated with me in the later stages of my research.

My special thanks to the employees of Santa Clara County, the City of San Jose, the City and County of San Francisco, and the San Francisco School District; also members of the American Federation of State, County and Municipal Employees Local 101; the Service Employees' International Union Locals 715, 400, and 1877; the California Nurses' Association; and also managers in Santa Clara Valley's hospital and building maintenance industries.

I received guidance in this study from a variety of people, including participants in the cases themselves. I was particularly fortunate to witness the exemplary work of Naomi Bowden, Nancy Elliott, and Maxine Jenkins, as well as that of other inspired pioneers in public service unionism and in social movement unionism more generally, especially Michael Harvey Baratz, Bill Callahan, Shirley Campbell, Leroy Chatfield, Peter Cervantes-Gautschi, Michael Johnston, Stephen Lerner, and Mary Rogers. I am also indebted to the participants and leaders of dozens of strikes and mobilizations by farmworkers, janitors, nurses, and others in the private and public sectors.

Others who helped guide my analysis (or at least moderate my mistakes) include Kim Blankenship, Michael Burawoy, Steward Clegg, Samuel Cohn, Pasqualino Columbaro, Daniel Cornfield, Paul DiMaggio, Joshua Gamson, Joan Goddard, Michael Hout, Deborah Minkoff, John Mollenkopf, Patricia

Morgan, Nancy Naples, James O'Connor, Charles Perrow, Timothy Redmond, Ian Robinson, Eli Sagan, Charles Tilly, Philip Trounstine, Kim Voss, Erik Olin Wright, and several anonymous reviewers.

Several people collected and generously shared indispensable documentary materials: Elizabeth Anello, Bill Callahan, Denise D'Anne, Mike Garcia, Joan Goddard, Maxine Jenkins, Marilyn Kenefick, Myra Snyder, Judy Sugar, and Jennifer Watson. For allowing me to use their extraordinary archive on the recent history of public sector labor relations in California, my thanks to the staff of the *California Public Employee Relations Journal* at the Institute for Industrial Relations in Berkeley.

During its development, this project was supported, in part, by fellowships or other support from the Institute for Governmental Studies at the University of California at Berkeley; by the Griswold Fund, the Cowell Research Fund, and the Social Science Research Fund at Yale University.

Languishing here so far from my beloved California, I am grateful for the hospitality of colleagues and friends in two resurgent institutions—the Department of Sociology and the Institute for Social and Policy Studies at Yale—and in one resurgent city: New Haven, Connecticut. I am still more grateful for the pride and pleasure of watching four young men—Jumiah, Tony, Jason, and Patrick Elliott Johnston—growing in goodness, wit, strength, grace, verve, and all-round competence in the kitchen.

Finally, this book was (finally!) produced by the inspired editorial staff of ILR Press at Cornell University. Andrea Clardy, Faith Short, and Erica Fox infused work with pleasure, and Frances Benson is a gift.

P. J.
New Haven

SUCCESS
WHILE OTHERS
FAIL

1 *"The Richness of Its Possibilities"*

Starting in the 1960s and peaking in the late 1970s, a wave of public workers' movements swept the United States. Typically, these movements crested in strikes. Political in nature and overwhelmingly concentrated in the cities, counties, schools, and other agencies of local government, these strikes were aimed at public officials and often disrupted public services.[1] They left in their wake new patterns of politics and labor organization in communities across the country. While other parts of the workforce were witnessing the decline of unionism, these movements strengthened the power of women and minorities in the public workplace and in local government and brought public workers, formerly excluded from the house of labor, to its forefront.

Then, a massive upheaval occurred in U.S. politics and policy. Centered in the public workplace, it was foreshadowed by the fiscal collapse of New York City in 1975, sparked by the passage of Proposition 13 in California in 1978, confirmed with the election of Ronald Reagan in 1980, and reinforced by the Professional Air Traffic Controllers' (PATCO) strike of 1981–82. Suddenly and sharply, strike activity in the public sector subsided. At the same time, the new unions that had been produced by the public workers' movements of the 1960s and 1970s emerged as key coalition-builders in defense of public services in local government.

The existence and unique status of public workers are of course common knowledge, and the strength of their social movements is familiar to those who lived through the 1960s and 1970s. But unlike other actors rooted in

[1]On the concentration of strikes in local agencies, see Lewin et al. 1988:326–27 and Mitchell 1988:154. Membership in federal unions is concentrated in the postal service, which is uniquely empowered by its distribution in every congressional district and was already highly organized (76 percent by 1960) before the emergence of the social movements that are our focus here.

public organization—state managers (Evans, Rueschemeyer, and Skocpol 1985; Block 1987; Pahl 1975), for example—or other urban social movements (Castells 1978; Fainstein and Fainstein 1974), public workers are scarcely visible in social theory. This book aims to draw attention to them and to their role in the United States.

The focus of this study is not public sector labor relations institutions, although they are important and do appear.[2] Rather, the focus is the public workers' movements themselves. They have changed, I argue, all public sector labor relations institutions: laws, wage relations, personnel systems, bargaining processes, unions, and employee associations. Moreover, because they also move *outside* the familiar collective bargaining system, they have made an enduring mark on politics and public life in the United States as well.

Where did these movements come from, and where did they go? Why did they surface, concentrated in local government, during the 1960s and 1970s, and why did they wane in the 1980s? What were their demands, and what were their resources? What can their history tell us about the promise and the pitfalls of public sector labor movements?

I argue here that public workers' movements are shaped by—and in turn shape—the distinctive context within and against which they operate: public organization. Consequently, their demands, their resources, and their historical roles differ in important ways from those of private sector labor movements. Public workers' movements are constrained to frame their demands as public policy—rational, universalistic, and, purportedly at least, in the public interest. They depend for power less on their market position and on coalitions in their labor market than on their political position and involvement in the coalitions that govern public agencies. These movements are involved not only in collective bargaining and lobbying over wages, benefits, and working conditions but also in broader political conflicts over the public agendas that guide and fund public sector work. Thus, the public workers' movements that swept American cities in the 1960s and 1970s must be understood as part of the ongoing conflict over our urban agenda.

Two Labor Movements?

In the world of industrial relations, law and public policy are closely intertwined with academic research; deeply embedded in the theories that guide work in all these areas is the assumption that workers and their unions

---

[2]There are three excellent collections on public sector labor relations institutions, edited by Benjamin Aaron, Joyce M. Najita, and James L. Stern (1988); Richard B. Freeman and Casey Ichniowski (1988); and David Lewin et al. (1988).

face *private firms*. Whether these theories concern labor market behavior (Commons 1909), industrialization (Kerr et al. 1960) or deindustrialization (Touraine 1986), political class conflict (Korpi 1978), or the capitalist labor process (Edwards 1979), for example, theories of the labor movement rely on core assumptions that implicitly exclude the public workforce.[3] This institutional legacy of private sector labor relations influences not only scholars but public sector unionists themselves. When they mobilize, they often lack clear ideas about their own goals and resources and so are disoriented, disorganized, and easily demoralized.

Because our conceptual tools for thinking about labor relations are so shaped by their origins in the private sector, my approach here is to examine similarities and differences between the private and public sector, using cross-sectoral comparisons.[4] The cases we will study involve workers in both the private and the public sectors, all of whom produced social movements that peaked in strikes or related mobilizations.

In all these cases, we observe learning processes. In each, unionists' and employers' assumptions and strategies collided with the conditions they faced. In each, participants adapted to new conditions and learned—sometimes through painful experience—what succeeds and what fails. Here, we will be as concerned with understanding those conditions—especially in the public sector—as in learning these lessons for success and failure. What succeeds and what fails depends, as we shall see, not only on participants' assumptions and strategies and innovations but also on conditions that are unique to each sector.

This process of learning, which is still unfinished, is a main feature of recent history in U.S. labor relations in both sectors. In both sectors, labor relations have sharply departed from past practices that had come to define scholars' and participants' basic assumptions about strikes and unionism. Suddenly, it seems, there are two labor movements in the United States, each uncertain of its future.

The most obvious evidence of two labor movements is the difference in union membership rates, beginning in the 1950s: "the ebb of private sector union membership and a meteoric rise in public sector membership" (Troy 1986:80). By 1993, slightly more than two-fifths of U.S. union members were public workers (U.S. Department of Labor 1994), compared with one-twelfth

[3]Luca Perrone's (1984) notion of "positional power" is an exception, although it also disregards sectoral location. Broad treatments of labor relations and occupational behavior typically fail to disaggregate by sector, analyzing trends on the assumption that all workers are employed by firms. Trends for public and private sector workforces frequently run in opposite directions, so that this approach blurs data on the private sector and obscures data on the public.

[4]This strategy was inspired by Michael Burawoy's related work (1979), which compares labor processes in capitalist and statist factories; the strategy allows for a combination of constant comparative methods—or grounded theory—and extended case methods—or reconstructing theory (Burawoy 1991).

three decades ago (Troy 1986); in 1991, fully half the workers covered by collective bargaining agreements expiring that year were public employees (Sleemie, Borum, and Wasilewski 1991). During the 1960s and 1970s, membership in public sector unions more than doubled, while rates in the private sector declined by more than half.[5]

Almost as obvious are the trends in strike activity—perhaps the best evidence of trends in labor movements. While strike activity in the private sector clearly varied with economic conditions—especially, in the period before the 1980s, with the rate of unemployment (Kaufman 1992; Western 1993; Franzosi 1989)—strike activity in the public sector followed a very different pattern. Figure 1.1, for example, compares the strike trends for California's public and private sectors with that state's unemployment rates. (The unemployment rates have been inverted for ease of visual comparison.) The correlation between the unemployment rate and the number of private sector strikes per million workers is obvious; by contrast, there is no apparent relationship between the unemployment rate and the number of strikes in the public sector.[6]

Other trends over time are equally curious. Both sectors passed together through periods of economic and fiscal growth followed by austerity and through years of favorable political conditions followed by political adversity. But instability in labor relations occurred earlier in the public sector—*before* the watershed years around 1980, when the new era of austerity and adversity was inaugurated—whereas the private sector had relative *stability* in that period. Conversely, the new labor relations environment of the 1980s brought relative *stability* to the public sector and *instability* or disruption of established relations to the private. In short, workers in the two sectors responded in opposite ways to more or less similar conditions. Between the 1970s and the 1980s, the center of crisis and change in labor relations switched from the public sector to the private.

---

[5]Data on these trends are notoriously incomplete and inconsistent (Chaison and Rose 1991; Burton and Thomason 1988; Freeman, Ichiniowski, and Zax 1988). The crux of the problem is that much union growth did not involve the formation of new organizations (as many scholars assume) but the transformation of existing employee associations. Scholars agree, however, on the sharp differences in these trends.

[6]From 1962 through 1985, the number of annual public and private sector strikes per million workers in California is uncorrelated ($r = -.02$). The correlation between unemployment and the number of private strikes is strong and negative ($r = -.56$ and significant at the .005 level), but it is weak and positive between unemployment and the number of public sector strikes ($r = .17$, not significant). Strike data sources: public sector 1969–90, *California Public Employee Relations Journal* (CPER); public sector strikes pre-1969 and private sector strikes through 1981, *Work Stoppages in California,* annual, California Department of Industrial Relations, Division of Labor Statistics and Research; private sector strikes 1982–85, *Report of Work Stoppages* (internal report of the California Employment Development Department).

Figure 1.1. *California's Unemployment Rate and Public and Private Sector Strike Trends, 1962 – 1985*

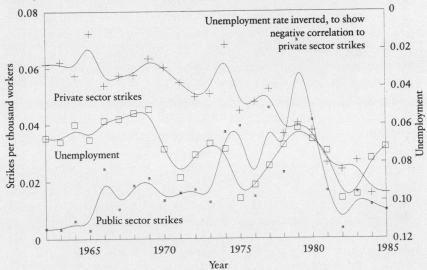

For a few years in the early 1980s, to be sure, strike rates in both sectors moved together: both declined sharply. But such a drop could signal very different changes in labor relations. Fewer and *shorter* strikes can reflect *lower* levels of conflict; fewer and *longer* strikes can reflect *intensified* conflict, more defensive strikes by more desperate unions, and a general fear of strikes. In fact, as figure 1.2 shows for California, during the early 1980s the strikes were longer and more bitter in the private sector; strikes were shorter and labor relations more amicable in local government.[7] It appears that the strength of management domination in the early 1980s left private sector unions hesitant to strike, even in the face of demands for concessions, and forced them into long and bitter battles when they did. But despite comparable political adversity and fiscal austerity in the public sector, the early 1980s produced new labor-management coalitions in much of local government, as unions allied with erstwhile adversaries—frequently, Democrats rallying resources against the Republican ascendance—in defense of public services.[8]

[7] Shorter strikes can also reflect a greater reliance on one-day "protest" actions; that is not the case here. Though public workers do engage in many more protest strikes than private workers, their rate of recourse to one-day work stoppages remained constant, at about 34 percent, from 1969 through 1985. Data sources same as in note 6. On longer defensive strikes, see Naples 1987; on shorter strikes, see Shorter and Tilly 1974, Shalev 1978.

[8] Important exceptions occurred in agencies where Reaganite politicians held local power: in Los Angeles County, for example.

Figure 1.2. *Duration of Strikes in California's Public and Private Sectors, 1962 – 1985*

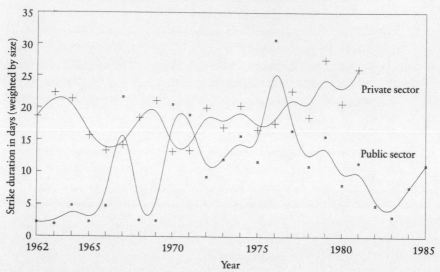

Similarly, although concession bargaining swept the private sector in the early 1980s, it was a "lesser force" in the public sector (Mitchell 1986). Further, although private sector unions won far larger pay and benefit increases than public sector unions in the 1970s, the increases in the public sector in the 1980s were more than three times larger (Lewin et al. 1988). Also in the early 1980s, public employers' resistance to agency shops weakened. Public sector unions in some states thus won legislation—often with the support of former adversaries—permitting agency shop provisions in contracts, which sharply increased these unions' revenues.

Perversely, then, although the latter part of the 1980s saw an increasing trend toward the privatization of public services, many local government unions gained the same organizational security and fiscal solvency during the Reagan years that industrial unions in the private sector gained during World War II. Also perversely, since the mid-1980s, the beleaguered *private sector* shows increasing promise of producing the next surge of labor innovation and mobilization. In short, in the 1970s and 1980s, the two sectors followed not merely different but *contrary* paths of change, despite generally comparable conditions.[9] These different trends in unionization and strike rates in response to the same historical conditions suggest that the terms "unionization" and

---

[9]Economists offer opposing interpretations of these trajectories: according to one influential scholar, they are converging (Troy 1984); according to another, they are diverging (Freeman 1988). The observation of *contrary* paths suggests that both scholars may be partially right: over time, they may converge, cross paths, diverge, and then converge again.

"strike" refer to different phenomena in the public and private sectors. If that is so, we need different theories to explain them.

Another difference between the two sectors is so obvious that it is also invisible, unremarked on and untheorized. Private sector unions organize within and against labor markets. They seek to take wages out of competition by creating alliances among similar workers, often across many employers in the same labor market. Public sector unions, by contrast, typically ignore the labor market. They focus on a single public organization. They seek to influence their terms of employment by creating alliances that represent a variety of interests—including, perhaps, those of other workers—across the political-bureaucratic division of labor, *within* the political universe of a public agency.[10] This difference has important strategic consequences for public workers' movements and suggests there are profound differences in the meaning of solidarity in the public and private workplace.

A related and equally important difference between the two sectors *is* widely recognized, perhaps because it conforms to economists' preferred image of public bureaucracy as oversupply or size maximization (Niskanen 1971; Downs 1967; Lane 1993). Scholars agree—often with alarm—that public sector unionism *increases* public sector employment by mobilizing political resources to influence the budget process in support of the functions the unions represent.[11] Private sector unionism, the theory goes, *decreases* employment through its effects on labor supply and demand. This formula is probably overly simplistic, since it neglects, for example, widespread union efforts in the 1980s and 1990s to improve productivity, among other strategies, to preserve jobs threatened by plant closings and contracting out. Nonetheless, based on the cases I have studied, political mobilization by public workers on behalf of the functions they perform does appear to play a central role in the public workers' movement. Though some may view this with alarm and others with approval, scholars all agree that public workers are, through their movements and their unions, state-builders. Similarly, students of the welfare state find that in recent decades the main advocates for human services have been neither liberal reformers nor clients but the organized human service workers themselves (Piven and Cloward 1988).

[10]The "political-bureaucratic division of labor" refers to a peculiar set of divisions intrinsic to public organization, including not only specialization and hierarchy within the workplace but also worker/client, client/constituent, constituent/politician, and politician/bureaucrat relationships.
[11]See Benecki 1978, Victor 1977, Spizman 1980, Freeman 1986, Freeman and Valletta 1988, Valletta 1989, and Zax and Ichniowski 1988 and 1990. Stephen J. Trejo (1991) says that part of the correlation between public sector unionization and higher employment rates may be due to the second attracting the first rather than the first causing the second; he argues, though, that this would reduce the magnitude of the latter effect rather than negate it.

One final set of questions will complete this preliminary comparison. How does one explain the fact that women have achieved greater status, pay, and power in the public workplace than in the private? Why have women's unions, women union leaders, and women's wage gains all been concentrated so heavily in the public sector? Why have claims to pay equity been concentrated—and progress toward pay equity still more concentrated—in the public workplace? (Riccucci 1990; Cook 1985 and 1986.) The same questions, with some variation, could be asked about racial equality. Why is it that not only white and nonwhite women but nonwhite men earn more for comparable work in the state sector than in the private sector (Smith 1983; Asher and Popkin 1984; Wines, Ley, and Fiorito 1986; Gunderson 1980)?

Public organization is, to be sure, a main carrier of the standards of formal equality that enjoin discrimination on the basis of race and gender (Jepperson and Meyer 1991). Administrative justice emerges, however, not as an automatic expression of democratic values but as a response to social movements and political conflict (see appendix). The convergence of public workers' movement with movements for racial justice and gender justice boosted the power of nonwhite and female workers in local government.[12] Martin Luther King's fateful participation in the Memphis sanitation workers' strike of 1968 is only one example of how "the civil rights and public-sector unionization movement became intertwined" in many cities (Burton and Thomason 1988:16); the comparable worth movement is an expression of the women's movement's similar convergence with the public workers' movement. How do we explain the apparent affinity between these movements? How were these parts of the public workforce empowered at this particular time and place to press their claims to administrative justice?

These questions refer to the central problem of this book: how did the character of public work combine with the historical conditions of the postwar era to produce public workers' movements concentrated in local government? This question has two parts: First, what are the effects of the peculiarities of the public workplace on the character of public workers' movements? Second, why did these particular movements occur in local governments in the 1960s and 1970s? Answering the first question requires that we generalize about the demands and resources of public workers' movements. The second directs our attention to the specific historical conditions shaping public (and especially urban) life and organization in these years, and it locates this surge of

---

[12]More precisely, as we shall see, sections of the mobilizing public workforce were both racialized and gendered; mobilizations of predominantly white and male parts of the workforce appeared as well—frequently as defensive responses to African-American (Piven 1972) and/or women's movements in and around the public workplace.

militancy in that context. The next two sections introduce the approach of this book to each of these issues.

Peculiarities of the Public Workers' Movement

The view developed here is that the public workers' movement has been decisively shaped by its emergence within and against political bureaucracy— just as private sector unionism in the postwar United States was decisively shaped by its contest with private sector firms. This sectoral influence can be seen in both the resources—or weapons—and goals—or demands—of movements in each sector.

The public workers' movement faces different strategic conditions from those facing private sector mobilizations, so that success or failure depends on the use of different resources. While private sector unionism mobilizes collective action and organization among labor market participants—chiefly, though not exclusively, workers employed across firms in the same labor market—public sector unionism mobilizes collective action and organization within a single organization. The labor market is generally ignored, and when it does come into play, it is typically a referent of bureaucratic procedures for setting salaries rather than a strategic context for either competition or coalition-building.[13]

Within the public agency, workers' status and opportunities for collective action depend heavily on their status in the bureaucratic classification structure and on their relationship to the agency's governing coalition and policy agenda.[14] The workers' strength rests chiefly on *political-organizational* resources: first, legal rights, organizational status, and established procedures; second, strategic alliances within the shifting political universe of the public agency, including clients, constituents, and other participants in that political universe; third, forms of voice that can help mobilize new organization, build or prevent alliances, and, by framing and appealing to "the public interest," put a potent political edge on the workers' demands.

In the private sector, by contrast, workers have relied mainly on *market* position for power. In the postwar period, the political and organizational context of collective bargaining has been important but—until the late 1970s— relatively constant (Kaufman 1982). When they do mobilize political and

---

[13]To be sure, many public employers have turned to private contracting to increase the flexibility and lower the cost of public work. Remarkably, though, public sector unions uniformly disregard organizing these competing workforces, relying instead on political means to limit privatization.
[14]As organizational sociologists have long observed, political coalitions also govern the internal life of firms (Cyert and March 1963). The public agency's relationship to its larger environment is organized primarily through its political regime, however, rather than through its market relations.

organizational resources in times of crisis—such as in the 1980s—these resources, even then, are used mainly to buttress market position. To the extent
that they go further, seeking to impose political jurisdiction over private property, the union movement becomes, in effect, a public workers' movement.

In the public sector, by contrast, political and organizational resources are
not reserved for times of crisis but are normal strategic weapons. Times of
crisis provoke the power of "voice" to mobilize new political-organizational
resources.[15] Accordingly, whereas some occupational groups with scarce skills
wield disproportionate power in the private sector, those groups with developed organizational and verbal skills have an edge in the public.

These different contexts for labor conflict and mobilization produce labor
movements that vary not only in their *weapons* but also in their *goals*.[16]
Despite surface similarities in the demands of private and public sector unions,
those of public workers tend to assume a distinctly *political-bureaucratic*
rather than a *commodified* form. Public workers' movements are constrained
to frame their claims as "public needs"—legitimate and administrable—and to
align with and even assemble coalitions around these public needs, turning
bargaining into a political debate over public policy. Even wage claims are
made in an appeal to principles such as administrative justice or bureaucratic
due process.[17]

The location of public workers' movements in public organizations gives
them a special relationship to the public agenda—especially in local government, where public workers most easily organize and most directly confront
their communities' needs. Public workers' views of the public interest almost
invariably complement their own private interests, and they are bureaucracy
builders. For better or worse, though, they are involved in public issues:
because they confront them face-to-face—at the point of production, so to
speak, of society itself; because their fate is closely linked to the status,

[15]Alfred O. Hirschman (1970), and after him Richard B. Freeman and James Medoff (1984),
describe the use of "vertical" voice, instead of exiting, to convey dissatisfaction to managers. I also
follow Guillermo O'Donnell (1986) in using "lateral" voice, emphasizing its importance in the
construction of collective identity. See also William Gamson (1988).

[16]These differences are complicated by the diffusion of institutionalized repertoires (Tilly 1992)
or models of unionism—including legal institutions, organizational forms, scholarly paradigms,
and so on—from the private sector to the public (described in chapter 2) and vice versa (described
in chapter 6).

[17]Harold Laski (1919) emphasizes this feature of "administrative syndicalism," especially its
historical continuity with democratic movements to limit the power of the absolutist state.
Institutional sociologists view the modern state as carrier of these universalistic norms of
bureaucratic rationality (e.g., Jepperson and Meyer 1991). Labor process theorists, by contrast,
frame these norms as political products of workplace conflict (Burawoy 1985; Jacoby 1985;
Clawson 1980). These seemingly alien arguments converge where public workers mobilize within
the state as workplace.

funding, and fate of their employing agencies; because the discourse of demand and response produces a dialogue about "what should be public policy." Thus, they are participants in the never-ending argument over "what is the public good" and join—and increasingly organize—coalitions on behalf of politically defined public goals associated with their work.[18]

This involvement in the contest over the public agenda is significant not only because it departs so sharply from unionism as we have known it in the United States but because the welfare state is in crisis. Public workers and their unions have played a pivotal role in our response to this crisis, and they may do so again. In twentieth-century America, the argument goes, economic, fiscal, and political trends are more and more closely linked. Economic crises regularly combine with fiscal crises to produce cycles of political instability. During these periods public workers and their unions become political lightning rods, key actors with unpredictable but potentially powerful effects on subsequent history. In their role as scapegoats—in the Boston police strike of 1919, in the mid- to late 1970s in local government, and in the early 1980s during the PATCO debacle—public workers can serve as a fulcrum for a lurch to the right in political life. In defense of their own status, wages, and working conditions, they can (and do) easily embrace interests that pit themselves against the urban poor and render them vulnerable to such scapegoating. At the same time, however, public workers' unions that are mindful of their political resources and employ strategies of public service unionism are uniquely positioned to build new alliances that defend and assert public needs. These possibilities are well worth examining in a society that systematically underproduces public education, child care, public health facilities, public transportation, and similar "public goods."[19]

This does not mean that public workers' movements will promote a "workers' state," abolish capitalism or the state, and so on. Different parts of the public workforce are likely to be implicated on different sides of every great social contest. The important point is that public workers' claims are framed

---

[18]Scholars on the left have properly emphasized the potential power of labor-community coalitions in public administration (O'Connor 1973; Johnston 1978; Lipsky 1980; Piven 1986; Reed 1994). According to this argument, however, groups of public workers may well mobilize coalitions on behalf of policy agendas that are decidedly less attractive to the left (e.g., racism, narrowly defined professional and bureaucratic interests, law and order); they are also likely to identify their interests in bureaucratic terms and so may well resist rather than promote radical reforms.

[19]The final chapter of James O'Connor's now-classic *Fiscal Crisis of the State* (1973) resonates with this argument, as does Frances Fox Piven and Richard A. Cloward's (1988) study of the role of organized public workers in limiting the Reagan assault on the welfare state. Unlike the "sectoral theory" associated with O'Connor's work (e.g., Hodson 1978), however, I do not reduce the state to a circuit of capital or, like Piven and Cloward, reduce it to a political apparatus. Rather, I emphasize the distinctive logic of state-organized production.

in certain common forms and that these workers rely on certain common kinds of strategic resources; beyond that, the significance of a particular movement depends on its historical context. As they frame their interests as administrable public interests, they are perhaps the quintessential "state-making" social movement (Bright and Harding 1984). In the United States in the current historical period, the significance of these movements may hinge decisively on whether they embrace and channel the politics of antibureaucratic reform before they become its target.

Here, I am especially interested in the problems and possibilities of the miscellaneous human service public workers' unions—those that combine large numbers of semiskilled blue-collar, clerical, professional, and technical workers. Often predominantly nonwhite and female, these workers are heavily concentrated in human service agencies in a wide array of local government departments and neighborhoods in cities and towns. The significance of this group of workers stems not only from the peculiarities of public work but also from these workers' potential role as central actors in new progressive urban coalitions involved in the struggle over the public agenda in the United States.[20]

Locating the Public Workers' Movement in History

Labor relations in the public sector—whether adversarial or collaborative, mobilizing or demobilized—are part of the larger constellation of political alliances and conflicts that surround and shape public organization. This political universe is less an external condition for labor relations behavior than an immediate field for labor movement activity. The public workforce itself is a tool and a political base for the public agency's governing policy coalition, which rests on a larger constellation of power based as well in other institutions. The relative position of different groups of public workers and their opportunities for successful mobilization depend in good part, then, on their position—mainly by virtue of the work they do—in that larger context. Change, conflict, and political realignment in this larger political-organizational field means change, conflict, and political realignment in public work and labor relations. The simultaneous appearance, then, of public worker militancy and other urban social movements and political conflicts in urban life in the 1960s and 1970s was no coincidence.

Explaining the concentration, timing, and character of militancy in local government requires that a bridge be created between two groups of re-

---

[20]Arguably, because of the increasing centrality of education in the informational society, teachers can play an equally significant strategic role.

searchers who have historically neglected one another: scholars of public sector labor relations and of urban political sociology. It also requires that urban sociologists direct their attention to the impact of gender dynamics on urban life and public organization.[21]

Public Workers and Urban Politics

Scholars who study urban life emphasize what might be called two faces of urbanism. On the one hand, public institutions are embedded in a local "growth machine" that pursues profit from property (Harvey 1973; Logan and Molotch 1987). On the other hand, the city is a setting for localized and increasingly politically regulated "collective consumption," including health care, education, housing, transportation, and neighborhood life itself (Castells 1978), through which public agencies subsidize the costs of private production while producing the "use values" of everyday life.

Different scholars place different emphasis on these two faces of urbanism; most describe a tension between them. While urban political regimes in the postwar era organized mainly around economic development agendas (Stone 1989), the politics of collective consumption provided a base for the main social movements—some composed of middle-class white liberals, some based in black and Latino communities—challenging the hegemony of these progrowth coalitions.

Using these or related conceptual tools, scholars have produced compelling accounts of the postwar histories of American cities. Focusing on the perennial issue of "who governs and how?" they describe the early heyday of progrowth coalitions and, more recently, the "neighborhood revolt" (Mollenkopf 1983) associated with efforts to build "new liberal dominant coalitions" (Browning, Marshall, and Tabb 1990). They focus on the economic and political aspects of cities—economic restructuring; the problems, sometimes racialized, of political conflict and coalition-building; relationships among key public officials and private interests associated with public policy agendas; social movements based in collective consumption; and, most recently, the impact of local political and economic institutions.

This recent work by urban scholars, however, has neglected the involvement of the public workforce in regime politics.[22] "Collective consumption," however, is also public production, and urban regimes are based not only in economic and political institutions but in the great networks of public organizations that *produce* public policy agendas. In John Mollenkopf's words,

[21]I skirt the matter of race in this analysis. See, on this, pp. 112n and 213 – 215 below.
[22]For an exception, see Shefter 1985.

"Each function of government has strong producer interests associated with it; to varying degrees, these interests contend with the mayor to shape agency work and practices and policy outputs" (1992:71). As Mollenkopf further notes, these producer interests include city workers organized through municipal employee unions, "stratified by civil service classification, agency, and the union that represents them" (73).

These producer interests are organized as well into clusters of interest and power associated with what I call above the two faces of urbanism, are typically segregated into different political bureaucracies (Friedland, Piven, and Alford 1977), and are governed by separate political networks. Different blocs of public workers depend on these competing public agendas. So these different blocs of workers and their organizations participate in the struggle over public needs in different ways: as repressed interests, marginalized in urban politics; as part of insurgent political coalitions; as participants in governing coalitions. This participation in coalition-building and conflict in American cities helps explain the timing as well as the content of public worker militancy.

In brief, the turn toward adversarial relations in the 1960s and 1970s and the subsequent turn away from adversarial relations in the 1980s were expressions of the politics of *growth* in the former period and of *austerity* in the latter. These were not direct economic effects, however. In the former period, public workers in organizations marginal to pro-growth regimes mobilized for inclusion, allied with the "revolt of the neighborhoods" against the urban growth machine; workers in more privileged positions mobilized to defend threatened status, pay, and power. In the latter period, political change gave some challengers a place in new political regimes, while the Republican ascendance and other external threats motivated a defensive labor-management coalition in local government. Trends in strike activity during this period were also influenced by learning processes, however, as both unionists and their adversaries at first drew upon strategic frames (Goffman 1974) or repertoires inherited from the private sector but soon discovered new pitfalls and possibilities in the public sector context and so adapted their routines.

This argument does not preclude the influence of more conventional factors on public worker militancy, such as inflation or the unemployment rate—although the latter is likely to be less important than in the private sector. It does suggest, however, that historical processes emphasized in recent urban sociology drove the rise and decline of public worker militancy from the 1960s through the 1980s. These movements also responded, however, to other historical processes neglected in much of this work: processes visible only when we recognize the essentially gendered character of urban life and public work.

Public Workers and Gender Relations

By the mid-1970s, the feminist movement had begun its long march through organizational life in the United States, including local government (Katzenstein 1990). To date, however, urban political sociology has obscured the effects of change in family life and gender relations (themselves partly driven by population mobility and workforce recomposition resulting from the economic development emphasized by some scholars of urban life) and the mobilizations of women responding to them. Feminist scholars, however, have documented the gendered character of the welfare state.[23]

The rise of the welfare state was accompanied, feminist scholars observe, by a massive set of changes in gender relations that had important consequences outside as well as within the family. These changes included increased public sector involvement in activities previously organized within the family and neighborhood (Hernes 1987). The result is a new structure of gender relations and a new political economy that links the public sector to family life, transforming women and children into clients and women into employees of new agencies that focus on gendered needs (Ferguson 1984).

The important point is that the two sides of urbanism that are the focus of the urban sociology described above have a gendered character. On the one hand, pro-growth coalitions and public work associated with development efforts assembled men in business, urban development, construction, and law enforcement to produce, to use Suttles's (1990) revealing term, "the man-made city." These projects remade urban life in the postwar period, with drastic consequences for community life, for families, and especially for women who do the work of care. On the other hand, the clients, workers, and even administrators and union leaders in human service agencies are disproportionately female, as are the participants in neighborhood organizations and slow-growth movements.

Compared with the privileged interests and agencies associated with the growth agenda, these female-gendered interests and agencies are *devalued*—in budget decisions, in their marginal position in policy-making, and in the wages of their employees. They are devalued not only because they are subordinated to the development agenda but because they are associated with women's needs and powerlessness. This gendered division of public work is an important feature of the "gendered economy" (Kelly 1991); intertwined as it is with the primacy of economic development interests over "use values" (Logan and Molotch 1987) or "social consumption" (O'Connor 1973), this gendered

---

[23]See especially Mimi Abramovitz (1988) and the collections edited by Anne Showstack Sassoon (1987) and by Linda Gordon (1990). For further discussion of this scholarship, see chapter 4.

division of public work serves as one basis for "men's resistance to gender equality" (Cockburn 1991) in public organizations.

The new public organizations targeting women and their families serve both as new structures of control (Pateman 1988) and as new resources for women (Piven 1990), so that women's relationships to them are deeply ambivalent. Regardless of their attitudes, however, new blocs of women workers (and their male co-workers), clients, activists, and local government officials assemble around the production, use, administration, and defense of social consumption resources (Piven 1990). In politics, in public organization, and, as we shall see, in the internal life of unions themselves, these blocs of women confront the entrenched power of men based, in part, in the hegemonic economic development agenda. Some recent mobilizations by public workers can be viewed, then, as movements by women workers defending and asserting the relative political worth of gendered public work. In the first case study, which focuses on San Jose, in the Santa Clara Valley or Silicon Valley, I discuss what may be the best-known grassroots movement for comparable worth in this light.[24]

Women's participation and leadership in social movements is not a new phenomenon. Manuel Castells's global survey of urban social movements (1983) suggests that active involvement has been the rule rather than the exception: "If the urban experience follows the hidden detours of civil society more naturally than the large avenues toward the state, then, at some fundamental level, there is an intimate connection between women and the city, between urban movements and women's liberation" (68). Historically, as Castells observes, women have mobilized on the level of everyday experience, in defense of their families' needs. With the rise of the new gendered political economy of the welfare state, however, gender issues have been imported in new ways into the perennial contest over the public agenda and into the internal life of public organization itself.

Strategy and Structure of This Book

This study grew from my own successes and failures as a labor organizer, mostly in the public sector.[25] Most of the evidence studied here, however, was gathered later through conventional research methods. Still, my origins as a

---

[24]I will use "Santa Clara Valley" to refer to the geographic entity and "Silicon Valley" to refer to the new social formation that currently occupies it.

[25]I started as an organizer with the United Farm Workers Union. After I was drafted into the army, I organized GIs and later veterans against the Vietnam War. Later I became a union activist in a private sector printing plant and, still later, was hired as a public sector union representative. In and out of staff jobs, I remained a public sector organizer from 1973 through 1982.

native participant call for attention to the problem of bias. So the next chapter locates the text—its questions, its argument, its writer, and also its probable critics—in the history under study, starting in the early days of public sector unionism in Silicon Valley and then focusing on the turbulent 1970s and early 1980s in the city and county of San Francisco.

San Francisco was also a birthplace of the new managerial strategies in public sector labor relations that would later be wielded with devastating effect across the country in the PATCO strike of 1981. Thus, the first part of chapter 2 frames the questions of this book as they surfaced as practical problems in that time and place. Chapter 2 cannot stand as a systematic study of this setting, however. Rather, it reflects my own understandings and practical dilemmas, inside the public workers' movement in that particular time and place. The second part of chapter 2 turns to the bias that stems from this status as a participant in the setting under study. It also considers the similar bias— less obvious but equally treacherous—that plagues more conventionally detached scholarship on this topic.

Chapters 3 through 7 comprise the case comparisons. The last of these returns to San Francisco; the question then becomes whether, informed by the conceptual framework developed in these case studies, it is possible to clarify the problems and explain the social movements that emerged in that city.

Throughout the book, I use *cross-sectoral comparisons* to examine the peculiarities of the public sector. Since developments in the private sector serve mainly as vehicles for comparison, they are studied less systematically than those in the public sector. The contrast between public workers' movements and market-oriented unionism in the United States is sharp and, to most observers, fairly obvious. We would be caricaturing the private sector movement, however, if we reduced it entirely to an economistic model. Varieties of social unionism surfaced in the private sector not only in the 1930s but throughout U.S. labor history, drawing on social movements and pressing for social change. The new labor relations environment since 1980 has stimulated diverse private sector union strategies and movements—only partially explored here—seeking to outflank labor's weakness in the labor market.[26] Given the uneven appearance of social movement unionism in both sectors, how can we tell whether observed differences reflect genuine differences in the private and public sectors? One solution is to compare public sector workforces with private sector workforces that have engaged in social movement unionism. Thus, this book turns in chapter 5 to the first private sector strike

[26]See Shostak 1991, Brecher and Costello 1990, all the issues of *Labor Research Review*, and chapters 5 and 6.

for comparable worth and in chapter 6 to movements among private sector custodial workers that unfolded into a "Justice for Janitors" movement.[27]

It is now common wisdom that a "paradigm shift in labor relations" (Price and Bain 1989:105) occurred or at least began in the early 1980s. By comparing cases that span those pivotal years, we can also consider whether the two sectors experienced *similar* or *different* paradigm shifts.[28] The cases suggest that by the late 1980s the public sector and some private sector labor movements were indeed converging toward more political unionism. Despite this convergence, however, these movements remain different. While social movement unionism was on the rise in the private sector, it had subsided in the public sector, leaving a strengthened political-bureaucratic interest group in its wake.

The best way to examine sectoral differences is through controlled comparisons, within and across sectors and within and across occupational groups. This requires focusing on groups found in good number and in more or less similar circumstances in both sectors but that differ on several theoretically relevant counts: race, gender, pay, education, industry, occupational status, and so on. With these issues in mind, I chose to compare the experiences of nurses and custodians.

Most of our understanding of work and labor movements emphasize factors associated not with sector but with *occupational groups,* which are assumed to operate similarly across sectors; for example, white-collar, service, or professional work is contrasted with blue-collar work (Oppenheimer 1985). Such occupation-related differences are likely to be emphasized in counterarguments to the sectoral explanation developed here. For example, by the early 1980s, more than 50 percent of the union members in the public sector were professionals and semiprofessionals, whereas the figure for the private sector was less than 10 percent. To some observers, this might account for the different character and course of labor relations in the two sectors. In fact, the reverse appears to be true: professionals and semiprofessionals employed in public sector bureaucracies unionize and, to date, those in the private sector fail to do so.[29] Sectoral differences appear to explain differences in union

[27]Justice for Janitors campaigns, organized for the Service Employees' International Union (SEIU) through its building services division, swept through many U.S. cities starting in the late 1980s. These campaigns are discussed in chapter 6.

[28]Lewin et al. (1988:1) locate the public sector's shift to fiscal constraint, political adversity, and hard bargaining as occurring at the beginning of the 1970s; I place it in the late 1970s. Though heralded at mid-decade by the New York fiscal crisis and events in San Francisco, it was accomplished only after the passage of Proposition 13 in California in 1978.

[29]By the early 1980s, professionals and semiprofessionals represented 53 percent of union members and 42 percent of nonmembers in the public sector versus 6 percent of union members and 20 percent of nonmembers in the private sector (U.S. Department of Commerce 1984).

organization and collective action by female workers and by clerical workers as well.

Commonalities associated with occupation, including race and gender, exist across sectors and indeed make a difference. For example, the female nurses and Mexican-American custodians I studied all revolted in part against the devaluation of their work. These revolts followed different paths in each sector, however. Race, gender, and occupational and other organizational factors have effects, but *different* effects, in each sector.

The four case studies involve public sector union movements in San Jose and in San Francisco, and two private sector workforces that mobilized in the same period in the Santa Clara Valley. The case study involving San Jose focuses on women workers in Local 101 of the American Federation of State, County, and Municipal Employees (AFSCME), whose movement peaked in a widely known comparable worth strike in 1981. Tracing the influence of the city's political-bureaucratic context for mobilization and its local politics and fiscal crisis, chapter 3 closely examines the *form* of the city workers' demands and the *nature* of their weapons or resources and arrives at a reinterpretation of that widely misunderstood strike. Chapter 4 also focuses on San Jose but now situates the comparable worth campaign and the mostly female workers' simultaneous mobilization in defense of human services in the broader politics and the shifting social foundations of public life in Silicon Valley.

Chapter 5 turns to the private sector, specifically nurses in the Silicon Valley who are represented by the California Nurses' Association. Their surprisingly unknown 1982 strike was the first strike for comparable worth in the private sector. It therefore provides a useful comparison with the city workers' strike. We shall find, for example, that the meanings in the claim to comparable worth mutated—from the logic of political bureaucracy, in the public sector, to that of market relations, in the private. Also in contrast to the city, and despite the nurses' intense personal engagement with meeting human needs, the public service orientation so prominent in the public workers' movement did not appear. And again in contrast to the city workers, the private sector nurses and their union relied on (and eventually succumbed to) market-based power relations, despite their seemingly strong labor market position, impressive internal organization, and culture of solidarity.

As we shall see, neither of these movements can be understood without paying attention to the independent effects in each sector of gender relations on work organization and of the feminist impulse on the labor movement. Conversely, these cases direct our attention to the neglected influence of the public workplace on the comparable worth or pay equity movement.

Chapter 6 moves to the far end of the occupational spectrum, to examine labor movements among public and private sector custodians. These include the custodians who work for the city of San Jose, mostly Latino men who had been key allies for the women of the city during their comparable worth campaign, but were the primary losers in its aftermath. The chapter compares their experience with that of the private sector janitors of the valley, whose revolt against their union leadership led to a powerful "Justice for Janitors" campaign.

In chapter 7, we return to the city and county of San Francisco. This shift is of particular interest because, whereas San Jose is an archetypal new "Sunbelt city," San Francisco is in some ways an archetypal "old city." Here we focus on the city nurses' strike of 1982 in what is now Local 790 of the SEIU. The question here is whether and in what ways the city nurses' experience was similar to that of the private sector nurses of Silicon Valley or to that of the public workers of San Jose. As in San Jose, the challenge is to locate San Francisco's city workforce and its labor movement in the changing context of urban life and politics, and to trace the effects of the city's political-bureaucratic system on the city workers' movements.

The concluding chapter summarizes my findings. I also suggest that the common historical trends in San Francisco and San Jose represent only one variation on the new politics of public work since the 1960s and, briefly, describe what would be expected under more conservative administrations and in more overtly racialized cities. I then discuss the implications of my results—empirical, theoretical, and practical. On the first, I outline several research agendas and briefly relate my qualitative findings to aggregate data on labor relations in California's local governments. On the second, I consider the implications of the public workers' movement for the broad varieties of social theory that intersect in the public workplace. On the third, I focus on problems and prospects today and for the immediate future for the social movements studied here.

Although this book is not focused on comparable worth, the first public and private sector comparable worth strikes do serve as two of the cases compared here. Accordingly, in a final appendix, I relate the claim to comparable worth to the arguments developed here—in particular, to the politics of internal alignment in public personnel administration.

Social Research and the Public Workers' Movement

Why has the public workers' movement attracted so little attention among social researchers? Around the 1960s, much U.S. scholarship shifted its gaze

away from industrial relations—to organization theory, to newer social movements—while industrial relations research narrowed its vision "as it meta-
morphosed from a broad coalition of . . . disciplines devoted to the study of
all aspects of the world of work to a much narrower field devoted to the study
of unions, collective bargaining, and the employment problems of special
groups" (Kaufman 1993:104). During the following decade, moreover, many
scholars who had focused on the problems of urban social change posed by the
great movements of the 1960s turned to more tractable fields of study. As a
result, the field of industrial relations is more closely linked to practitioners—
personnel officers, mediators, and union officials—than to other scholars. It is
insular, oriented mainly to policy questions and professional training, committed to the collective bargaining institutions that it helped design and, more
recently, to the agendas of labor-management collaboration for productivity
enhancement that interest many of its practitioners. The field is also generally
unaffected by much recent work in state theory, urban political sociology,
organization theory, feminist theory, and the study of social movements. In
turn, not surprisingly, work in related fields is uninformed by industrial
relations research.[30]

At the same time, in the strand of political sociology that studies social
movements, the labor movement is "the old social movement," buried and all
but forgotten, or at least counterposed to resource-mobilizing advocacy
groups or new identity-oriented social movements.[31] In the analysis developed
here, public workers' movements appear as a unique type of *urban social
movement*. Unlike those organized, according to Castells (1978), around
urban social consumption, these are the social movements of those who
produce, in effect, city life.

Industrial Relations and the Public Workers' Movement

The main exception to the insularity of industrial relations research
stems from the work of economists, who *have* devoted attention to public
workers' movements. So, much work on public workers' movements relies
heavily on economists' conceptual tools, and the main arguments reflect

[30]Thus, though the uniquely political character of public sector labor relations is a truism in all
public sector research, I have found even this distinction controversial among colleagues in
sociology. Despite the steady accumulation of research on the uniqueness of public organization
(Rainey 1992), many organizational scholars remain wedded to generic views of bureaucracy.
Even industrial relations scholars routinely neglect the public sector (Cornfield 1991) and aggregate public and private sector data in their analyses (Western 1993), despite "accumulating
evidence that some key explanatory variables either play different roles in the private or public
sectors or are relevant only to one sector or the other" (Chaison and Rose 1991:10).
[31]See, for example, Alain Touraine's (1986) epitaph for the labor movement. Rick Fantasia's
Cultures of Solidarity (1988) is a welcome exception.

disputes within that discipline—typically, between institutional economists and "political choice" theorists more wedded to neoclassical assumptions.

Researchers who study public workers' movements have long agreed on one essential point: "Public employment relations . . . operate in an environment the very essence of which is politics. This more than anything else determines the nature and direction of public employer-employee relations" (Spero and Capozola 1973:235).[32] This "political essence" is often viewed, however, through economic eyes: public officials, union leaders, members and nonmembers are treated as utility-maximizers, and the defining feature of public life is a shortage of market competition (or, perhaps, the presence of political markets, with public sector unions appearing as monopolists threatening to distort those more or less competitive markets). Alternatively, for those more friendly to collective bargaining in the public sector, the state is an untheorized actor, appearing perhaps as a source of legislation or other policy that scholars may evaluate but are unlikely to explain (Adams 1992). Either way, the study of public sector labor relations remains by and large uninformed by the great body of recent research on the state.[33]

By the early 1970s, a paradigm had emerged in public sector industrial relations research reflecting the economist's "government as pernicious monopoly" perspective. In this view, public sector unions would grow and enjoy excessive power because they share in the monopoly power of their employers (Wellington and Winter 1971; Summers 1976). As a result, some scholars feared, the political influence of public workers or their monopolistic position in the "political marketplace" would result in the excessive allocation of resources to public needs—if not in wages, then in excessive public employment and thus excessive provision of public services. This led economists to view public employee strikes with great alarm; the most influential work in this tradition, in fact, proposed that they be banned (Wellington and Winter 1971).[34] Though institutional economists were likely to share these concerns, they dissented from this conclusion, arguing that conflict is inevitable and that

[32]Ironically, this observation concludes a chapter that argues that "although distinguishing characteristics may be enumerated, there are actually more similarities than differences between the majority of public and private sector employees" (312). It would appear that sympathy for public workers' right to collective action—and, perhaps, industrial relations scholars' attachment to a bargaining model closely coupled to the status of their own discipline—overrode Spero and Capozzola's essential insight.

[33]See Alford and Friedland 1985 for the most far-ranging and synthetic review of this work and also Carnoy 1984 and King 1986. Strikingly, the public workforce never appears in these texts.

[34]Curiously, they do not consider that other interests—private firms, free riders of various sorts—may have already reduced public allocation below the hypothetical optimum. For a critique of this early paradigm, see Cohen 1979.

legislation creating proper institutional arrangements could contain and channel this conflict more constructively.

The public workers' movement that unfolded in the 1960s and 1970s challenged this whole line of thought. As participants acted out more or less conventional private sector scripts for collective bargaining and strike action, public employers discovered surprising new political resources. The result was a learning process that led to very different conclusions from those deduced by economists. This process unfolded with great force on the national scene when President Ronald Reagan, applying a strategy already honed in local government, crushed the PATCO strike. The result for public sector industrial relations scholars, in any event, was dwindling support for the "public worker as monopolist" perspective (Lewin et al. 1988:86 – 88). Echoes of this view lingered, however (e.g., Burton 1982; Freeman 1986; Troy 1984), perhaps because no compelling theory that explained and predicted developments in the public sector emerged to take its place.

One perspective that is more oriented to political processes has focused on "multilateral bargaining" (Kochan 1974), in an effort to explain the power of public unions based on their access to the multiple decision makers in political agencies (and thereby, in effect, warning managers to limit this access). Though somewhat uneven in its results, research based on this theory has underlined the importance for union bargaining power of political strategies that take advantage of the dispersal of influence over decisions in public organizations; it has drawn particular and well-deserved attention to the fact that divisions in this management can increase union power and to the coalition-building process more generally (Kochan 1974; Kochan and Wheeler 1975; Anderson 1979).

The question remains, however, coalition-building by whom, with whom, and for what? Opportunities for coalition-building depend not only on management structure and bargaining arrangements but, more important, on the shifting alignment of interests in— and outside— *governing policy coalitions*. The actual workings of bargaining arrangements are more effects than causes of these political alignments. To understand opportunities for union power, then, we need a vision that locates particular workers within the changing political structures resulting from coalition-building, regime formation, and political transition. The question, then, is not "Coalition or no coalition?" but "What coalitions?" and whether and why they isolate or empower particular public workers.

Recently, industrial relations scholars seeking to explain changes in public sector bargaining power have embraced a "good times, bad times" argument, which emphasizes the effects of fiscal stress on the politics of public organization

(Lewin 1986; Horton 1986). Because it refers to growth and austerity, that account is at least superficially similar to this one. But although both perspectives point to the impact of changing fiscal conditions, there is a fundamental difference between them. The "good times, bad times" theory is an economic argument; its reasoning is that fiscal constraints weaken the bargaining power of unions by increasing competition for scarce resources. I emphasize, by contrast, an argument based on the *politics* of growth and austerity. The consequences of growth and austerity for the politics of public organization are unintelligible[35] unless we consider the political alignments associated with growth or austerity in a given historical context. On the matter of wage outcomes, we need look no further than the case of San Jose, where, as we shall see, the women of the city secured substantial comparable worth adjustments in the midst of fiscal crisis, while at the same time the city's Latino custodians found most of their jobs privatized at half the pay.

Most recently, debate among public labor relations researchers has revolved around the claim by institutional economists that the growth of unionism in the 1960s and 1970s was an effect of labor laws, which, they argue, promoted unionization and collective bargaining.[36] This argument is supplemented by the observation—widely accepted since Harry H. Wellington and Ralph K. Winter, Jr.'s influential book *The Unions and the Cities* (1971)—that public sector employers offer less resistance to unionization than private sector employers. The opposing argument—persuasive to this writer—is that, despite its apparent influence, labor legislation is more the effect than the cause of labor movement activity (Burton and Thomason 1988; Bronfenbrenner and Juravich 1994).[37]

Based on the evidence examined here, legal institutions *can* serve as either resources or constraints for mobilization. Legal institutions being equal, however, certain groups still mobilize while others do not. And, important for my purposes here, the bases for conflict that drive adversarial relations in the private sector are indeed largely absent in the public sector; this tells us little, unfortunately, about what *does* drive militancy in the public workplace or explain changes in the levels of labor-management conflict over time. In sum,

[35]For example, Raymond D. Horton's study of New York City (1986) found a *decline* in labor's share of the public budget in the expansive early 1970s but found several indicators of *increased* strength for labor as a whole and for nonuniformed, lower-waged workers in particular in the later era of retrenchment.

[36]See, for example, Burton and Thomason 1988, Saltzman 1985, and Freeman 1988.

[37]This view is supported by important historical studies that demonstrate the effects of prior worker unrest and union mobilization on the passage of labor laws. See, for example, Vosloo 1966 on John F. Kennedy's Executive Order 10988; Crouch 1978 on California law; Bellush and Bellush 1984 and Maier 1987 on New York City; and Donovan 1990 on the New York State Taylor Law.

a great body of research, driven largely by economists' models of labor relations, has produced many false starts but no compelling theory of the public workers' movement. The list of explanations produced by industrial relations scholars for the eruption of public worker militancy in the 1960s and 1970s is longer still: (1) the disparity in public and private sector wages (Stieber 1973); (2) the upsurge in activism among college-educated youth (Kassalow 1969); (3) organizing efforts by the AFL-CIO (Gitlow 1970); (4) the "proletarianization" of public work (Levi 1977) (e.g., the bureaucratization of social work); (5) the decline of public trust in the political community (Nisbet 1976); (6) "changed public attitudes" that led to greater acceptance of unions in the public sector (Karper 1990); (7) the effects of poverty programs on urban administrators' transaction costs (e.g., federal funding of local agreements to raise wages in model city programs (Kurth 1983); (8) the racialization of urban centers (Lentz 1983); (9) the passage of collective bargaining laws (Freeman 1986); (10) the less adversarial nature of public sector versus private sector labor relations (Freeman 1986); and (11) the prior existence of employee associations (Levitan and Gallo 1989).

Each of these explanations has compelling counterarguments. Briefly, (1) most studies show that during most of the period of union growth and militancy compensation of state and local government employees was roughly equal to that of private sector employees—higher if fringe benefits are considered (Mitchell 1988); (2) the activism of the 1960s failed to take root in demographically comparable private sector workforces, in health care and electronics, for example; (3) many of the new AFL-CIO unions originated in employee associations, and employee associations also turned militant in the absence of AFL-CIO affiliation; and if (4) "proletarianization," or (5) "the decline of public trust," or (6) "changed public attitudes" accompanied the increase in unionization in the public sector, they obviously also accompanied *decreasing* unionization in the private sector. The "transaction costs" argument (7) refers to the special fiscal status of federally funded War on Poverty programs and is hardly relevant to the broader turn toward militancy in the rest of the workforce. The "racialization" argument (8) cannot explain the simultaneous surge in militancy among predominately white workforces facing white administrations in predominately white communities. Collective bargaining laws (9) were at least as much an effect as a cause of public workers' movements (Saltzman 1985). And neither the (at times) less adversarial character of public sector labor relations (10) nor the preexistence of employee associations (11) can explain the issue at hand: the changes that took place over time *within* the public workforce in militancy or labor movement activity; nor can they explain the *timing* of those changes. Moreover, since 1980, all such explanations must account not only for the unexpected *turbulence* during the 1960s and 1970s but for the unexpected *stability and decline* of public sector militancy since then.

Small wonder, then, that industrial relations scholars have settled for essentially descriptive accounts (Lewin et al. 1988). Small wonder, too, the bemused conclusion of two recent reviewers that "in light of the demonstrated inability of scholars to anticipate . . . [these changes] . . . any prediction of the future of public-sector bargaining is of questionable value" (Burton and Thomason 1988:2). Rather, it seems, some still-unnamed processes of historical change are at work here, driving labor unrest among some workers, driving the transformation of some unions and associations into adversarial organizations (and then back again), and driving the passage of labor law.

Public Workplace as Context for Collective Action

In the view developed here, the strike wave of the 1960s and 1970s—along with a host of related changes in public law, organization, and politics—was the product of a distinctive social movement, which was shaped by its emergence within the peculiar context of state and local government in the United States. "Unionization" was less a set of individual decisions to join together against the labor market than a change in the character of *existing* organizations. The strike wave was a marker of this movement, roughly reflecting the emergence of an inchoate—but, for a time at least, adversarial—new group identity within an already organized workplace.

The public workers' movement is hard to locate in social movement theory because it appears related both to the "old" labor movement and to newer social movements. Emerging within and sometimes against public bureaucracy, it bears some relation to the *antistatist* movements of Europe and Eastern Europe; asserting the interests of public workers as public workers, it also appears as a *state-building* movement. Some currents intertwine with the civil rights movement of the 1960s; some are feminist; in others, white men and sometimes women form defensive enclaves within segments of public bureaucracy comparable to the urban and suburban ethnic neighborhoods in which they live. Public workers' movements can serve as powerful vehicles for each of these interests and a variety of others, refracting each through its lens, as it were, and imposing on each a common form of demand and common kinds of resources.

Understanding this "form of demand"—and grasping the peculiar power of certain kinds of demands as weapons in public organization—requires paying attention to symbolic practices familiar to students of new social movements and also considering their diffusion from one time and place to another. Grasping strategic resources—explaining why some succeed while others fail, identifying organizational resources for collective action (McCarthy and Zald 1977), and identifying the shifting political alignments that open up (and later close) political opportunities (Jenkins 1987; Perrow 1979) that make collective action more viable at one time than another—also requires paying attention to "resource mobilization" traditions in social movement research. Taken together, these traditions allow us to conceptualize a complex and contingent learning process that has produced variations in social movement activity between sectors of the labor movement and over time.[38]

The first step required is a broader recognition among social movement scholars that social movement activity is far from dead among the millions of American workers in unions and the millions more who would like to be in them. It will perhaps come as the greatest surprise that this is especially true of workers in the private sector; there, unionism as a social movement was indeed in decline during three decades of "good times," before the "hard times" of the 1980s gave a new generation of organizers painful lessons in how to fight.

If the public workers' movement is different in any essential sense from the movement in the private sector, it is because of its peculiar context for mobilization: public organization. This observation requires—as the second step toward understanding public workers' movements—that we relate both the *forms of social movement identity*—best expressed as the boundaries of collective identity and the cultural construction of demands—and the movement's *arsenal of resources* to this structural context. (Later, we will historicize this perspective by introducing the conditions of urban life in postwar America.)

For politically oriented resource mobilization scholars, resources are shaped not only from familiar stocks of experience (influenced, that is, not only by institutional processes) but also by strategic context (Tilly 1992). A resource is only a resource, as participants are liable to learn through painful experience, if it taps levers of power. So, rather than *assuming* pervasive and generic political domination and resistance (Tilly 1978), or pervasive and generic competition for resources (McCarthy and Zald 1977), one must pay attention to the peculiarities of the context in which mobilization occurs.

Features of public organization, on the one hand, and of the labor market, on the other, *do* create radically different contexts for mobilization: different bases for labor-management conflict, different bases of power or resources,

---

[38]In Aldon Morris's terms, "Concepts such as 'collective identity,' 'master frames,' 'packages,' and the like should be solidly rooted in their relevant structural contexts. . . . What needs to be analyzed and identified are the main structural and cultural determinants of collective action and how they interact. . . ." (1992:369).

different imperatives for alliance formation, and so on. Charles Tilly's own account of workers' resources implicitly recognizes this, since he focuses exclusively on factors that affect market relations in commodity production—assuming, as most analysts do, that all workers are employees of capitalists (1988:455). The question, then, is, What other kinds of repertoires evolve in the public organization, where such market leverage has little effect? The answer developed here emphasizes three resources: first, established rules; second, coalitions across the bureaucratic division of labor; and, third, what I term the power of voice.

In discussing cultural practices, scholars have drawn attention to variations in "meaning construction" by participants—variations in the significance of superficially similar actions, the different interests animating social movement behavior, and the different collective identities expressed by social movements in different historical or structural contexts (Mueller 1992)—and to actors' increasingly reflexive awareness and use of this cultural contingency (Touraine 1986). Because of the racialization of collective identity in American political life, and because of the importance of gender relations in urban change, both public and private sector movements today draw not only upon inherited repertoires of unionism but also upon these two sources of collective indentity and action, among others. In each sector, however, unique structural and historical conditions also impose their own form upon these movements.

Organized as it is around the production of *politically defined and administrable public goods*, public organization constrains claimants to frame their claims—including continued funding for their jobs and including wage claims—as (1) in the general interest and as (2) administrable. In contrast to the capitalist labor market, moreover, public organization is a crucible for social movements displaying a distinct pattern of collective identity or solidarity. Solidarity in the private sector typically reaches out into a labor market, is organized across organizations, and expresses homogeneous self-interest; in Émile Durkheim's term, it is mechanical. Solidarity in the public sector is far more organic, tenuous, and complex: it attempts to align fragmented interests across the bureaucratic division of labor within the political universe of a single organization.[39]

If we are to locate this social movement in its structural context, we need, of course, a theory of public organization. The scraps of such a theory are present

[39]In recent years private sector workers *have* formed more coalitions across diverse occupational groups (see, e.g., Walsh's 1994 study of the airline industry) but, typically, to address common economic problems like employer bankruptcy, corporate buyouts, or allocation of wage concessions. And public workers *do* occasionally form coalitions across different agencies; typically, again, to deal with common policy concerns at higher levels of government.

in the last paragraph. The state of state theory is such, however, that developing a theory of public organization would take more than a few more paragraphs. In the interest of progress, I limit discussion here to a brief definition and come back to it again later.

I view public organization as the political solution to the problem of collective action. Public organization claims a monopoly, for a defined jurisdiction, on the ability to set and implement collective goals. *Economic* analyses of the state (and of collective action more generally) take such goals for granted; in that view, public goods as well as private interests are "goals" because they meet private preferences (Olson 1965). Action by a *public* organization, however, requires policy decisions that are framed (Goffman 1974) or defined as in the interests of the collective. This "definition process," scholars have recently acknowledged, requires close attention (Klandermans 1984; Feree 1992). This process is a complex cultural act, not merely a matter of creating a persuasive definition of the situation facing a group, but an evocation of collective identity and agency, through some legitimate decision-making process that defines the "official" policy for organized collective action. Implicit in this process, in fact, is the whole ensemble of institutions— including not only public bureacracy but structures of political participation, governance, and public consumption—which I refer to here as "public organization."

Given diversity, inequality, domination, and change, these "interests of the collective" are always elusive and usually downright false. Government policy reflects prevailing power among private agendas—including, importantly, agendas rooted in public organization itself—framed via governing coalitions or political regimes as the "public interest."[40] In the endless contest over the official definition of the public good, the purported public interest is important not because the public good can ever be truly defined but because the pivotal focus of political conflict is how and by and for whom public goods, for the purposes of policy, shall be defined. Class interests, gender interests, and political-bureaucratic interests must pass together through this lens or squeeze into this mold, since they are framed as "universalized" claims. Formal bureaucracy and scientific knowledge are especially useful in this process, because—among the many other services they provide—they are self-legitimizing, in part because they appear to abstract from private interests. Unfortunately, we have no term to refer to these "politically defined, bureaucratically administered common

---

[40]In other words, the significance of the civil service is not that it *is* a "universal class" but that it must *claim* to be. This view is consistent with Karl Marx's analysis (e.g., 1963, 1964) except that Marx failed—tragically—to consider the state bureaucracy as itself one base of societal power.

interests" around which public agencies are organized; I will call them "public needs."[41]

What set of institutions is required to accomplish and sustain this monopoly over public needs? One such institution, among many, is the public workforce. For some part of that workforce to pursue its interests, whatever they may be, it must frame those interests as public needs, and it must work the levers of power peculiar to public organization.

I will argue in the next chapter that most public sector industrial relations scholarship implicitly identifies with the regulators, the legislators, the managers, and at times the adversaries of the public workers' movement. Not surprisingly, public worker militancy is treated more as an effect than a cause, more as a dependent than an independent variable: something to be explained, and also regulated, legislated, managed, contained. These are valid positions from which to examine the evidence. I suggest, however, that it will also be useful to consider the movement as a collective *actor*. By considering it as an occasionally independent variable, so to speak, we may not only strengthen our explanations but help inform the movement itself.

[41]Marxists, ex-Marxists, neo-Marxists, post-Marxists, and recovering Marxists will have an advantage here if they consider this the statist counterpart to the commodity form. By contrast, the economist's "public good" is an aggregated individual utility function; like the Marxists' "social use value" (Wright 1985; Offe 1985), "public good" neglects the political and cultural construction of common interests for the purposes of policy.

2 *Inside the Public Workers' Movement*

Public sector labor relations in San Francisco in the 1970s attracted the attention of unionists as well as public officials and scholars not because they were unique but because they were exemplary. These developments mirrored those elsewhere, but the city also served as a "testing ground" for innovations on both sides of the bargaining table (Katz 1984:4).[1]

San Francisco was also the scene of my last few years—and of my involuntary retirement—as an organizer in the public sector labor movement. So, in several different ways, it is the starting point for this investigation: first, because events there posed the practical questions that led to this study; second, because those events led to some answers and permitted me to test them in practice; and, third, because those events resulted in my leaving union work, freeing me (or, it sometimes seems, condemning me) to study and write about it.

My personal involvement in these events invites suspicion that I am lacking in objectivity. It should, because I am. This poses a real dilemma for me: whether I mask my involvement or whether I allow it to run through the text, I am vulnerable to criticism that this is a partial history and a slanted interpretation. But so, I shall suggest, are my more conventionally detached colleagues. And although the appearance of objectivity may make an account more persuasive, it also tends to conceal (from the writer as well as the reader) the effects of one's involvement on one's research as well as on the setting under study.

[1]Katz's study of the San Francisco case reaches similar conclusions to some of those emphasized here. He found that city workers' wage relations were the result of political processes and argued that changes in union power were the result of changing political alignments. Less convincing are his warnings about the danger of private sector workers joining city workers in a general strike over city workers' issues.

This study not only originated in the setting it examines, it remains in that setting—although I sometimes took on more passive roles, examined aggregate data on behavior, and used other "objectivizing" methods. The research itself is an act of participation in the public workers' movement, influenced by and, perhaps, influencing it. There is, I observe, no radical departure here: despite its scientific and objective stance, more conventional research on public sector labor relations is embedded in this history as well.

In this chapter I locate this book in its history. I begin by describing, from the inside, problems and learning processes faced by participants in the public workers' movement. Then, writing as an observer who is also a "chastened participant," I discuss how my participation has affected this study.

"Testing Ground" in San Francisco

The early 1970s found me working as a field representative for Local 715 of SEIU, the major public workers' union in the Santa Clara Valley, some sixty miles south of San Francisco.[2] Local 715 was a new union. It had originated as a county civil service association, within which a group of union-minded members and staff had mobilized in the early 1970s. The group won leadership in the association, affiliated with the Service Employees' International Union in 1972, and began to organize other public workers in Santa Clara and San Mateo counties (*CPER* 12:39).[3]

Local 715 grew mainly by affiliating with employee associations in other local agencies and then conducting "internal organizing campaigns"—department by department, work group by work group. These campaigns centered on workplace rights[4]; occupational identity and recognition[5]; pay inequities among low-paid workers, typically women and minorities; and job reclassification schemes that provided more rewarding work, training, and better upward mobility.

[2]We called ourselves "field reps" to differentiate ourselves from the "business agents" who staffed the unions that surrounded us; our new union was, we believed, more progressive, more democratic, and less corrupt than those others.
[3]SEIU began as a private sector union for building maintenance employees in 1921 but went on to organize health care and public employees, making it the largest public employee union after AFSCME. Thanks to pioneering organizing by social workers and an aggressive affiliation strategy, by the mid-1970s SEIU was the largest public employee union in California and, after the Teamsters, the largest in the state's public or private sector.
[4]This mainly meant targeting abusive supervisors while negotiating departmental agreements establishing formal rules in place of arbitrary authority—introducing, for example, bidding procedures for desirable work and shift assignments—and rewriting civil service rules in enforceable contract language.
[5]This mainly meant coalition-building by creating structures that assured each major group its own voice in union leadership and bargaining.

The diversity of these workplaces was a defining factor in how we conducted our work. For example, the forty-five-hundred – person jurisdiction that formed the core of Local 715's membership included six different bargaining units—clerical, blue collar, and several administrative professional and technical groups—distributed across various departments of the county government. Our biggest challenge—and Local 715's major accomplishment—was to organize each group around its own issues—by job classification and classification group, by bargaining unit and department—while creating a culture of solidarity based on mutual support and a few shared issues. An eighteen-day countywide strike in July 1975, for example, involved dozens of unit-specific issues and a countywide demand for proportionately higher pay raises for the lowest-paid workers—mostly women and Latinos—through "flat dollar" rather than "percentage" pay increases (*CPER* 26:68).[6]

Despite its strength, the strike produced little more than symbolic gains. Through this experience, however, I became increasingly interested in problems of strike organization and strategy, so I paid close attention to public sector strikes whenever they occurred in the region. I visited other unions' picket lines and strike headquarters, interviewed participants, often worked on strike efforts, and compared notes with other organizers to develop a more effective model of strike organization and strategy. When I observed events in San Francisco, it was from this perspective.

The New Antiunion Strategy

A series of controversial strikes in San Francisco captured my attention—and that of every other public sector unionist in the region—in the mid-1970s. Involving almost every part of that city's thirty-thousand – person workforce, the strikes achieved notoriety with the appearance of media reports damaging to the workers and their unions. Recriminations grew as unionists crossed one anothers' picket lines in a cycle of nonsupport and union defeats.

In 1976, now a single parent with a small child to care for, I left my position with Local 715 for a part-time job in the rank and file. With a mixture of fascination and dread, I continued to follow San Francisco's series of strike debacles. (After the passage of Proposition 13 in 1978, attracted by the challenge of helping to resist a menacing trend, I would take a job with San

[6]This complex alliance required both countywide and group-specific union meetings and negotiating teams and a master contract with unit appendixes. The strength of this alliance was best expressed during the 1975 strike in the "flying squads," which would descend on a picket site for a burst of activity, "pull off" most picketers into a caravan, and gradually grow from site to site into a stream of hundreds of exhilarated clerks, custodians, heavy-equipment operators, accountants, and nurses.

Francisco's largest civil service union and so observe developments at far closer quarters.) I was not the only one taking note of events in that city. According to economist Harry Katz:

> City officials across the nation look to San Francisco for guidance in the formation of policies to be implemented in their own cities. . . . During its latest two strikes, in the fall of 1975 and the spring of 1976, San Francisco received substantial national attention as an alleged testing ground for policies directed at limiting the influence of public employee unions. Evaluating the success of those efforts will provide assistance to cities across the nation in their efforts to deal with the pressing demands placed upon them (1984:x)

This interest in evaluating the success of efforts to limit the influence of public employee unions nicely captures the managerial bias in much research on public sector labor relations. An examination of these efforts can also be useful, however, from the point of view of the labor movement against which these innovations were directed.

Why was innovation on the agenda in the first place? What had given rise to the shift in tactics?

By the time public sector unionism erupted in the 1960s, much of "unionism" in the United States had come to mean some variation on "business" or "market" unionism. Workers and their employers formed alliances with other workers and employers in the same labor and/or product markets and engaged in economic bargaining, and unions relied on economic resources to produce economic results in workers' paychecks. The defining act and the single central resource for the union was the economic strike, or the withdrawal of labor power. By the late 1960s, this unionism and the whole set of internal and external institutions associated with it had achieved a taken-for-granted status. In the common view at the time, "a union was a union was a union"—more or less militant, perhaps, more or less democratic, but still, fundamentally, a business union.[7]

As students of social movements (Tilly 1978), strikes (Waddington 1986), and organizational behavior more generally (DiMaggio and Powell 1983) have

---

[7]The United Farm Workers' Union was the critical exception in California's private sector. Since 1980, moreover, economic unionism itself has been in crisis and new unionisms are germinating in the private sector; we will return to these themes in later chapters. Social workers were an important exception in the public sector. The expansion of social work in the 1960s drew in many young radicals who pioneered grassroots labor coalitions in alliance with the welfare rights movement. Typically, however, they were insulated from the rest of the public workforce. California's social workers pioneered militancy in the state and partly for that reason were "hived off" into a single statewide local, SEIU Local 535. On Chicago's social workers, see Schutt 1986; on New York, see Maier 1987.

observed, actors tend to rely on familiar repertoires or behavioral scripts when faced with new conditions. Not surprisingly, then, as public worker militancy erupted in the 1960s, most participants automatically turned, at first, to the inherited scripts of business unionism.

It is one thing to imitate a well-established script in a new setting; it is another to sustain it in a context alien to its logic and assumptions (Powell 1991). Inevitably, many of the new public worker unionists and their adversaries in management were surprised by the unanticipated effects of their actions. As they stumbled across new dangers and, occasionally, new opportunities, participants on both sides of the bargaining table began to reconsider their assumptions and to cast about for new strategies. Nowhere was this learning process pursued with more interest and effect than in San Francisco.

As Katz observes, labor's adversaries in San Francisco learned to take advantage of the political backlash against public sector unions and strikes. Management and its allies could direct blame for the fiscal crisis, tax increases, and urban social problems away from public officials and corporate power and toward public workers and their unions. The most resonant image in this campaign was the "$17,000 streetsweeper," held up by conservative politicians and their supporters in the media and Chamber of Commerce as a symbol of the overpaid civil servant.

While spotlighting the wages of building trades union members, this campaign spearheaded a broader counterattack on the growing strength of unions in the entire city workforce. The major target of this attack was the "miscellaneous" human service workers' union, Local 400 of SEIU—San Francisco's largest city workers' union and an upstart in city politics.[8]

The antiunion campaign was led by members of the San Francisco Board of Supervisors, including Dianne Feinstein, John Barbagelata, and Quentin Kopp.[9] Among the tactics used were deliberate provocations of strikes, aggressive responses when they occurred, and skillful public relations that blamed unions for ensuing problems. These conservative public officials, allied with the Chamber of Commerce and major media sources, reaped both fiscal and political benefits by "rounding up the wagons" to defend the public treasury from the "greedy unions." In 1974, for example, a strike by teachers and miscellaneous city workers resulted in the release of raw sewage into San Francisco Bay. Public officials responded by castigating city workers and their

---

[8]This account relies on my own observations but accords with that of Katz 1984 and Boehm and Heldman 1982.
[9]Barbagelata and Kopp split from Feinstein because they refused to support her package of reforms on public employee compensation and labor relations.

unions. In the same period, Supervisor Dianne Feinstein advanced a series of antilabor ballot initiatives banning collective bargaining, sharply limiting fringe benefits, imposing salary formulas that ensured that most city workers' pay would stay below market rates, requiring the termination of strikers, and prohibiting the restoration of their seniority if they were reemployed.[10]

Elsewhere in the state, public officials monitored the debacle in San Francisco. They concluded that a public workers' strike could be a fiscal and political windfall, saving payroll costs while mobilizing a broad constituency against the union.[11] Katz concluded that

> it appears that public employee strikes are becoming a negotiation tool less attractive to employee unions and more attractive to city officials. The experience in San Francisco certainly substantiates that trend. This leads one to conclude that the Wellington/Winter argument in favor of a strike ban should be turned on its head. The choice of taking a strike may be an option that city officials are hard-pressed to do without (1984:95 – 96).

The $17,000 streetsweeper strategy was widely adopted, and public officials began to "take strikes" with increasing assurance. Strikes, which by the mid-1970s came in waves at the start of each fiscal year, surged in frequency. As John Kenneth Galbraith noted in an address at AFSCME's national convention in 1978, the vilification of public workers became a popular theme in public discourse: "Politicians now have a license to condemn all bureaucrats as a class. It is the only form of racism that is still reputable in the United States. No similar immunity is accorded the orator who condemns women, blacks, Chicanos, farmers, carpenters or even lawyers" (*CPER* 38:50 – 51).

This condemnation of public workers was a constant theme in the rhetoric of former governor Ronald Reagan as he prepared for his presidential campaign of 1980. The theme would also become important in California's "tax revolt," launched in the same period and directed in good measure against public workers. Finally, the same tactics would be deployed against federal workers during the PATCO strike debacle of 1981. That episode would prove

[10]Readers interested in the details of developments in the mid-1970s are referred to Katz's (1984) account. Randolph H. Boehm and Dan C. Heldman's (1982) somewhat jaundiced book on the same period documents the role of the Chamber of Commerce, the *San Francisco Examiner*, and members of the board of supervisors in the campaign against union power. Chapter 7 provides more details on the San Francisco case, including the years after the passage of Proposition 13 and emphasizing, for the sake of controlled cross-sectoral comparison, the mobilization of nurses in the city's health department in 1981.

[11]The neighboring towns of San Rafael and Vallejo, for example, passed measures calling for the termination of strikers immediately after San Francisco did so in 1975 (Boehm and Heldman 1982:211).

to be a pivotal event in U.S. labor history, changing the basic parameters of *private sector* labor conflict, which had been relatively constant in the postwar period.

The Promise of Public Service Unionism

Those of us who were involved in or closely observing developments in San Francisco in the mid-1970s had no inkling, of course, of what the next several years would bring. Strikes in San Francisco and similar experiences in other local governments, however, forced some of us to ask the urgent questions that launched this book: Could the walkout—the single most important weapon at the core of U.S. trade unionism—have lost its sting? This was more than a theoretical question: for unionists whose entire strategy revolved around negotiating and enforcing a contract relying on the threat of a strike, losing this weapon was an immediate practical concern. What had permitted such setbacks in that fabled "union town," San Francisco? How could we avoid them elsewhere? Was it simply that the leadership was inept and inexperienced and therefore unable to organize and conduct the strike properly? Or were the pitfalls represented by the San Francisco experience deeper and more dangerous still? Were there differences between the public and private sector terrains of labor conflict, such that this inherited model of the strike—and the unionism that depended on it—might be dangerously unreliable?

It was easy to believe that incompetence played a part in the debacle. Most public workers had no strike experience, and many of their leaders were beginners as well. Some of us, however, concluded that the problem ran deeper. This conclusion was forced on me in part, as the social scientist would say, after I tested the alternative hypothesis. Along with a circle of other public sector unionists in northern California, I learned, through experience, how to organize stronger strikes. We rediscovered lessons learned by strikers in the 1930s—lessons that were also emerging from the experience of the farm-workers' movement in California at the same time. We learned how to organize, staff, and sustain a powerful strike by tapping into the organizational capacities of the strikeforce itself—by involving strikers in building and running their own organizations. We became competent.[12] Still, more often than not, we failed to win strikes—finding ourselves fortunate, after a long and strong strike, simply to return to work with our union intact.

Not all strikes ended in defeat. Some strikes succeeded, I found, when they were able to mobilize sufficient political resources on their side and their

---

[12]The SEIU strike manual, written by the brilliant strike coordinator Shirley Campbell (1977), reflects this learning process.

adversaries failed to do the same. They lost when the reverse was the case. "Political resources" usually meant alliances: with other workers in the same political universe, sometimes with certain managers or certain politicians, and, most important, with citizen and client groups in the local political community. Workers in the same labor markets were usually irrelevant and never active players. (The private sector members of unions that operated in both sectors, for example, limited their interest to public decisions that would increase their employment opportunities, such as public contracts with unionized employers.)

Thus, employees in Alameda County generated political power (and buttressed their own morale) in a 1976 strike by emphasizing one demand: the need to increase the nurses' staffing levels so as to improve service in the public hospital's emergency room (*CPER* 32:42). Likewise, in 1979, city workers in San Mateo won a strike after they crossed their own picket lines to prevent the town's sewage treatment plant from spilling sewage into San Francisco Bay. They had learned from the widely publicized and painful experience of the miscellaneous workers in San Francisco.

As these cases suggest, these public sector unionists learned that the issues they emphasized and the manner in which they framed them were of central importance, in part because they saw how politicians skillfully used issues against them. All organizers and political activists are aware, of course, that framing issues in certain ways (for example, in the interests of the whole group) and posing questions and facilitating decisions are essential steps in mobilizing collective action. These unionists learned, however, that issues framed as in the public interest could carry weight not only with the union membership but in the larger sphere of political discourse within and around the public agency. They could not—or, at any event, did not—appeal to similar workers in the community on the basis of their common interests as workers or as members of a given occupation; rather, they allied with others in or around their agencies by appealing to other issues. Teachers and school bus drivers, for example, formed coalitions with parents more so than with other teachers or other bus drivers and built their coalitions by emphasizing common concerns about the quality of education and the safety of children.

Appeals to common concerns proved effective not only in coalition-building; they also had a direct impact on management decision-making in bargaining, on organizing efforts in workplaces, on the impact of public hearings, and so forth. While narrow economic claims could be a political liability, the same demands framed, for example, as "comparable worth" could serve as a "club" with almost palpable power.

Increasingly, then, we conducted strikes not as economic actions but as political mobilizations. Annual elections and "the battle of the budget," which annually set levels of staffing and service as well as pay, became as important as contract negotiations. While the familiar model of unionism emphasizes the need to form coalitions within labor markets, we found ourselves relying on coalitions across diverse work groups within public agencies and on labor-community coalitions in defense of public needs.

Wage demands remained important, to be sure, but they were typically framed as rights rather than as a bargained price for labor. For example, early and effective resistance to Feinstein's prohibition on collective bargaining in San Francisco came from women in the city workforce who argued that the prohibition would prevent reforms to correct gender-based inequities in wages.[13]

Campaigns conducted around election time and during budget deliberations became as important as mobilizations for strikes. Labor-management relations were not necessarily adversarial, however; that depended on what coalition governed the city agency and what alliances a union was able to join. Where circumstances permitted, alliances with elected officials were an attractive option, although relations might well be adversarial with other political forces.[14] In any case, where adversarial relations prevailed, adversarial tactics with a *political* edge were required.

Based on our observations of the events transpiring in San Francisco, I and other local public worker activists arrived at a notion of "public service unionism" that was radically different from the unionism that had been transplanted from the private sector (Johnston 1978). Thus, public workers' unions in San Francisco emerged, increasingly, as key players in the coalitions that sought to articulate the public good and shape the budget in local government. I would later learn that this unionism had surfaced again and again—especially in social workers' unions—elsewhere in the United States as early as 1965 (Maier 1987; Schutt 1986) and had received theoretical treatment in the final chapter of James O'Connor's seminal book, *The Fiscal Crisis of the State*, in 1973.

In the turbulent politics of San Francisco, the new tactics for public sector unionism were tested under very adversarial conditions indeed. In 1976, just as Dianne Feinstein's antilabor legislation seemed to be putting an end to civil service union power, hopes of a comeback rose with the election of Mayor

---

[13]Feinstein's main antagonist was an organizer for Local 400 named Maxine Jenkins (see the *San Francisco Examiner*, Oct. 13 and Oct. 24, 1974). We will meet her again and again in these cases.
[14]For example, during Moscone's tenure, city workers had nonadversarial relations with his office and adversarial relations with the bloc spearheaded by the county supervisors and the Chamber of Commerce. During the 1980s, many local government unions had nonadversarial relations with their immediate employers and adversarial relations with state and especially federal powers.

George Moscone, who represented a coalition of the city's multicultural neighborhoods and progressive unions, especially Local 400. By 1978, hopes faded with the passage of Proposition 13, which seriously cut revenue for state and local services. Hope died later that year when Moscone and Harvey Milk—the first openly gay elected official and the strongest friend of progressive unions on the county board of supervisors—were assassinated by a conservative member of the county board. (The murderer, Dan White, was a former firefighter and police officer who enjoyed a strong base of support— even after the assassination—among Irish and Italian employees in the city's fire and police departments.) Under the terms of the city charter, Moscone was automatically replaced as mayor by another conservative—Supervisor Dianne Feinstein, who had previously tried and failed to win that office by election. Remarkably, public sector unionism emerged and flourished in this adverse climate.

Public Service Unionism at the Housing Authority

One dramatic instance of the emergence of public service unionism occurred at the San Francisco Housing Authority, a microcosm of the larger city workforce. In November 1979, a labor-community coalition of housing authority workers and tenants in public housing projects struck immediately before the mayoral election. The strike was launched by plumbers and was joined immediately by other building trades work groups—each represented by its own craft union—whose relatively high wages had been targeted by city officials.

Circumstances looked grim for the unions: the housing authority had a deep budget deficit, Proposition 13 had recently been passed at the state level and other antilabor laws at the local level, the workforce was already demoralized, and the different groups of workers in the housing authority—as in the city itself—had developed a tradition of mutual scabbing. In early 1979, the housing authority in Alameda County, across the bay, had successfully imposed pay cuts on building trades employees while crushing an abortive strike by the isolated craft workers. Now the officials of San Francisco's housing authority aimed to do the same.

The hand of Dianne Feinstein—now mayor—was evident in this effort. After the assassination of the city's most prominent progressive leaders, Moscone and Milk, Feinstein had positioned herself as a centrist in her contest with conservative challenger Quentin Kopp. Thus, she sought to continue her offensive on the craft workers' wages while wooing black support by promising trainee positions in maintenance to residents of the city's public housing.

Unlike the strike in Alameda County, however, clerical and professional employees in San Francisco represented by Local 400 and led by black women, some of whom were former tenants of housing projects themselves, broke the cycle of scabbing and honored the craft workers' lines. Circumventing officials of the building trades unions, the professional and clerical employees extracted a pledge of reciprocal support directly from the craft workers. Then, a week later, they launched a strike of their own.[15]

Although the strikers made several demands, from higher wages to improved health and safety at work in the projects, they emphasized one issue: *mismanagement*. They labeled the housing authority "the worst slumlord in San Francisco" and demanded a voice in its reform. They accused their employer of incompetence and of being unable to carry out the agency's mission. They defined their strike, in other words, as a campaign for safe and decent housing in San Francisco's decaying, crime-infested projects.

Meanwhile, the Public Housing Tenants' Association (PHTA) joined the fray with a rent strike (an easy task since the rent collectors were among the strikers) and announced its own set of demands for better security in the projects. The association's participation added the political weight of some twenty thousand tenants to that of the few hundred housing authority workers already on strike, and the union members were grateful. In the middle of the strike, the housing authority's police force—seeing the direction events were moving—enrolled in Local 400 and also joined the strike.

The timing of the strike could not have been better, beginning as it did two weeks before the election between Feinstein and Kopp. Feinstein desperately needed the support of SEIU and of the African-American community, both of which supported the strike by the workers at the housing authority.

After a raucous two weeks, Feinstein capitulated, first to the demands of the craft workers and then to those of Local 400. On the eve of Election Day, more than one hundred exhilarated members of Local 400 crowded into Roosevelt Hall in SEIU's headquarters. Word was out that city officials had surrendered to the strikers' demands.

The meeting was called to order by Barbara Winters, president of Local 400's housing authority chapter and manager of a project in the Hunters Point neighborhood. She called on the negotiating committee to deliver its report for discussion and ratification. Then Mary Rogers—a social worker in the projects and a longtime community organizer with a fearsome reputation in political circles—rose to take the floor.[16] Rogers was not on the negotiating

[15]I served as staff coordinator for this strike, and this account is based on my recollections.
[16]Rogers appears as a neighborhood activist in John Mollenkopf's (1983:187) account and as a

committee but had taken charge of the food committee, which supplied victuals to the picket lines. "Madam president," she began, "a point of information. What about the tenants' association? Has the city negotiated with them yet? Have they reached a settlement?"

Representatives of the PHTA, present as observers at the meeting, as they had been at strike-related meetings and negotiations over the past weeks, now stood up. A representative told the gathering that city officials had refused even to meet with them. Rogers resumed: "In that case, madam president, I move that we not hear any report from the negotiating committee, and we not vote on any settlement, until the tenants' association has got an agreement of their own with the city."

Rogers's motion was unanimously adopted and the meeting adjourned. The housing authority workers (and I, their bemused strike coordinator) trooped back out to the picket lines. We remained there for two more days, while the mayor's representatives met with and finally satisfied the tenants' representatives. The city's union leaders were astonished, and the leadership of the craft union particularly perplexed, as their members voluntarily observed picket lines maintained by members of Local 400 in support of a rent strike by tenants of the city's projects.

With this turn of events, the morale of the workforce of the housing authority was, at least for a time, radically transformed. Union membership— previously below 50 percent—shot up to more than 90 percent. One clerical employee who emerged as chief picket captain and who subsequently served as chief shop steward recounted how "we used to chase after people to join the union and they'd say, 'I don't know, what's the union going to do for me?' Now they come to us and say 'Can I join?' and we say, 'I don't know, what you going to do for the union?' "

Another striker, a clerical employee and a former resident of the projects, marveled:

> I can't believe I'm actually proud. I mean proud of being in the union and
> what we did in the strike. We wasn't just doing something for ourselves,
> you know, but for the people in the projects, to make things the way they
> oughta be. Can you believe being proud you work at the *housing author-*
> *ity?* God, we was always *embarrassed* before!

It is difficult to imagine a more drastic departure from the recent history of public sector unionism in San Francisco or a more hopeful episode from the standpoint of public sector unionists. Furthermore, the strike was not

housing authority administrator in Richard Edward DeLeon's (1992:143 – 44) report of neighborhood resistance to redevelopment projects in San Francisco.

an isolated event in San Francisco. In 1981, the same brand of public sector unionism would emerge in a very different context: the city's five-thousand – employee health department. There, hospital-based medical interns and residents would conduct a creative "strike" against understaffing among the nurses and other health care employees. While continuing to care for patients, the doctors picketed between shifts, refused to process billing documents, and smuggled press people into the hospital to expose the medical impact of "mismanagement." Here again, the new tactics of public service unionism proved potent. The settlement agreement promised improvements in the quality of patient care—in part, by hiring more nurses and other hospital employees. It also set the stage for the nurses' strike mobilization, discussed in chapter 7.

The Reagan Realignment

Neither the new antiunion strategy nor the response of public service unionism would be sustained, however, in the following decades. Starting in the late 1970s, with the passage of Proposition 13, a substantial realignment occurred in local government politics and labor relations in San Francisco and subsequently, with the triumph of Reaganism, in the rest of the United States. Suddenly and sharply, labor-management conflict diminished. Democrats rallied the troops against Republican power, and former adversaries set aside their weapons and made common cause in defense of local government resources against fiscal constraints and political assaults from above and below.

In San Francisco, beginning in 1979, city officials, civil service unionists, and neighborhood activists joined together in defensive campaigns against annual state and local tax-cutting measures modeled on Proposition 13, or in lobbying efforts to increase state revenue-sharing or "bailouts" for local government. These campaigns created fertile conditions for the birth of new labor-management coalitions in local government.

This realignment was particularly dramatic in San Francisco because Mayor Dianne Feinstein set her sights on the Democratic vice presidential nomination for 1984. The national leadership of SEIU embraced her as its candidate for vice president; Feinstein in turn granted city locals of SEIU an agency shop clause, tripling their dues revenue.[17] Then, in 1982, the SEIU fired its staff—

[17]When a union has an agency shop clause, nonmembers must pay the union a service fee in lieu of union dues. Because only one-third of SEIU's San Francisco jurisdiction voluntarily belonged to their unions, this clause tripled the union's revenue from dues. Although some employers required (and some unionists preferred) a vote of all affected workers before the implementation of such a clause, Feinstein agreed to its implementation in San Francisco without a vote. Some of these developments are treated in more detail in chapter 7.

myself included—associated with adversarial labor relations, public service strikes, and related mobilizations.

These developments interrupted the emergence of the progressive coalition in city government. Furthermore, SEIU, the city's most politically potent and progressive union, lost much of its capacity for mobilization and alliance with community organizations. Instead, it spent the early 1980s in uneasy alliance with a conservative mayor. As we shall see, this would have fateful effects on the progressive agenda in that city.

Fault Lines in the Public Workforce

Throughout my experience in the public workforce during the 1970s and early 1980s, I confronted what appear, in retrospect, to have been consistent gender-based divisions and conflicts. During the early 1970s in Local 715 in Santa Clara County, for example, an insurgent group of higher-paid, mostly white blue-collar workers rebelled against the "bunch of *women,* nurses, and clerks" who had taken over the county employees' association and turned it into a union. The insurgents aimed to decertify Local 715 and replace it with "a real man's union," such as the Teamsters or Operating Engineers. My first assignment as a member of Local 715's staff was to contain this revolt, which was centered among several hundred men in the road maintenance division of the public works department. ("Some guy on a forklift truck," I was told, "tried to run down the last union representative who went out there.") By recruiting mostly Latino custodians, groundskeepers, park maintenance workers, and other lower-wage blue-collar workers to the unit, we were able to weaken the insurgency. It was weakened further as new leadership stepped forward among the public works employees who were willing to work with a diverse union. The insurgency was not defeated, however, until—shamed by the militancy of the women in the county's social service department—the men in public works joined Local 715's countywide strike in 1975.[18]

The ascent of women workers in Santa Clara County and their pivotal alliance with the lower-wage, mostly minority blue-collar workers in their contest with public works employees parallel events in other public sector cases we shall examine. Though they found allies (and provoked opposition) across the entire job classification structure, women in female-dominated occupations were the movers in the countywide strike. The same women played a similarly decisive role in the late 1970s through the 1980s as Santa

---

[18]The conflict still simmered, however. In *Paul Johnson v. Santa Clara County and SEIU Local 715*, public works employees' challenge to affirmative action for female and nonwhite employees would eventually reach the U.S. Supreme Court (*CPER* 64:46).

Clara County workers and their union emerged as a main political force in Silicon Valley and as the central coalition-builder in defense of the public services they produced.

The relationship between these gendered patterns of power and change in union politics and community life did not become evident until—as a sociologist—I found similar patterns in the comparable worth movement in San Jose. Then those earlier experiences in Santa Clara County—and similar experiences in the interim, as a participant in San Francisco—would take on new meaning.

One small episode in San Francisco assumed particular clarity. It occurred in 1978, immediately after the passage of Proposition 13 and immediately after I moved from San Jose to San Francisco to become a business agent for SEIU's Local 400, which serves the mostly female and/or minority "miscellaneous" workforce of the city.[19] It was not a particularly dramatic incident, but it has come to symbolize for me the contrasting trajectories of such mostly female and/or nonwhite "miscellaneous" local unions as Locals 715 and 400 compared to those in the building trades.

In the aftermath of Proposition 13, the state legislature and then-governor Gerry Brown decreed that local governments had to freeze their employees' wages as a condition of receiving state "bailout" dollars in 1978. A rare gathering of the leaders of all the city's unions, including the craft unions, the police and firefighters' unions, and the larger but lower-status miscellaneous locals, assembled in Mayor Feinstein's office to discuss the crisis with Her Honor and the president of the board of supervisors. As we waited for the city officials to arrive, the police, fire, and craft union officials began complaining about how difficult it had been to "get to" some of the members of the board of supervisors on this problem.

At first their gripes made sense: some supervisors' doors were always open to our union; others were always shut. At that point, the lawyer for the unions recalled "the old days," when "you could get to everyone on the board, and you didn't get people with these kinds of attitudes." Confused, I paid closer attention. "You can't talk to these new people," he went on. "These new guys and girls, the neighborhood types who came in with Moscone—they're all antilabor."

The officials of the craft unions muttered their agreement. The recently elected neighborhood activists on the board of supervisors were particularly obnoxious, they complained, in their opposition to downtown development. I

[19]My jurisdictions in San Francisco included clerical and blue-collar school district employees; clerical, professional, and law enforcement employees of the housing authority; and, later, clerical, professional, and technical employees in the city's health department.

was startled to realize that they were talking about our friends—women, minorities, a gay man—elected by neighborhood coalitions and by members of our union, along with members of the social workers' and hospital workers' unions. The friends of the craft unions were our foes, and their foes were our friends. As this realization sank in, the mayor and her retinue swept into the room and we turned to the business at hand.

Had I not been new to San Francisco, these differences might not have startled me.[20] Much later, however, I considered the differences as a research problem: Do different groups of public workers follow different trajectories of change in their labor relations?[21] If so, why? How does one explain the much earlier unionization and relatively favored position of building trades workers in local government? What is the difference, if any, between their position and that of miscellaneous human service unions?

The Observer as Chastened Participant

There is a convention in studies based on participant observation of including methodological appendixes in which the author steps out from behind the scenes after the performance to converse with the audience about the script and its production. Our increasing self-consciousness about cultural practices, however, includes not only a sensitivity to the traditional concerns of the participant observer, which I share,[22] but an increasing awareness of how reality is socially constructed—how the identities of actors and the definition of "the problem" are framed in social research and in public policy discussions, as well as in social movements and everyday life. As this self-consciousness grows, we become aware that the production of an account—such as this—is itself an act of participation, regardless of the degree of physical presence or "direct" involvement in the setting. Social research itself becomes participation in the field, with known effects. From this point of view, reflection on the researcher's role may belong less in a postscript and more in the center of an account.

As this chapter suggests, there is a good deal of continuity between the efforts I made to understand and respond to practical problems encountered as a participant and the research reported here. Lessons drawn in that past life were modified and supplemented, but they still appear here. Interests driving

[20]These differences run through Boehm and Heldman's (1982) account.
[21]By contrast, David Lewin (1986), for example, discusses the case of municipal sanitation workers based on the assumption that it is typical of all local government workers.
[22]How did my involvement—through my role in the setting and through the conceptual equipment I brought with me—influence what I learned? How did it direct my attention? What was concealed by this influence? What bias was introduced through its effect on the questions I considered, the answers I entertained, the data I observed and those I ignored?

that earlier effort—to clarify possibilities as well as pitfalls in the path of the public workers' movement and to help fashion a self-understanding and strategic sense to achieve the former and avoid the latter—remain as well. Although "clarifying the goals and resources" of a social movement is a justifiable analytical strategy, it can also help define and orient the movement for itself, as a collective actor. In sum, this book is an act of participation in the setting it studies, as concerned with addressing its practical problems with providing a theoretical explanation for events.

Perils of Participation

I am not the first one who has hoped to help arm a labor movement with self-consciousness. The tragic outcome of the Marxist project stands as a warning to anyone who would attempt this. The dangers suggested by the Marxist history of participation in the history about which it theorizes are similar to the dangers emphasized by sociologists who warn against "going native": (1) idealization of those with whom we identify in the field, (2) limited access and insight with respect to those in conflict with those with whom we identify in the field, and (3) the likelihood that we will join participants in taking for granted what they take for granted or lose our sense of "detached wonder" (Miller 1969:88; McCall and Simmons 1969:64). Furthermore, participants' roles influence their construction of who is an actor, what is a problem, what causal relations are important, and how to explain events—typically, in a manner that mirrors the intentional structure of their own activity in the field and precludes critical reflection on their own practice. The institutional economist, for example, might trace the episode of militancy that culminated in San Jose's 1981 strike, described in the next chapter, to the passage of labor law (probably written by an institutional economist). For the feminist comparable worth scholar, the same episode might be traced to the practices of feminist activists. As a former union organizer, my own first inclination is to attribute the strike to the work of union organizers. Coincidence? I think not.

This last point suggests that the questions we ask in a given role tend to flow from or reflect the practical stance implicit in that role. We are likely to frame certain participants as autonomous actors and others as stereotypes, as constrained by structure or as the objects of action. We are inclined to frame the choices of our preferred actors as independent variables and the outcomes of interest to them as dependent variables.[23]

---

[23]I found, for example, that accounts given by parents, teachers, union officials, school principals, and central administrators of a teachers' strike—won by the teachers, apparently because of a

These biases certainly haunted this study. My own history as a "native" of this setting is reflected in the research problems framed here. These effects were not all negative, by any means. Years of participation in negotiations, strikes, classification studies, organizing campaigns, and day-to-day representation of every kind of worker in a diverse public workplace provide an almost tactile feel for the setting and the process under study here. Insider knowledge directed my attention to processes and events that have not drawn the attention of other observers: to the shifting repertoires of public unionists like myself, for example, as we adopted and adapted models of unionism. Work among custodians, construction workers, and other blue-collar workers in several diversified workforces directed my attention to underlying patterns of alliance and conflict that have eluded other observers. Similarly, given my history as a "native" in the Santa Clara Valley's labor movement, I was naturally cognizant of the private nurses' strike over comparable worth issues, which had escaped the attention of other scholars who had visited the valley to study the San Jose city workers' strike.

The crucial challenge in taking advantage of this mass of insider's knowledge is in gaining the distance and perspective to "know what I know," on the one hand, and to "know what I don't know," on the other. It is one thing, for example, to be able to gather a collection of passive and relatively powerless individuals in fragmented job classifications into a collective actor capable of defining a common interest and wielding power to achieve it; it is another to conceptualize that process as something requiring explanation; it is still more difficult to include in that explanation things taken for granted and thus invisible from the standpoint of the participant.

Contrary to my early assumption that practical experience provided all the insight I required, much of my learning for this analysis depended on detachment, which developed over a period of time as I explored the field in ways foreign to full participants: by moving out of my active role, sifting through aggregate data, conducting fieldwork on unfamiliar cases in the role of a more neutral observer, interviewing managers and nonstriking workers as well as strikers and their leaders, absorbing work in a variety of related research traditions, attempting to apply different conceptual frameworks to the same setting, and so on.

---

parent boycott in support of the strike—told the same story but gave five different explanations. The explanations varied as members of each group attributed causality to things they did or things constraining their efforts. Teachers cited their efforts to communicate their problems to parents; administrators cited constraints on hiring substitute teachers (which produced turmoil in the schools and promoted the boycott), and so on (Johnston 1984).

Through this process, I found my image of the setting shifting in subtle but important ways. It seemed natural, for example, that after working to mobilize the public workers' movement—articulating its aims among workers, recruiting and training activists, wrestling with its goals and strategic problems, "staffing it"—I would construct public workers, their unions, and their social movement as key actors. That perspective still defines what is presented here. This point of view gradually changed, however, with a growing awareness of the structural and historical constraints that influenced public workers' behavior.

For example, I initially attributed the turn toward labor-management collaboration in the aftermath of the tax revolt and the 1980 presidential election to unprincipled or incompetent leadership; only with distance and observation of similar trends in many agencies did I grasp the historical realignment that drove these new alliances. Similarly, I grasped the significance of gendered fault lines of organization and conflict in the public workforce only when my unexpected confrontation with the comparable worth movement in fieldwork forced me to reflect on the common patterns of gender relations that I had encountered as a participant in other incidents.

Also, while I was in the midst of the public workers' movement, I idealized it. As I was drawn with that movement into the dramatic public sector politics of the period, and as I glimpsed possibilities for the creation of powerful new urban coalitions centered around this extraordinarily diverse workforce, I thought I saw a chance for the realization of that old Marxist-Hegelian dream of earthly salvation, collectively organized social self-reproduction. To be sure, I had seen enough fragmentation and conflict—public workers mobilizing in their bureaucratically defined self-interest against their clients, as well as police riots, racial exclusion, and misogyny—to know that there was nothing inevitable about this vision. The point, from my actor-centered point of view, was to help make the good things happen while avoiding the bad.

As I became more able to distance myself from my prior role, or to objectify the public workers' movement, the image of the movement as a universalistic, collective actor was supplanted by a more complex and less idealized image of the status and historical role of public workers. I make an argument here that is more consistent with these observations and more consonant with what we know about bureaucratic organization. Public workers do make universal claims, and their movement may advance us closer to a universalistic way of life. They remain, however, state-builders, pursuing political-bureaucratic self-interests even when framed as public needs; in short, they remain a flawed universal class.

Perils of Objectivity

In general, I support the rule espoused by social researchers: "Be wary of identifying . . . symbolically or emotionally with a particular group," especially in situations involving controversy (Miller 1969:88). In principle, this is sound advice. On the one hand, participation conceals even as it reveals, and it *is* easier to ask questions about a setting when we are detached from roles native to it. On the other hand, this rule offers little help for those, like myself in this case, who identify with the participants they study.[24] Further, objectivity lays a trap for the more detached social researcher, who is influenced, of course, by the taken-for-granted assumptions of *that* role—including the fatal assumption that with "objectivity" self-monitoring becomes unnecessary.

Too often, the stance of objectivity conceals deep connections between the research agenda, on the one hand, and interests located in the setting under study, on the other. Even absent overt participation or identification with one or another set of protagonists, we easily import the self-consciousness of the setting we study into our own conceptual schemes (Jepperson and Meyer 1991; Alford and Friedland 1991). Research is more readily framed and funded, of course, on the problems of more legitimate and powerful actors—in the case of public sector labor relations, legislators and managers. *Their* problems—in this case, the behaviors of workers and their unions—become our research problems, or dependent variables. Managers and legislators appear, implicitly at least, as our actors, while "those others" are more likely to be "constrained by social structure."

According to Bruce E. Kaufman, most industrial relations researchers who study strikes are well insulated from the participants:

> With the exception of a few case studies, I found no indication in all of the strike literature of the 1980s that the author's theoretical or empirical work was in any way informed by personal observation or participation in a strike, interviews with company or union officials, case studies of strikes, or descriptions of strikes in the popular press. Again, I recognize that a person can make a significant contribution to science without having experienced the event he is writing about. It also seems apparent, however, that much of the strike literature is sadly divorced from reality because the researcher has not the slightest experience or practical familiarity with the subject (1992:118).

As I've argued, even the researcher who lacks personal experience with the setting under study is not protected from the taint of involvement. The

[24]It also offers little help, of course, to the participants themselves, unless they can secure the services of a suitably detached professional researcher.

concepts we use typically reflect and reinforce the more legitimate and conventional perspectives of the more legitimate and powerful actors in the field. To the extent that our work contributes to the self-understanding of participants, justifying, influencing, even driving policy, we are actors in the field, no matter how far removed we might keep ourselves. Our choice of social research problems and conceptual strategies still frame some people as problem-solvers and others as "problems."

Despite their mainstream status, all the dominant perspectives on the public workplace are deeply involved in the setting, often to the point of explicit identification with crucial actors under study. Most of the literature in this field speaks—again, explicitly or implicitly—from the standpoint of the adversaries, managers, or regulators of the labor movement and not that of the labor movement itself.[25] Most proponents of organization theory identify with managers, to the extent that they recognize actors at all; followers of public administration theory embrace the public administrator; industrial relations scholars and institutional economists usually identify with managers, legislators, and mediators who would reconcile labor and management; and advocates of neoclassical "political market" theory identify with the privatizers of the Reagan era.

Public as well as private sector industrial relations researchers have taken especially active roles in the settings they have studied, as advisers to public officials and as authors of laws to regulate labor relations. Thus, during the early postwar era, then-influential institutional economists developed a special relationship with those lawmakers who enacted their own favorite variable: labor law. Not by chance have the fortunes of industrial relations scholars followed those of their carefully cultivated collective bargaining laws and institutions.

The "neutral" stance of lawgiver or regulator is comfortably consistent with both the image of objectivity and the dual career of academic and "manager of discontent": consultant, commissioner, and author of public sector labor law, and so on. New York's repressive Taylor Law, for example, was named for George Taylor, its primary author and one of the preeminent industrial relations scholars of the postwar era.[26] In the 1970s, as described in chapter 1, industrial relations scholars produced a great body of literature on what had to be done to limit the power of the public workers' movement (e.g., Wellington and Winter 1971; Summers 1976), and that task was subsequently accomplished. We still lack a literature, however, on strengthening the public workers' movement.

[25]Exceptions are rare and usually marginalized—Maier 1987, O'Connor 1973, and Laski 1919—and feminist students of comparable worth (e.g., Blum 1991).
[26]Two of the four other members of Taylor's drafting committee—John Dunlop and Frederick Harbison—were coauthors, with Clark Kerr and Charles Myers, of the paradigmatic *Industrialism and Industrial Man* (1960) (Donovan 1990).

From the perspective adopted here, these connections to practical issues are not fatal flaws—as long as scholars recognize how their attention has been directed and consider what is revealed and what is concealed in the process. These connections imply, though, that this book departs from conventional work less in its identification with participants than in which side it is on.

Maxine Jenkins challenges Dianne Feinstein. In 1974, San Francisco County Supervisor Feinstein proposed a ban on collective bargaining for public workers. Jenkins's campaign argued that market-based salary formulas would stand in the way of comparable worth adjustments for women in San Francisco, and the proposal was defeated. Feinstein (right rear), now U.S. senator from California, achieved prominence in the mid-1970s in a campaign against public workers' unions. Her proposal, passed in 1975, helped launch the movement that led to the passage of Proposition 13 in California and helped define the script for Reagan's handling of the PATCO strike of 1981. (See chapter 2.) Jenkins went on to lead the first strikes for comparable worth in both public and private sectors. (See chapters 3 and 5.) Photograph by Cathy Cade, courtesy of Maxine Jenkins.

San Jose city workers picket City Hall. They had already won comparable worth adjustments before their 1981 strike but used the demand as a political weapon in their strike to win a higher pay increase for all city workers. At the same time, they mobilized a labor-community coalition in defense of human services in the aftermath of Proposition 13. Despite weak organization and low participation, the strikers won. (See chapters 3 and 4.) Photograph courtesy of AFSCME, AFL-CIO.

The first private sector strike for comparable worth. Led by Maxine Jenkins, nurses struck four Santa Clara Valley hospitals in 1982. In contrast to the city workers' comparable worth campaign, the nurses did not challenge market standards but appealed to "the laws of supply and demand" in the larger RN labor market. Despite strong organization and high participation, the strikers lost. Above, Pat Smith, Candy Ascension, and Martha Sutton picket outside O'Connor Hospital, which hired permanent replacements and later decertified the union. (See chapter 5.) Photograph by Deborah Foster, California Nurses' Association.

Explaining "nurse burnout." A banner in front of O'Connor Hospital displays the formula that striking private sector nurses used to justify a market-based solution to their problem of "nurse burnout." (See chapter 5.) Photograph by Deborah Foster, California Nurses' Association.

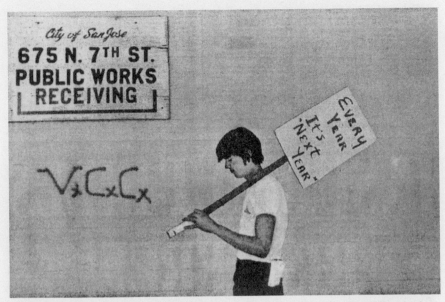

San Jose city custodians losing ground. San Jose's mostly Mexican-American city janitors served as key allies in the women's contest with public works employees for leadership in their union and in their campaign for pay equity. But although the women achieved their goals in the 1980s, most of the custodial positions were contracted out—with lower pay and without civil service or union rights—in the same period. Here, a city custodian walks the picket line at the San Jose Public Works Department. (See chapter 6.)

Public service unionism at the San Francisco Housing Authority. San Francisco Housing Authority workers and tenants conducted a work stoppage and a rent strike together in 1979. They framed their campaign—against living conditions in the projects and against a wage freeze, cuts in benefits, and layoffs—as an attack on mismanagement. After the unions won their demands, they remained on strike for two more days in support of the tenants' demands. Here, workers and tenants march to City Hall, where they deposited bags of garbage, which had accumulated in the projects, on Mayor Feinstein's doorstep. (See chapters 2 and 7.) Photograph by Charles Bolton, courtesy of Elizabeth Anello.

"Justice for janitors!" In San Jose's private sector, the custodians' revolt against an undemocratic union, weak leadership, declining wages, and disrespectful treatment by employers led to the emergence of the "Justice for Janitors" campaign in the Santa Clara Valley. They reorganized their industry and rebuilt their union, relying on labor-community coalitions, flexible strike tactics, and corporate campaigns targeting core firms such as Apple Computer. Here, 120 mostly Mexican-American janitors march through the city's downtown development district, before conducting an all-night vigil, demanding that public subsidies for redevelopment be accompanied by union recognition for janitors. (See chapter 6.) Photograph by Jim Gensheimer.

3 *The Women of the City*

My earlier involvement in labor-management conflict and controversies within labor unions in San Francisco stood in the way of my new role as social researcher, limiting my access to many informants and my ability to conduct research in that city. So, in 1986, I decided to return to San Jose, after an eight-year absence. At first I hoped to study my favorite union, SEIU Local 715, based mainly in the county workforce in the Santa Clara Valley. I quickly learned that, despite the passage of time, my earlier work on the staff of that union stood in the way of gaining full access in my new role. I reluctantly turned to AFSCME's Local 101, based mainly in San Jose's workforce.

I knew of Local 101 only indirectly, as the unenergetic union downstairs from my office in Local 715's old San Jose headquarters in the early 1970s. I recalled that during those years Local 101 had been dominated by members of the city's powerful public works department, who enjoyed a cozy relationship with the pro-growth coalition that controlled city government. Though I had followed the local's short, well-publicized comparable worth strike of 1981, I also knew that, because of the division of labor between cities and counties in California, San Jose had few of the human service workers who had played so powerful a part in Local 715, in San Francisco's Local 400, and elsewhere. I was therefore not confident of finding material suitable for a study of the public workers' movement or patterns comparable to those I had witnessed in Santa Clara County, San Francisco, and other local government agencies.

I was not to be disappointed, however. During my absence from San Jose, Local 101 had indeed undergone dramatic changes—unique events, but also changes that directly paralleled developments in other agencies.

The public workers' movement emerged late in San Jose, surfacing in the late 1970s and peaking in July 1981, in what is widely regarded as the first strike for comparable worth. This chapter provides a brief account of the comparable worth movement; it then closely examines the claims made by different groups of city workers and the resources they found effective. Chapter 4 expands the argument, seeking to explain the turn toward and then away from adversarial labor relations in the city—and to explain its distinctively gendered character—by locating it in the larger urban context. Chapter 5 compares the city workers' movement to the first *private sector* strike for comparable worth, which erupted among nurses in the Santa Clara Valley less than a year later.

The women of San Jose and their allies achieved their remarkable gains at a remarkable time: during the years immediately after the passage of Proposition 13, in the first year of the Reagan presidency. Those years were marked by an atmosphere of palpable hostility toward public employees, as exemplified by the PATCO strike of 1981. They also brought the sharpest recession since the 1930s, which intensified the fiscal crisis in local government and increased the threat of unemployment for would-be strikers.

The comparable worth strike itself was surprisingly unimpressive: it was poorly organized, had a low participation rate, and was ready to collapse after a single week. By all accounts, though, the women were successful in meeting their demands, and by all accounts the strike was a victory for the union against seemingly impossible odds. How does one account for such success? How did they win?

Again and again, scholars mistakenly refer to San Jose as the city where workers won comparable worth reforms through a nine-day strike by its employees (e.g., Shostak 1991; Freeman and Leonard 1985; Waste 1989). In fact, the leaders of the various groups of striking workers had a clear agreement that comparable worth was *not* a strike issue; they struck for a larger across-the-board wage increase. A comparable worth package had already been won before the strike through extended mobilized action—including two one-day strikes, which were in fact the first strikes for comparable worth. Only minor changes were made in the original package during the strike that followed. More progress on comparable worth came in later years, through political action that also produced a new labor-management coalition in the city. Why, then, is the strike of 1981 identified so closely with the claim to comparable worth?

Popular misunderstandings about the history of the strike are no accident, since comparable worth served as a potent *strike weapon*; misinterpretations of the strike reflect the fact that city workers used it as such. Behind the events of the strike, we shall see, lay a delicate process of issue articulation and coalition-building—skillfully accomplished by San Jose's comparable worth activists and other leaders in the city workforce. Through this process, these women wielded power while addressing the problem of unity in their extraordinarily diverse workforce. To understand how the comparable worth activists *did* win comparable worth gains in this difficult period, how they also made the claim to comparable worth into a potent weapon, and what other resources the women brought into the fray, we shall look carefully not only at the comparable worth campaign but at these women's involvement in broader political coalitions and conflicts in city government.

The account that results does not diminish the importance of the long and skillful process of mobilization by the women of the city. Rather, it shows how, in what appear to have been extremely unfavorable conditions, the women brought about a revolution in their union, secured substantial comparable worth gains, and moved from a marginalized status in city politics to being strong and welcome participants in San Jose's governing coalition.

Despite its fame, several features of the San Jose story have escaped notice. These include, for example, the history of conflict—starting long before the strike—inside the city's major union: between the women in libraries, parks, and other departments and the men in public works. This observation, which is critical to my argument, is developed in both this chapter and the next and links the comparable worth movement and the turn toward (and later away from) adversarial relations more generally to underlying tensions in the valley's changing political economy.

Another group composed mostly of male workers also makes an appearance in this account: the city's custodians. The grievances of the women of the city—and especially the librarians—had to do mainly with their status relative to that of other city workers. By contrast, the custodians, most of whom were Latino, were generally dissatisfied with conditions at the workplace. They served, moreover, as essential strategic allies to the women of the city. Unfortunately, despite their important role, *these* "symbols of solidarity" escape notice in other accounts of these events.

Also neglected in accounts of the strike is another set of achievements: the same women also mobilized to defend jobs and services in the same period—the aftermath of Proposition 13 and the early years of the Reagan administration. As this chapter and the next will show, the public workers' movement did not stick solely to collective bargaining processes in San Jose; nor did the movement revolve entirely around wage demands. Rather, it also mobilized for the *public needs* associated with the work of the mostly female parts of the public workforce.[1]

---

[1]These are some of several respects in which this account differs from the most important published study of this comparable worth movement. Linda M. Blum (1991) characterizes the public works group as a symbol of the possibility of solidarity around feminist demands, while disregarding the role of the custodians. She holds that the conflict between the city's female workers and the men in public works did not emerge until after the strike and assumes that the conflict occurred because assertive females bruised male psyches (173).

Like other organized human service employees in the early 1980s, these workers found themselves in the midst of a great political struggle over the basic direction of local government. Thus, as they were challenging the relative pay and hegemony of public works employees, the comparable worth activists were also central actors in labor-management-community coalitions asserting the political worth of their work—against well-entrenched priorities championed by public works officials and other development interests, on the one hand, and the tax-cut movements of the post – Proposition 13 era, on the other.

In this light, both the city workers' movement and the claim to comparable worth appear to have been part of a broader assertion of "the worth of women's work." The women's success culminated, moreover, in a new labor-management alliance—in which the comparable worth activists, rather than the public works employees, occupied the privileged position.

Several historical questions implicit in this account will form the basis for the next chapter's broader examination of the San Jose case. Why, for example, did this movement erupt in the late 1970s? Was it because of the earlier passage of collective bargaining law? How does one explain the very different status and roles of the mostly female human service workers, on the one hand, and the mostly male public works employees, on the other? Why did this particular movement, with its appeal to gender equity, emerge in this particular public workplace? Until we examine these historical questions closely, we will not fully understand these events. The next chapter addresses these questions by examining the relationship between the city workers' movement and the dramatic and broader developments in politics and social life in Silicon Valley. Also set aside for closer examination in a later chapter is the fate of the city's custodians.

After a summary of the case, this chapter addresses two questions: First, what were the *demands* of the city workers' movement? We know that the conventional demand for higher wages was framed as a claim to gender justice. What other influences left their mark on the workers' demands? How were wage claims, as well as the feminist impulse itself, shaped by the movement's emergence in this particular setting? To what extent did the workers limit themselves to the scope of issues inherited from the private sector, "wages, benefits, and working conditions"? What, if anything, do these demands tell us about the demands made by public workers' movements?

Second, what *resources* did the city workers' movement use? How, under adverse conditions, did the workers launch a successful campaign for comparable worth and succeed in winning their strike? This question also addresses the *strategic context* within which this movement operated, because resources are only resources—can only serve as a basis for power—in a structural context within which those particular resources carry weight. Also, because of what we might call the *power of voice* to frame the situation, define issues and interests, evoke collective identity, motivate collective action and fashion alliances, and because the assertion of demands in public organizations is itself an exercise of this power, these two questions are closely connected.

The Mobilization of the Women

AFSCME's Local 101 had its origins in San Jose's civil service employee association, the Municipal Employees' Federation (MEF). With slightly fewer than seven hundred members, the MEF affiliated with AFSCME in 1972 to form Local 101. The new union grew by incorporating other AFSCME chapters representing other public employees in the region (*CPER* 14:48, 67; *CPER* 18:41).

Until 1978, the MEF chapter of Local 101 (and, before affiliation, the association) was dominated by a well-organized bloc of about 150 employees of the public works department in San Jose. In that city, it represented a bargaining unit of about nineteen hundred clerical, professional, technical, and semiskilled blue-collar workers. The MEF remained a passive organization, however, and its membership sank over the next five years from around seven hundred to five hundred members (interviews, William Callahan, Sept. 30, 1986, and Maxine Jenkins, Aug. 20, 1986).

In 1974, Janet Gray Hayes won the city's mayoral election on a slow-growth agenda, making her the first female mayor of a large American city. In 1975 and 1976, two independent committees of mostly female employees began to organize for a greater voice in employment relations—City Women for Advancement (CWA), based in City Hall, and the Coalition of Library Activist Workers (CLAW), based in the library department. The latter group would play the more important role in the next several years and eventually assume leadership in the union.[2]

CLAW was formed to advocate for the interests of library employees and for "library issues" (e.g., funding matters and preventing censorship), and from its inception it enjoyed the tacit support of management in the library department. The library department also maintained Friends of the Library groups at every neighborhood branch, frequently led by CLAW members.[3]

CWA and CLAW included both union and nonunion members. Generally, they were critical of the union, viewing it as ineffective, dominated by the

[2]The account of CLAW's early days is based on interviews with Joan Goddard, librarian, July 29, 1986; Pat Curia, librarian, Oct. 5, 1986; David Turner, personnel analyst, Oct.7, 1981, and Oct. 14, 1981; and Mike Ferraro, library technician, Sept. 29, 1986.
[3]For an account of the development of these committees, see Blum 1991:57 – 67.

public works group, and uninterested in issues of importance to the CWA and CLAW. In 1977, increasingly beleaguered by this criticism, union officials appealed to AFSCME's regional office (or district council) for help in handling women's issues. AFSCME dispatched Maxine Jenkins to San Jose.

Jenkins had extensive experience organizing female public sector workers in San Francisco during the mid-1970s. As organizer for SEIU Local 400, she had led a successful campaign in 1974 to defeat Dianne Feinstein's first package of legislation outlawing collective bargaining for city workers, which Jenkins had defined as an attack on working women because it would obstruct comparable worth reforms.[4]

Jenkins quickly drew members of both CLAW and the CWA into a union affirmative action committee (the Women's Committee, as it became known), which she staffed. In 1978, the committee produced a position paper demanding action on working women's issues, including career ladders, comparable worth, bilingual pay for clerical workers using Spanish on the job, job sharing, flextime, and child care (Jenkins and members of Affirmative Action Committee 1978).

Reinforced by Jenkins's forceful organizing and supported by the disgruntled custodians in the same chapter of AFSCME, activists based in the libraries, parks, and City Hall gained strength in the union. Jenkins describes the change in characteristically blunt terms:

> There was a revolution in that union while I was there. The professionals run the union now, but it had been run by the public works groups, the engineering techs. They gave pretty short shrift to women . . . so I worked with the women and the custodians, and we overthrew the public works rule (interview, Jenkins, Aug. 20, 1986).

The decisive moment came during the 1978 union elections, when a male librarian won the office of president of the MEF chapter of Local 101. Public works employees responded by withdrawing from the union en masse (interviews, Tony Cokeley, engineering technician, Oct. 9, 1986, and Ferraro, Sept. 29, 1986).

[4]Jenkins was fired by Local 400 in the following year, after her organizing helped spark a rebellion by Local 400's previously quiescent clerical members against the domination of that union by supervisory, managerial, and professional groups. The biography of this trailblazing leader has yet to be written. Born in 1936 to sharecropper parents in rural Mississippi, Jenkins was a clerical worker in Berkeley, California, during the Free Speech movement; her first organizing efforts launched AFSCME's union local on the university campus in the 1960s. In the early 1990s, after the episodes described in this study, she would pioneer grassroots women's political action in California's Democratic Party. Jenkins passed away in October 1994.

Emergence of the Claim to Comparable Worth

The new union leadership immediately faced serious problems. In July 1978, the California electorate passed Proposition 13, sharply limiting the property tax revenue going to local government and launching a climate of fiscal conservatism. State "bailout" dollars, drawn from an accumulated surplus in the state treasury, were shared with local agencies on the condition that public employees' wages be frozen in fiscal year 1978 – 79. San Jose's compliance with this condition resulted in a difficult and extended negotiation process with Local 101, which remained fruitless until the following spring.

During the same period, City Manager James Alloway initiated a citywide job classification and salary standardization study of management positions by Hay Associates, the country's major firm that consults on personnel systems. Included in the study were managers in both the traditionally male-dominated agencies, such as public works, as well as units dominated by lower-status females, such as the library. Although not a systematic comparison of occupants of male- and female-dominated job classifications (and although the managers in both groups studied overwhelmingly were male), in a sense this was the first comparable worth study in the city of San Jose (interview, David Armstrong, personnel analyst, Sept. 30, 1986, and Jenkins, Aug. 20, 1986). It would provide a strategic opening for Jenkins and the new leadership of Local 101 to launch their comparable worth campaign.

On April 6, 1979, city officials agreed to enter into a new contract with Hay Associates that would focus on nonmanagement classes in Local 101's jurisdiction (interviews, Jenkins, Aug. 20, 1986, and Goddard, Oct. 2, 1986). The agreement was reached during a one-day sick-in by workers, most of whom were female, concentrated in City Hall, the library, and the parks department, and led by Maxine Jenkins. This work stoppage—involving eighty or two hundred workers, according to management and union sources, respectively— was the first strike for comparable worth in the United States.[5] Interestingly, the sick-in coincided with an unrelated sick-in on April 6 and 7 by San Jose's independent Peace Officers' Association. On the same day that the women were winning a skirmish in their battle for an upward revaluation of their work, the city police were waging a rearguard action to restore a lucrative pay formula that had been in effect until 1975 and to preserve past-practice language and other workplace rights in their agreement (*CPER* 41:31 – 32).

The next battle the women fought focused on how much the union would participate in the job evaluation process and the weight to be given in setting

[5]Because union officials freely admit inflating numbers for political effect, the city figure is probably more accurate.

wages to conventional *market standards*, based on external wage surveys, as opposed to comparisons of the job contents *across disparate occupational groups*. The city manager preferred market standards, while the union advocated the latter approach. These issues were addressed and resolved in the union's favor in a dramatic city council meeting, described below, during the city's 1979 budget hearing.

Maxine Jenkins resigned from her position in early 1980.[6] She was replaced by William Callahan, a former gardener in the San Jose Unified School District and a strong supporter of the agenda Jenkins had fashioned with the members of the Women's Committee. Callahan and the other comparable worth activists in the union's leadership hoped to bring the public works employees back into the union fold. They also hoped to complete the potentially divisive comparable worth process before it complicated wage negotiations in mid-1981.

Frances Fox, the new city manager, refused to reopen negotiations for that purpose. Then, in July 1980, city officials implemented the recommendations of the first Hay study by granting large wage increases to Fox and other city officials—immediately after raising service fees and mobilizing public opinion against a tax-cutting successor to Proposition 13 on the grounds that the city was broke. Callahan took advantage of the public protest that ensued to force Fox to agree to reopen negotiations (interview, Callahan, Nov. 12, 1986).

In December 1980, the results of the second Hay study added force to the claims of the comparable worth activists. The gender gap in wages was particularly dramatic in job classifications more than 15 percent above and more than 15 percent below the "trend line" that related compensation to job requirements: of the thirty-two classifications in the higher category, twenty-seven were male-dominated, while one was female-dominated; of the forty-six classifications in the lower category, thirty were female-dominated and only one was male-dominated (Farnquist, Armstrong, and Strausbaugh 1983).

The San Jose City Workers' Strike

The comparable worth activists in union leadership positions had hoped to arrive at a quick agreement on the comparable worth adjustments before regular negotiations began for the whole bargaining unit. By March 1981, however, as those negotiations loomed, little progress had been made. The process of mobilization intensified. On Friday, March 27, union leaders organized yet another work stoppage—"Hay fever," they called it—primarily among library

---

[6]Jenkins worked for the California Nurses' Association in southern California and then returned to the Santa Clara Valley in the aftermath of the city workers' strike to lead the comparable worth strike in 1982 by nurses in the Santa Clara Valley's private sector hospitals. This strike is discussed in chapter 5.

employees (John Spalding and Betty Barnacle, "Women Workers Strike City Hall," *San Jose News*, March 27, 1981). Though publicly described as a "wildcat strike," it was actually a union action—the second strike for comparable worth in the United States (interview, Callahan, Nov. 12, 1986; Scott Herhold, "San Jose Workers Walk Off Jobs in Pay Protest" *San Jose News*, March 28, 1981).

During the same weeks, the city was conducting budget hearings for what would be another difficult fiscal year. On the following Tuesday morning, two hundred city employees left work to demonstrate at a city council budget meeting against cutbacks and in favor of comparable worth (Philip J. Trounstine, "200 City Workers Press Equal Pay Demand," *San Jose News*, March 31, 1981).

In the following weeks union officials issued a public strike threat, although privately they had no intention of conducting a full-blown strike. They did, however, use the strike threat as a bargaining tactic. They formally requested strike sanction from the Central Labor Council, set a strike deadline of May 5, and publicized that action in a press release to local and national media in which the emphasis was on the issue of comparable worth (interview, Callahan, Nov. 12, 1986). The union generated a great deal of media attention to the strike threat, using the charge that the "feminist capital of the world" was making only a token commitment to comparable worth.

Elsewhere in the city workforce, support for the comparable worth claim was uneven. Among the mostly Latino custodians, it was unhesitating and fairly strong. They were alienated from the public works group that had controlled the union for so many years, generally disgruntled with their working conditions, and had supported the librarians' bid for leadership (interviews, Callahan, Sept. 30, 1986; Jenkins, Aug. 20, 1986; and Glenn Heath, former shop steward for the custodians, Oct. 22, 1986). The custodians' support was facilitated by their concentration at the same physical sites as the employees in the predominately female classifications and their advocacy groups: City Hall and the main library.

The custodians' grievances centered on their authoritarian supervision and a general sense of offended dignity. Also, a threat to contract out custodial positions had surfaced in early 1981, after the massive layoffs of employees hired under the Comprehensive Employment and Training Act (CETA).[7] Because custodians were among the few city classifications with wages low enough to qualify under federally imposed ceilings on CETA workers' pay, city officials had used CETA-funded jobs to expand custodial services.

[7]Funded through the Public Service Employment Program of the federal CETA program, these workers were hired by public and nonprofit agencies during the late 1970s. This part of the federal program was abolished by the Reagan administration in 1981.

The CETA cuts hit the custodians hard: approximately 15 percent were laid off and replaced with workers on private contract. Now city officials were planning to privatize more custodial jobs. In return for their support of the women's bid for power in the union and their claim to comparable worth, the custodians counted on their allies to resist these encroachments on the custodians' jobs.

Clerical workers composed the largest bloc in the bargaining unit and were the major beneficiaries of the comparable worth claim, but they participated in all these developments less than the blue-collar, professional, and technical work groups (interview, Callahan, Nov. 12, 1986). According to Callahan, the comparable worth movement and the revolt in the union more generally was led mainly by professional or semiprofessional women:

> Though they were the targeted group, clerical workers never did join the union or participate in large numbers, earlier or in the strike. We won comparable worth in spite of them. The clerks were last as far as activity goes in the membership, even behind the custodians (interview, Callahan Nov. 12, 1986).

The other major bloc in the unit was the engineering technicians or "techs" in the public works department. A semiprofessional group, the techs were overwhelmingly male, disproportionately Italian, and drawn mainly from the construction trades. They conducted building inspections and provided surveying and drafting services on local construction and development projects. This is the group that had collectively withdrawn from the union in 1978 when their representatives were displaced from leadership.

As the contract date approached and comparable worth bargaining intensified in the spring of 1981, the public works group mobilized, suddenly appeared at the April 1981 membership meeting to elect the contract negotiating committee, and rejoined the union, en masse. By packing the meeting, the techs intended to seize control of the bargaining process from the women. Completely controlling the voting process—they outnumbered all others present by a ratio of at least four to one—the public works group filled three of the four elected seats on the negotiating committee with its own representatives and the fourth with a custodian. (Two additional seats were reserved for representatives of the "confidential" unit—management secretaries and so on). The comparable worth activists were completely excluded. In an effort to counteract the takeover, union officials declared that elected chapter officers would serve on the negotiating team as well (interviews, Cokeley, Oct. 9, 1986; Ferraro, Sept. 29, 1986; Callahan Nov. 12, 1986).

In spite of their differences, the leaders of the different work groups succeeded in accommodating one another. Within the negotiating committee, the public works representatives traded their support for the comparable worth demand for support for special internal adjustments in key engineering technician classifications[8] and for a commitment to a satisfactory general wage increase for all employee groups represented by the union.

Among themselves, the leaders of the different occupational groups agreed that comparable worth would not be a "strike issue." This was no secret among the members; actually, it was an important factor in sustaining the public works employees' support. Thus, rather than progress on comparable worth, the critical bargaining goal and eventual strike settlement issue became, in a brilliant sleight-of-hand, the *inclusion of the predominately male employees* in the settlement. Recognizing the political impact of the claim to comparable worth, however, union spokespersons did not emphasize this to the press (interview, Callahan, Sept. 20, 1986).

On May 5, the union "postponed" the threatened strike. At this point, union demands amounted to $3.2 million in comparable worth adjustments over four years; the city was offering $350,000. In exchange for an agreement to combine comparable worth negotiations with regular negotiations, the city promised to increase its offer.[9] By late May, union officials had promised the male-dominated work groups that there would be no strike over comparable worth.[10]

In June 1981, to their own surprise, members of Local 101 voted unanimously to authorize a strike. This action was less a serious strike decision than a strategy to bring pressure to bear in hopes of a settlement.[11] Then, just before the July 1 contract expiration date, the Supreme Court ruled in *Gunther v. The County of Washington* that comparable worth claims could be the basis for lawsuits. Local 101 immediately filed a complaint with the Equal Employment

---

[8]The union's lead negotiator, Bill Callahan, later explained these special adjustments: "Those specials for the public works classes were totally arbitrary . . . just the price of their support for the strike" (interview, Nov. 12, 1986).

[9]According to Philip J. Trounstine ("San Jose, Union to Resume Negotiations on Pay Parity," *San Jose News*, May 6, 1981), this agreement was brokered by Mike West, now a mediator with the California State Conciliation Service. In the early 1970s, as chief staffer for the Santa Clara County Employees' Association, West had guided that organization's affiliation with SEIU and its transformation into Local 715.

[10]This important and perhaps controversial point was affirmed in interviews with Goddard, July 29 and Oct. 2, 1986; Callahan, Sept. 20, 1986; Ferraro, Sept. 29, 1986; Cokeley, Oct. 9, 1986; and Diana Wirt, Oct. 13, 1986.

[11]Conducting a strike vote several days or a week before the deadline for a strike is a common bargaining tactic; to the extent that management fears a strike, the strategy strengthens the hands of the negotiators. Informally, members are reassured that this is a bargaining tactic, told that the best way to avoid the need for a strike is visibly to prepare for one, and, if necessary, promised that another vote on management's final offer will be taken. This maneuver has the effect of creating momentum and making the decision to strike easier for otherwise reluctant workers.

Opportunity Commission (EEOC), the first step in such a suit. City officials considered this to be an act of bad faith and broke off negotiations on the comparable worth issue (interview, Armstrong, Oct. 7, 1986).

In retrospect, the city was probably justified in its reaction, since negotiations were well advanced and significant progress had been made on the comparable worth agenda during June. The union, however, was unprepared to settle because members were generally dissatisfied with the across-the-board wage offer. Filing the complaint with the EEOC was a bargaining ploy intended to gain support for the union's main objective at that point: getting a higher across-the-board increase (interview, Callahan, Nov. 12, 1986).

The strike commenced on July 5 and lasted until July 14—seven workdays.[12] In organizational terms, the stoppage was weak. Although union statements and most published reports placed the number of strikers at 1,500, the actual number was between 350 and 450: no more than 25 percent of the 1,900-person bargaining unit.[13] In the opinion of its leaders, the strike probably lacked the strength to last through its second week (interview, Callahan, Nov. 12, 1986). The strike leaders also lacked internal organization, so that one staff person attempted to coordinate both bargaining and picketing simultaneously, while rank-and-file negotiators simultaneously attempted to lead field activity.

Despite its weaknesses, however, the strike was politically strong. It drew national public attention through intense media coverage, which dominated the local news, and drew prominent attention nationally (*CPER* 51:2).

The key unresolved issues at the outset of the strike were the amounts of the general wage increase, the comparable worth adjustments, and the other special wage adjustments or "internal alignments" for individual classifications, including the engineering technicians. The formal city offer that the strikers rejected would have provided 4.5, 5.0, and 5.5 percent general wage increases over three years; three days after the strike began, they also rejected an offer of 6 percent for each of two years.

The union also refused an offer for comparable worth adjustments over two years, variously valued at between $1.3 and $1.5 million, which would have brought the wages of workers in female-dominated classes halfway up to, or within 10 percent of, the trend line. City and union representatives agreed, in general, on the terms; they also agreed that full pay equity should be achieved

---

[12]Strike developments are described in *CPER* 49:16 – 18 and 50:18 – 20.
[13]See, for example, Stephen Magagnini, "Equal Pay for Women: 1,500 City Workers Walk Out," *San Francisco Chronicle*, July 6, 1981; "San Jose's Equal Pay Issue Spreads to S.F.," *San Francisco Examiner*, July 8, 1981; and Ed Pope, "Strikers Vote Down Latest Proposal," *San Jose News*, July 8, 1981.

through another set of adjustments during a second two-year period. The city proposed to negotiate the further adjustments in the subsequent two-year agreement, whereas the union maintained that the current agreement should specify adjustments for the third and fourth years.

Also important—though less public—was the union's concern that the comparable worth study had justified large adjustments for workers in some female-dominated classifications with whom the union enjoyed little support—such as the accounting technician classification—but relatively small adjustments for others with whom it enjoyed strong support—such as account clerk II (Farnquist, Armstrong, and Strausbaugh 1983:365). Again, the union's negotiators and strike leaders had clearly agreed among themselves that problems related to comparable worth would not be allowed to stand in the way of a settlement.

The final settlement was a two-year agreement that contained 7.5 percent and 8 percent general pay increases (in contrast to the rejected prestrike offer of 4.5, 5.0, and 5.5 percent over three years) and comparable worth adjustments valued at $1.45 million.[14] The earlier management offer had been changed slightly to favor employees in more highly unionized classifications; it also included extra pay adjustments for some male-dominated blue-collar/technical jobs. A tentative settlement, reached after five days on strike, would have extended the city's commitment to make comparable worth adjustments for two more years; however, the city council rejected that proposal (interview, Callahan, Nov. 12, 1986; Armstrong, Oct. 7, 1986; Goddard, Oct. 2, 1986). Finally, then, although the strike was the climax to a successful campaign for comparable worth, its main accomplishment was that it led to increases in the city workers' general wages.

Aftermath of the San Jose City Workers' Strike

Labor-management conflict in San Jose was not over when the strike was settled. After all, the city had committed only to moving the women in the city's workforce to within 10 percent of the trend line identified with gender equality. Further, immediately after the strike and in the throes of the "Reagan recession" of 1981, the city faced its most drastic fiscal crisis. The mayor and the city manager, against whose leadership the strike had been directed, proposed that the agencies whose employees were most visible during the strike—specifically, the parks and recreation department and the library department—be merged into one agency (interview, Ferraro, Sept. 29, 1986).

[14]Subsequent budget data showed the real cost of these adjustments to be only $1.124 million. As Janet A. Flammang (1986) notes, the $1.45 million projection was inflated because it assumed a zero vacancy rate in city positions.

The city officials underlined the expendability of these departments by proposing that the new agency be called "Leisure Services" and that the total funding be 59 percent less than the former budget for the two agencies combined. "It was sheer vindictiveness," according to then vice mayor Jerry Estruth. "The top city staff recommended we go after the programs that would hurt Local 101 the most" (interview, Estruth, Nov. 4, 1986).

This assault galvanized groups in and around these departments, especially the Friends of the Library, based at most branches, the leaders of the now highly mobilized union, and the management of the new agency. The labor-community-management alliance that emerged had the capacity to turn out hundreds of citizens to crucial budget hearings. The proposed reorganization was defeated, and reductions were rolled back to 10 percent for the library and for the parks and recreation department (interviews, Goddard, July 29, 1986; Ferraro, Sept. 29, 1986; Estruth, Nov. 4, 1986).

At the peak of the intense budget negotiations with the city council, the union cemented an alliance with Tom McEnery, a city council member who emerged as a mayoral candidate to succeed Janet Hayes. In intimate communications during the budget battle, union officials and McEnery arrived at an understanding: if elected mayor, he would implement comparable worth adjustments for a third and fourth year, restore and protect funding for the libraries, and adopt an agency shop plan requiring nonmembers to pay service fees to the union (interviews, Callahan, Sept. 20, 1986, and Ferraro, Sept. 29, 1986).

In the election, McEnery faced Claude Fletcher, a conservative member of the city council associated with the growth-at-any-cost cabal in city politics. He had been adamantly opposed to the union and to the comparable worth concept during the strike the previous year.

Relying in part on the heightened capacity for mobilization evident during the strike and the budget crisis and on the Friends of the Library neighborhood infrastructure, the union galvanized a large cadre of volunteers to work for McEnery. Fielding fully half the precinct workers in the campaign, the union emerged as an important political player.

The local was able to claim some credit in the subsequent victory and to hold McEnery to his commitments. Thus, in 1983, the new mayor continued the process of comparable worth adjustments, restored lost positions in the libraries, and adopted a "modified agency shop" provision.[15]

[15]The modified agency shop provision adopted in San Jose requires only new employees, as opposed to all nonmembers, to pay a service fee in lieu of union dues. The result is a steady increase in union revenues with normal turnover and minimal resistance, since dissatisfied employees do not have to join the union.

After the election, lobbying and collaborative problem-solving prevailed over adversarial relations, and no serious strike threat was made in subsequent contract negotiations.[16] When I visited San Jose in 1986, Local 101 was ratifying a new agreement that included $541,685 in pay equity adjustments, to be implemented over the subsequent two years. The adjustments were intended to bring women in the female-dominated classes to within 2.5 percent of the trend line, which the parties agreed would amount to pay equity (*The Moose* [internal union bulletin], July 1986). The agreement also included another quid pro quo for those in the public works classifications: $282,399 in internal adjustments for workers in blue-collar and related positions in construction and purchasing.

After McEnery's election, the union returned to a stance reminiscent of its preunion days as an employee association and its early days as a nonadversarial union. Now, however, leadership was centered in the groups associated with the old CLAW and CWA and their allies, rather than with the men from public works. Also during this time, the city continued to contract out custodial positions as they became vacant, so that by 1986 the custodial workforce was reduced to only 30 percent of its size five years earlier.

By the early 1980s, the alienation of both the custodians and the public works employees from the union's leadership was such that both groups soon sought, in separate developments, to have the union decertified (interviews, Cokeley, Oct. 9, 1986; Heath, Oct. 22, 1986; and Goddard, July 29 and Oct. 2, 1986). The public works employees withdrew—again—en masse, whereas the custodians remained in the union during the decertification campaign, which was led by their shop steward.

In both cases, city officials determined that the work groups did not possess sufficient community of interest to merit their own bargaining units, and, accordingly, their petitions for decertification votes were denied.[17] In the case of the custodians, the union leadership also abolished their right to elect shop stewards, and city management transferred the disgruntled former shop steward out of the bargaining unit.

Making Demands on Public Organization

Claims made by social movements reflect the context within which and against which they emerge. Content aside, demands are framed in distinctive

[16]For information on this period, I relied on interviews with Callahan, Nov, 12, 1986; Armstrong, Oct. 7, 1986; Ferraro, Sept. 29, 1986; and Goddard, Oct, 2, 1986.
[17]Under California's local government collective bargaining law, the employer doubles as a regulatory agency or surrogate for the National Labor Relations Board (NLRB); consequently, the employer rules on the appropriateness of proposed bargaining units.

forms, reflecting the institutions within which needs are defined and met, or the way of life within which they are produced and reproduced. Social movements are influenced as well by other familiar institutions that frame needs in other forms. In San Jose as elsewhere, for example, the public workers' movement inherited a set of operating assumptions about appropriate union claims from the dominant economic model of the union formed in the postwar private sector of the United States. The public workers' movement was notable, however, in that it departed from these assumptions.

The notion that there is a peculiar form of demand native to the public workplace does not mean that other influences will leave no mark.[18] It does imply, however, that there will be a tendency for claims to reflect the assumptions embedded in public organization; that claims will meet with management responses, both favorable and unfavorable, which will assume a form peculiar to the public workplace; and that public workers are *constrained*, by this dialogue of demand and response, to frame their claims in terms native to the public workplace.

The gendered content of the claims of city workers cannot be explained without reference to the specific historical conditions within which the claims emerged. At the same time, the demands assumed a form that reflected the more general logic of public organization common to public workers' movements under other conditions. In San Jose, for example, claims were framed as appeals to univeralistic or otherwise legitimate norms, including formal-rational or administrable policies, and as demands to sustain, improve, or expand provision of the public services associated with the mission of the agency involved.

Wage Claims in Political Bureaucracies

Even before the arrival of Maxine Jenkins, and before the emergence of the claim to comparable worth in San Jose, the women's demands reflected the features noted above. Upon its formation, for example, CLAW defined itself as advocating for "library issues," including the occupationally rooted, universalistic "public good" widely embraced by librarians—freedom from censorship—and maintenance and expansion of library services.

CLAW's first campaign was for special salary adjustments for employees in some senior clerical and paraprofessional classifications. The claim was justified on the basis of salary compaction, which had been caused by the creation and insertion of new classes in the classification structure (interviews, God-

---

[18]City workers' repertoires also echoed the influence of older civil service associations, the civil rights and antiwar movements, the California farmworkers' movement, neighborhood movements, and, of course, the feminist movement.

dard, July 29, 1986, and Ferraro, Sept. 29, 1986). As a demand for an "internal adjustment," this pay demand was framed—specified and justified—in the quintessential bureaucratic logic of position classification and salary standardization. The demand referred, that is, not to prevailing wages in the labor market but to the relative standing of those in these job classifications within the civil service bureaucracy.

Similarly, when the public works employees who controlled the 1981 negotiating committee in San Jose exacted their quid pro quo for comparable worth, they framed their claims based on these politics of internal alignment. Demands for such internal adjustments are characteristic of demands in public worker bargaining, reflecting an orientation not to the labor market but to the politically defined, administratively regulated universe of the bureaucratic classification structure.[19]

From the beginning, the women's demands were framed as appealing both to these norms of administrative due process and to gender justice. In its 1978 position paper, the Women's Committee produced a set of claims for advancement, higher wages, and other changes in work arrangements in the interests of women and working mothers in particular (Jenkins and members of Affirmative Action Committee 1978). Most of their demands were for modifications in the system of personnel administration; thus, they had to do with career ladders, comparable worth, job sharing, flextime, and the designation of bilingual skills as a competency meriting additional pay. Each claim also appealed to norms of gender equality, which had become highly legitimate in the country's first large city with a female mayor and, by 1981, a female majority on the city council.[20]

Framing their demands in terms of norms of gender justice helped mobilize the women of San Jose while also serving as a political weapon. Again and again, Mayor Janet Hayes found herself called upon to give substance to her oft-quoted remark that, given the gender distribution of its public officials, San Jose was now "the feminist capital of the world."

Why did *comparable worth*, of all these claims, assume a special significance in the next several years?[21] And later—given that the main strike issue in

---

[19]The appendix discusses the relationship between classification and salary standardization in public employment and comparable worth.

[20]Interestingly, the main conceptual framework reflected in the 1978 position paper was not feminist theory or comparable worth literature but Harry Braverman's (1974) Marxist labor process theory, which emphasizes the degradation or proletarianization of clerical work.

[21]Linda M. Blum (1991) answers this question by referring to the women's disillusionment with affirmative action. In fact, the Women's Committee also proposed upward mobility/affirmative action. Blum underestimates, in my view, the importance for women of "upward mobility agendas" in the public workforce and the potential significance of those agendas for restructuring work, learning, and advancement in public organizations. Her account is oriented to a debate in feminist theory (e.g., Gilligan [1982] versus MacKinnon [1989]) in which comparable worth is related to

1981 was the across-the board wage increase, while leaders of different occupational groups explicitly agreed *not* to strike for comparable worth—why was that strike nevertheless framed as a strike for comparable worth?

There are strategic and institutional answers to these questions, rooted in the internal politics of public bureaucracy. There are also historical and structural answers, rooted in the larger political-economic context. The political force behind the claim to comparable worth in the public sector derives in good part from its link—often unrecognized, even by participants—to a broader mobilization of interests associated with gendered human services and neighborhood resources. Equally important, however, is the affinity between the claim to comparable worth as it has emerged in the public sector and the public sector's own distinctive political-bureaucratic personnel system. Through the claim to comparable worth as it appears in the public sector (including legal challenges to private sector wages), the feminist impulse harnesses bureaucratic personnel administration to challenge the gender-biased labor market.[22]

Reflecting its affinity with public organization, the comparable worth movement in the public sector is partly led by professional personnel analysts (Johansen 1984). The receptivity of the public sector personnel system to the claim to comparable worth was evident in San Jose in the role played by the primary personnel analyst staffing comparable worth activity on the *management* side of the table.

During the long process of mobilization and bargaining leading up to the comparable worth study, during the study itself, during the subsequent negotiations and strike, and during the equally important aftermath to these developments, personnel analyst David Armstrong bore major responsibility as technical staff person on the city's management team. According to one researcher, Armstrong's participation in the process was the single indispensable element that led to the successful adoption and implementation of comparable worth principles in the city (Flammang 1986).[23] Comparable worth

---

"valuing women's difference" and (falsely, in my view) counterposed to affirmative action.

[22]The early emergence of comparable worth efforts in the private sector under the "statist" aegis of the War Labor Board during World War II is a case in point (Milkman, 1987). For further discussion of this issue, see the appendix. Compare this view with that of Joan Acker (1989), Sarah M. Evans and Barbara J. Nelson (1989), and Linda Blum (1991), for whom comparable worth represents the intersection of capitalism, patriarchy, and the resistance evoked by each, while public organization appears only as an untheorized context.

[23]Curiously, Flammang does not consider the role of nonmanagerial participants, such as Bill Callahan or Gerry Brown, both of whom played essential roles in the comparable worth effort; they were responding, though, to the initiative of Jenkins and the small circle of women and men who assumed leadership in Local 101 in the late 1970s. I have encountered enough people like Armstrong to suspect that, although his presence was essential, similar individuals can be found in most major public agencies. Jenkins was a rarer breed.

activists themselves agreed, in retrospect, that Armstrong's involvement was crucial to the success of their efforts (interview, Goddard, Oct. 2, 1986).

Armstrong's neutrality and his adherence to the norms of rational personnel administration were among the reasons his participation was so useful to the comparable worth movement. In an interview (Oct. 7, 1986), he told me:

> Our job was technical: to implement, not to make policy. We were willing to apply whatever standards management settled on for salary setting. . . . We don't make the rules here; we just follow them. If the city wants to change the criteria, fine; if that's what they want, that's what I'll do. They want to use market rates, we use market rates. They want to do comparable worth, we do comparable worth.

But despite this stance of principled neutrality, Armstrong and others in the city's personnel department had their own stake in the comparable worth project. First, staff analysts, who were in a predominately female job classification in the personnel department, anticipated that they would share in the wage adjustments. Second, Armstrong and his staff were eager to learn through the Hay Associates study about "state-of-the-art" job analysis and evaluation methods. Third, Armstrong and the rest of the staff of the personnel department wanted to overhaul the old patched-together classification system for non-managerial as well as managerial ranks. Conducting a citywide study provided not only a basis for cross-benchmark salary standardization but an opportunity to clarify and "clean up" its classification structure, which had become "messy" as a result of decades of growth and change. Implementing a comparable worth agenda provided the personnel department with the resources to rationalize the classification system and strengthen its own position in the process.[24]

In sum, the city workers' wage claims were directed at the bureaucratic personnel system. They appealed to *legitimate standards*, in this case, unbiased job evaluation, equal treatment, and gender justice. Other wage claims in public organizations—for internal alignment, for example—appeal to some of the same authority. Even the more familiar demand for prevailing wages should be seen in this light: the claim to "prevailing wages" is asserted less as a market standard than as a principle of "good government."

In asserting the women's claims to comparable worth, moreover, Jenkins repeatedly denounced what she termed "the market standard." This theme

[24]As Elaine Johansen (1984) notes, the network of women working in personnel administration at the state and federal as well as local levels was an important channel for the comparable worth or pay equity movement (see also Freeman 1973). This movement displays the pattern associated here with public workers' movements: here too the feminist impulse is expressed within the logic of political bureaucracy, and here too public workers assert public needs associated with their own work—in this case, personnel administration.

was particularly clear during a turning point in the comparable worth campaign, the dramatic city council meeting in July 1979.

Among the items under discussion was the contract with Hay Associates for the study of nonmanagerial employees. In making his case for the proposed study, the city manager emphasized that labor market wage comparisons would be an integral part of the study and that consequently it would not resolve the concerns of "some women." In other words, the city manager planned to use labor market standards to set wages in the city, rather than rely on cross-series comparisons of different city worker jobs.

Next, Maxine Jenkins rose to speak for "the women of the city." The seven-person council she addressed was chaired by a female mayor, two other women, and four men, two of whom considered themselves feminists.[25] Jenkins delivered an eloquent appeal for gender equality and denounced "the market standard": "comparing depressed wages to depressed wages that are artificially depressed not because of the value of the labor but because most of the people doing the work happen to be women." She also appealed to the "objective, scientific" validity of comparing the relative worth of workers in disparate job classifications.[26]

By repeatedly posing pointed questions, Jenkins virtually took over the meeting, requiring the mayor, the council, and the city manager to respond and justify their position regarding use of the market standard. The mayor equivocated, sided with the city manager, and finally said that market wage comparisons should be in the study but "deemphasized." By then, however, Jenkins had gained a public commitment from the majority of the council to disregard the market standard.

Equal Treatment

The city workers' wage claims all appealed to standards of procedural justice and equal treatment among workers, through the unbiased application of formal procedures for setting salaries. The same standards could also be used to challenge racial inequality; that issue, however, was largely ignored during this history. The issue surfaced only in a position paper by the affirmative action committee on the need to recognize and pay additional wages to

[25]None of the women called themselves feminists. That's one of the characteristic features of what I call "grassroots" feminism. By the time of the strike in 1981, the council was restructured, with the implementation of district elections, so that its twelve members included seven women and five men.
[26]Blum (1991) aptly relates the claim to comparable worth to ideologies of science and rationality and notes the force of discursive practices in the movement. My argument—based on a comparison of this case to the private sector nurses' strike—is that these ideologies are particularly powerful in public organizations and that these practices carry a special force in public sector labor conflict.

workers who were bilingual.[27] When layoffs were imposed in the early 1980s, however, city management, not the union, moved to make bilingualism a factor in layoff, thereby protecting some lower-seniority Spanish-speaking employees (interviews, Rita Torres, library employee, July 23, 1986, and Goddard, July 15 and July 29, 1986).

The demand for equal treatment of managerial and nonmanagerial employees proved to be essential to progress on the comparable worth agenda. Alloway's decision to conduct the citywide study of management, for example, provided a natural opening for the members associated with the Affirmative Action Committee, now in union leadership, to demand a study of nonmanagers using similar methods (interview, Jenkins, Aug. 20, 1986). Thus, the first strike for pay equity between men and women, on April 6, 1979, was also a strike for equal treatment of nonmanagerial and managerial employees.

A comparable moment, which arose as the study of nonmanagerial employees was being completed in 1980, demonstrates not only the force of the demand for equal treatment but the power of publicity and the extent to which developments involving Local 101 were affected by the broader politics of public services and the fiscal crisis in San Jose. Because the current bargaining agreement would expire in mid-1981, bargaining for the entire unit would begin again early that year. Union officials were painfully aware that if negotiations on general raises and on comparable worth raises were combined, any special increases could well be interpreted as subtracting from the general raise, with disastrously divisive effects. Negotiations over comparable worth raises, they feared, could undermine their efforts to induce the public works constituency to rejoin the union. Also, on January 1, a new council, elected under the new system of district elections, would be seated, replacing the older body and quite possibly not bound by the previous city council's public commitment to comparable worth. Union leaders hoped, therefore, to commence and complete negotiations for comparable worth adjustments, based on the second Hay study, outside the regular bargaining process and by the end of 1980.

In mid-1980, the union proposed to city officials that there be a wage "reopener" to address the results of the Hay study on nonmanagerial workers. Frances Fox, the new city manager, rejected the proposal. Further, he refused to agree that the recommendations of the study would be negotiable or even published, much less implemented. Not surprisingly, he wanted to keep these cards to play in the 1981 round of negotiations (interview, Armstrong, Oct. 7, 1986).

[27]The change in the name of the union committee from the Affirmative Action Committee to the Women's Committee may imply, as Blum suggests, frustration with the affirmative action agenda. It also affirms, of course, that racial discrimination was a neglected issue.

Then, in mid-1980, the comparable worth project received a strategic boost and upper management's political legitimacy a severe blow. In the June elections, California's public sector faced Proposition 9, a Proposition 13 – style tax-cutting initiative. Throughout the state, local government officials, public service advocates, and organized public employees mobilized to oppose the measure. In San Jose, city officials, citing the already severe fiscal crisis, imposed stiff new user fees on public services and predicted an even worse budget deficit and service reductions if Proposition 9 was passed.

Proposition 9 was defeated. Immediately afterward, city officials discovered that there was a surplus in the city's budget after all—enough, in fact, to finance the pay increases for management that the Hay study had recommended. On Fox's recommendation, the city council acted to raise managers' pay to 10 percent *above* the trend line "in order to attract and retain the best managers." These raises, granted in addition to the annual pay raises all city employees received, ranged from 2 to 30 percent and averaged 14.7 percent; Fox received an annualized raise of $13,000 ("Big Bucks for the Brass at City Hall" [editorial] and "Here's What Top City Execs Will Make after Pay Hikes," *San Jose News*, July 3, 1980). The juxtaposition of the pay raises and the increase in user fees for public services provoked widespread public outcry, which climaxed when thousands of San Jose residents for the first time had to pay four dollars to see the city's Fourth of July fireworks display. (See, for example, "Letters to the Editor," *Mercury-News*, July 6, 1980, under the heading "City That Cried 'Wolf' Spends Surplus in Fat Cat Raises.")

According to Callahan, this created a strategic moment for the union to demand and win "equal treatment." Then Local 101's chief negotiator, he stormed into Fox's office and confronted him with a copy of a newspaper article describing the public anger over the managers' raises. Again according to Callahan, he threw the newspaper down on Fox's desk and threatened to return with a crowd to Fox's office and hold a press conference there denouncing the raises—unless Fox signed a letter of agreement committing the city to negotiate on comparable worth raises upon the conclusion of the Hay study. Callahan had brought a letter of agreement with him, and Fox signed it (interview, Callahan, Nov. 12, 1986).

Public Needs and the Battle of the Budget

The mobilization around the issue of comparable worth—and around collective bargaining more generally—was only one dimension of the public workers' movement in San Jose. The late 1970s and early 1980s were also, of course, the era of Proposition 13 and its aftermath: the "taxpayers' revolt," the assault on social services and public workers, the rise of Reaganism, the era of fiscal austerity. City workers thus found themselves deeply involved in the battle of the budget. Whereas internal conflicts around wages and working conditions tended to appeal, as we have seen, to formal standards of due process in public administration, on the budget front workers asserted public needs associated with their own work.

Like the comparable worth campaign, the workers' movement to protect human services can be traced to the mid-1970s. The earliest efforts had emerged spontaneously in San Jose's newer neighborhoods, as residents— mostly women—organized to get more city services.

The staff of the new facilities that emerged as a result of this effort— community centers, parks, libraries—became leaders during the fiscal crisis. Librarians and recreation directors—the same people who, along with several women in the less-organized clerical workforce, would become the vanguard of the drive for comparable worth—worked closely with department managers to set up the neighborhood-based Friends of the Libraries and Friends of the Parks, which were able to mobilize major crowds at budget hearings (interviews, Goddard, July 29, 1986, and Ferraro, Sept. 29, 1986).

In the immediate aftermath of Proposition 13, and again with the economic downturn of 1981, San Jose's city budget was once more operating at a deficit. Also, increased local reliance on annual budgetary decisions at the *state* level—always uncertain until the last moment—combined with a series of annual efforts to deepen the tax cuts through new voter initiatives and with annual projections of massive layoffs to create an *atmosphere of crisis* around the budget. In particular, as city revenue fell with the economy during 1982, and San Jose's major industry, electronics, reeled under the impact of new foreign competition, massive layoffs were imposed. According to union leader Mike Ferraro, the library department alone lost 20 percent of its positions from 1979 to 1983. As described above, labor-community coalitions against these cuts absorbed much of the union's energy in this period.

Political mobilization in defense of jobs and services came to define Local 101's agenda in this period. Even in the midst of the comparable worth negotiations, the budget battle remained important. The achievement of comparable worth under these crisis-ridden conditions makes the power these workers and their union wielded all the more significant.[28]

---

[28]Blum minimizes the city's fiscal crisis, suggesting that its strong fiscal position explains the comparable worth victory in a time of general fiscal crisis. However, city employment had reached 4,303 by the 1977 – 78 fiscal year; by 1979 – 80, it had been slashed to 3,842. The state bailout and other measures allowed some positions to be restored in the next few years, but by 1982, employment was cut again, to 4,024 (U.S. Department of Commerce, *City Employment*).

By the end of the 1970s, union activists based in the libraries had assumed top leadership roles in Local 101. Not surprisingly, then, preventing layoffs and protecting the library budget became a high priority. Ferraro recalled: "It became clear to us that the budget was becoming the real battleground, more than the negotiating table. If they can eliminate big pieces of your membership and your leadership, what you do at the bargaining table is not all that important" (interview, Sept. 30, 1986).

During the era associated with the comparable worth gains, the battle of the budget did become at least as important as issues on the bargaining table. Annual budget hearings provided a visible arena for the convergence of claims made on both fronts. For example, four days after the "Hay fever" work stoppage of March 27, 1981, some two hundred city employees left their jobs to fill the city council chambers for a hearing on the pending budget. The mostly female clerical and semiprofessional crowd demonstrated, chanted, and vigorously applauded their representatives as they spoke in favor of funding for the services city workers provided and in favor of comparable worth pay adjustments (interview, Callahan, Sept. 30, 1986). The buttons they wore succinctly summarized how these issues converged: "I am a budget priority" (Philip J. Trounstine, "200 City Workers Press Equal Pay Demand," *San Jose News*, March 31, 1981). In sum, because of the threat to their jobs, the interests of the city workers became identified with the defense of the public needs they produced.

Wielding Power in Public Organization

Not only the demands but also the *powers* of social movements reflect the context within and against which they mobilize. Differences in "what delivers power" for contests in different sectors of employment can be as sharp as, for example, the strategic differences in military contests fought on different kinds of terrain, or on land versus sea. Differences in the levers of power—how decisions are framed, how resources are allocated, how conflicts are decided—depend on differences in the strategic terrains of contest. There is no assurance that participants will use strategies suited to the terrains they face; frequently, they do not, as scripts for strategic action rooted in other institutional settings influence participants' assumptions and behavior. But if all participants involved share assumptions—even false assumptions—about what delivers power and act accordingly, threats to use those resources will indeed deliver results—at least for a time.

The powers of the public workers' movement are closely related, then, to the anatomy of public organization. These powers include, first, formal rules and rights defined in official policy; second, strategic alliances within a given political universe; third, what I call here, to use Albert O. Hirschman's (1970) term, "voice." This last resource plays a peculiar part in public organization and related settings, since it is used to participate in public discourse: to define policy and interpret law, to direct attention toward certain questions and away from others, to frame questions and influence decisions about them, to evoke collective identity, and to inspire collective action. The force of voice in this setting depends, in part, on the movement's ability to define private interests in universalistic or otherwise legitimate terms by framing them directly (e.g., need for libraries and clean air) or indirectly (e.g., due process, good government) as public needs.

The women and men who mobilized in defense of city services were also capable activists. The core group from CLAW had no private sector union experience, but some had participated in other social movements. They displayed a keen grasp of their own strategic terrain even before Jenkins's arrival. Their turn toward militancy took place relatively late compared with other local government agencies in California, and they benefited from their late involvement. By 1978, when the women were gathering steam, they reaped the lessons of a decade of militancy by other public workers. Maxine Jenkins, for example, brought to San Jose a wealth of experience in public sector organizing from her days in San Francisco.

CLAW's first campaign displays these activists' early understanding of the strategic context of political bureaucracy. Though based mainly among librarians, it focused not on the status of librarians as an occupational group but on achieving an internal wage adjustment for workers in some clerical and paraprofessional classifications. In this small campaign, the group used all three of the resources noted above. First, they appealed to formal standards or official rules for the alignment of related classifications in the civil service system. Second, according to participants, they selected the issue of alignment in a deliberate effort to broaden CLAW's base by allying workers in professional and nonprofessional job classifications. Third, they demonstrated how the articulation of a demand can serve as a strategic resource—in this case, for coalition-building.

Again and again in the next several years, the activists involved in the public workers' campaign displayed their effective strategic repertoire: finding themselves in a fragmented workplace, they sought to build their organizational base by carefully defining issues in a manner that both drew on legitimate principles or rules and that built intergroup solidarity. Their impressive grasp of their strategic options helps explain their success in the campaign for comparable worth, in the defense of city services, and in the brief and tenuous yet politically powerful unity they achieved in the strike of July 1981.

The Status Quo of Power

Established rules, rights, legal authority, and policy position are the "coin of the realm" in public organization. Consequently, public workers mobilize not to change the terms of economic contracts but to change policy. The status quo of rules empowers employees in some positions and disempowers others, while also defining the terrain on which conflict occurs. Thus, rules themselves can be a source of power for public workers' movements, although they are more likely to empower public workers' adversaries. Knowledge of the rules—usually concentrated in the hands of a few pivotal actors—is itself a source of power.

In the founding days of Local 101, for example, the old leadership of the MEF affiliated with AFSCME not as part of a turn toward militancy but to take advantage of Article 20 of the AFL-CIO Constitution, which prevented other AFL-CIO unions (such as Local 715, already on the prowl for organizing targets in 1972) from raiding its jurisdiction, even if its members had wanted to change representatives. So, rather than representing a turn toward more adversarial relations with management, affiliation with AFSCME buttressed the position of the MEF staff (and, through an AFSCME subsidy, augmented the MEF's income) until they were finally deposed during Jenkins's "revolution in the union."

Similarly, as comparable worth bargaining approached its climax, leaders of the public works group drew on their knowledge of union rules to seize control of the negotiating committee. Also in the early 1980s, disgruntled custodians expressed their anger with both the union and management by filing numerous grievances, civil service appeals, and discrimination complaints. Later, Local 101's executive board invoked its power under the union's bylaws to withdraw the custodians' right to elected shop stewards. And, of course, from the earliest days of CLAW to the latest comparable worth adjustment, union activists honed their skills as personnel technicians, learning how to maneuver in the maze of civil service rules and principles of job classification and salary standardization.

The status quo of power is likely to be a target as well as a weapon, as mobilizing workers seek to change rules to produce new resources. The campaign by the women of San Jose to change the basis for salary standardization is an excellent case in point. Though later efforts were necessary to win the implementation of pay equity, earlier victories in the conflict over the rules that would guide the study (e.g., reliance on internal comparable worth comparisons versus external market standards for salary setting) were essential preconditions for that later progress. The union's victory on that issue in the April 1979 city council meeting produced a new set of rules for salary standardization that deemphasized market standards and assured union participation in the job evaluation process. Capitalizing on these new resources, however, required skillful and determined use of other resources as well: alliance, the weapon of publicity, and the power of voice.

Alliance as Weapon

When I asked Maxine Jenkins to compare her experience organizing labor movements in the public and private sectors, she immediately brought up "the problem of unity"—a problem I recognized well from my years doing similar work. Jenkins and the other activists in San Jose were part of an extremely diverse workforce, composed of clerical, semiskilled blue-collar, skilled blue-collar, technical, professional, and administrative workers, spread out over many departments, and producing radically different products for very different constituencies. In her private sector work, by contrast, she faced a relatively homogeneous group of nurses (see chapter 6).

Both the nature of power in public organizations and the sheer diversity of the public workforce elevate the importance of alliances among disparate groups associated with the same agency. Necessary, of course, is solidarity within groups that share a similar relationship to an agency—clients, residents, or, in this case, occupational groups. This is not an automatic process but rather an occasional achievement, requiring mobilization. Beyond this, there is a world of divisions and potential conflicts: with other occupational groups in the workplace, with broader occupational groups associated with different functions of the agency, with the supervisory and managerial ranks to whom workers are subordinate, with clients on or for whom they perform their work, and with various blocs of the agency's constituents and its taxpayers.

Coalitions in this world of political bureaucracy are typically tenuous and difficult, especially when they run counter to the coalition that serves as the basis for the governing political regime. Overarching the whole agency, defining its mission and organizing its power relations, is the governing policy coalition, which is defined by a circle of exclusion as well as inclusion.[29] The status of a given occupational or functional group of workers in relation to

[29]Coalitions among people with power govern firms as well, to be sure (Cyert and March 1963). But in firms the circle of participation is relatively closed, hierarchical, and limited by private ownership and thus excludes workers, much less the constellations of power in the broader social formation. Such openness, of course, is a peculiarity of public organization.

that coalition is decisive in determining the fortunes of the occupational or functional group—as decisive as the labor market position of occupational groups in the private sector.

Unlike the "combination of workers" within and against a single labor market that defines unionism in the private sector, alliances in the public sector reach across the political-bureaucratic division of labor. Some do not even include other workers; building trades workers, teachers, and police, in fact, are more likely to ally with private construction interests, parents, and supporters of law and order, respectively. Because of this diversity, alliances in the public sector are likely to be difficult, tenuous, shortlived and less likely to display the effervescent shared culture of solidarity Rick Fantasia has described (1988). They depend for their success not only on their members having shared interests but, to some degree, on acknowledging members' different interests, all of which are related to the overall policy agenda (or to a vision of a reformed policy agenda) for the agency in question. Tenuous as they are, then, members' shared understandings are likely to be more complex than those among private sector unionists: rather than asserting a single corporate self-interest, public sector workers must weave different self-interests together around more general principles.

The San Jose case demonstrates the array of public sector alliances that are possible and their implications for the fortunes of the groups involved. The alliances wielded by the women of San Jose, for example, includes (1) a coalition of professional, paraprofessional, and clerical workers based mainly at the central library and City Hall, mobilized around their common opposition to the devaluation of their work both in the battle of the budget and in the arena of comparable worth; (2) formal and informal coalitions with users of neighborhood libraries, community centers, and parks, representatives of neighborhood organizations, participants in Friends of the Library and Friends of the Parks groups in different neighborhoods, assembled around the use of those services and mobilized to defend and expand their budgets; (3) a coalition with the custodians, whom the women promised inclusion in union leadership in exchange for political support; (4) a coalition with managers interested in sustaining their budget allocations and other policies favorable to their departments; (5) a labor-management coalition with Mayor McEnery, which gave him political support in exchange for the restoration of positions and the completion of the comparable worth adjustments; (6) coalitions with both public works and custodial groups for the 1981 bargaining and strike action, based on common interests in achieving a higher across-the-board wage increase, in return for support for their special issues and, in the case of the public works group, a promise not to allow comparable worth issues to stand in the way of a settlement.

Each of these coalitions played a strategic role in San Jose in the early 1980s. The first coalition established CLAW's base in the library department; similar attention to clerical issues over the next several years secured the leadership role of the professional and semiprofessional groups over the larger clerical workforce.

The second set of coalitions—with neighborhood-based users of services—served not only as a resource in the battle of the budget and in defense of public service employment but, by producing a neighborhood base for precinct operations and other political action, radically strengthened Local 101 in all its dealings with elected officials. In the aftermath of the 1981 strike, as the city administration began to seek vengeance for the humiliation of that experience, this new political apparatus guaranteed a commitment from mayoral candidate McEnery to restore positions, to adopt an agency shop provision (despite membership levels that remained at less than a third of the bargaining unit), and to proceed with the second stage of the comparable worth adjustment.

The third coalition produced the voting majority the women required in the union, by aligning two of the three major voting blocs, and thereby enabled them to defeat the entrenched power of the representatives of public works in internal union politics. Later, the custodians would offer unhesitating support for the comparable worth claim and for the 1981 strike. The fourth coalition produced cooperative relationships on workplace issues, tolerance of union activity elsewhere in the city, and long-term collaboration on budget issues. The fifth coalition enabled the new leadership group in Local 101 to enter the inner circle of decision-making on personnel issues in the city. Not surprisingly, the sixth coalition was the briefest and most tenuous of these alliances, since it bridged a bitter conflict over power in the union and reached across the gendered divide in city politics—between neighborhood interests and human services, on the one hand, and development interests, centered in the Department of Public Works, on the other.

The participation of a single circle of public worker activists in all these coalitions was no accident. These coalitions were not spontaneous formations but accomplishments by a single small group that used coalition-building strategies to establish its base and power. Most of these coalitions were created on the initiative of the CLAW activists, with the assistance of two particularly gifted union staffers—Jenkins and Callahan. Typically, they got support by giving support—or at least by promising it.

There were, however, coalitions in which the unionists did not wield all the strategic control, namely with their department managers and, eventually, with the mayor. Forming an alliance with management—especially likely when an agency or a section of an agency faces an outside threat—introduces a set of issues for public employee movements as well as their unions that are familiar to participants in "mature" unions of the private sector. Will such partnerships induce the union to demobilize, stop its drive to expand workers' rights, curtail its own members' rights within the union, limit alliances with other progressive groups, and encourage the defense rather than the reform of public organization? Does such political realignment spell the end of the public workers' movement as a movement, leaving instead an organized interest group in its wake? In San Jose (as in San Francisco), the answer to these questions appears to have been yes.

The Power of Publicity

The comparable worth strike was, in Callahan's words, a "polite" strike; in personnel analyst Armstrong's words, it was "one of the nicest strikes you'd ever want to see" (interview, Callahan, Nov. 12, 1986, and Armstrong, Oct. 7, 1986). This "niceness" may have reflected San Jose's small-town informality, but it also was cultivated through self-conscious posing before a public audience. The strike was, as one pair of observers noted, a "comparable worth media event" (*CPER* 51:2).

One striker recounted a moment, four days into the strike, that illustrates this point. The city council had just rejected a tentative settlement reached by its negotiator, at which point the outraged union negotiating team stormed toward the closed chambers where the city council was meeting. They were halted by a police officer at the door. "Just a minute," the officer said. The group then stopped and chatted as a television crew got a camera properly positioned to cover the team's entry. When the officers cheerfully signaled for the negotiating team to proceed, the group then resumed its angry demands for admission (interview, Goddard, Oct. 2, 1986).

The strike probably garnered more publicity at the national level than any other public sector strike in that period, with the exception of the strike by the federal air traffic controllers. The coverage centered, of course, on the comparable worth issue: a compelling news topic, combining as it did political conflict, drama, and the war between the sexes.

After months of brinkmanship and intense publicity on the comparable worth study and with budget negotiations in process, the media stage had been set for the strike to receive intense national attention. When it began, Callahan and Mayor Hayes flew—together—to New York City to appear on NBC's *Today* show. The *San Jose News* (Lincoln Smith, "San Jose

Strikers Send Ripples across the Nation," July 8, 1981) reported that "the chants of San Jose's striking municipal employees are being heard across the nation" and that a sampling of city administrators across the United States were watching the strike with sentiments ranging from trepidation to enthusiasm.

The comparable worth campaign evidently struck a responsive chord among the staff of the San Jose *Mercury-News*, which monopolized the valley's newspaper market. Never known as a pro-union paper, in the 1970s the *Mercury-News* began to take progressive editorial positions on social issues and to hire relatively progressive young reporters who were sensitive to issues of gender justice and positively disposed toward public sector action. During the year prior to the 1981 strike, for example, the paper published many commentaries such as "Employers Ignore Working Mothers' Woes" (Dianna Diamond, *San Jose Mercury*, July 2, 1980), "The Ongoing Battle against Discrimination" (Bob Schmidt, *San Jose News*, March 31, 1981), and "Free Enterprise Isn't the Cure for Human Suffering" (H. Bruce Miller, *San Jose News*, March 31, 1981). During the period in 1981 between the one-day strike on March 27 and the end of the strike on July 15, the *Mercury-News* published sixty-nine articles on comparable worth, most of them sympathetic to the comparable worth argument and many on the front page.

All this coverage affected the events themselves and so was used strategically by those aware of this impact. The union leadership had a solid grasp of how public interpretations could be used as political weapons,[30] and, as a result, the newspaper record is deceptive. Beyond the emphasis on comparable worth, this is reflected in the consistent overstatements of the number of workers involved. The low participation rate was obscured by the concentration of strike participants at the more visible, large, central locations. Media reports indicate that there were as many as seventeen hundred strikers and that most were clerical workers (see, for example, *San Francisco Chronicle*, July 6, 1981; *San Francisco Examiner,* July 8, 1981; *San Jose News*, July 8, 1981). Callahan admitted that this was not true:

> Yes, we said that 1,500 people were on strike, and it was the media's job
> to check it out, and they didn't. We probably never had more than 500
> people out, and just between you and me it might have even been less
> than that. But hey, that's politics. . . . Smoke and mirrors, right? As long

[30]See Michael Marmo's excellent studies (1983, 1984) of the use of symbolism in public sector labor relations. His arguments—based on Murray J. Edelman's (1967) work—differs from my own in that although Marmo distinguishes between material and symbolic rewards, I view all demands and responses as symbolically framed in important ways.

as they think it's true, then it is true. That's politics (interview, Nov. 12, 1986).[31]

"The Power of the Word"

Voice plays a key role in all social movements and a particularly central role in movements that emerge within and against public organizations. In this case, voice can not only define the interests and collective identity of participants but invoke potent claims to procedural justice and galvanize political alliances, while undermining adversaries' ability to do the same. These powers are intensified by the presence of public forums for articulating, justifying, and debating the definition of public needs, and the presence of actors skilled in the use of their voice and self-conscious of its power. Invariably, powerful discourse appeals to legitimate norms—to the mission of the public agency, to norms of good government, and to the value of procedural justice and technical rationality.

Maxine Jenkins used what she calls "the power of the word" (interview, June 28, 1994) with a self-conscious confidence, born of years of work as an organizer. Her performance in the pivotal budget hearings of July 1979 was a case in point. There, she appealed both to gender equality—a highly legitimate norm given the time and place—and to the "objective, scientific" validity of cross-benchmark salary standardization, as against employers' discriminatory bias as expressed in market wages. In the process, she helped constitute a new collective actor—"the women of the city"—while injecting new meaning into what would otherwise have been an unproblematic decision on whether to do the Hays study.

Jenkins was speaking as much to the women activists in her audience as to the city officials, helping to frame a powerful collective identity for them. While the city manager sought to frame the comparable worth agenda as that of "some women," Jenkins insisted on speaking for all the women of the city and even for all women "for thousands of years." Beyond asserting a new definition of the public good—the appropriate way to set wages—she was articulating a collective need—and, implicitly, a collective identity—to and for "the women of the city." Again and again, she resorted to the device of identifying her voice with that of the women, defining "the way the women of the city feel about [the need for comparable worth]." At one point, she turned, gestured to the crowd of unionists, and said, "All right. Our women representatives back there asked this question." She described these women as "so

---

[31]Blum's account reveals the same political manipulation of the numbers (1991:87).

determined" and as having been working on this now for years. "They will not turn back," she said.

Jenkins exercised a more subtle form of power by undermining the premises that routinely guided decision-making on public employees' salaries. In San Jose, as in other cities across the United States, no question surfaced regarding the then-accepted standard of using prevailing wages to set salaries until "the women of the city" posed it. After the issue was raised, however, the process would never be the same again, because the women had placed a now-unavoidable issue before the city manager and elected officials.

Finally, the city workers' use of the claim to comparable worth as a *strike weapon* is a dramatic example of the power of voice in public organizations. The women had effectively won their comparable worth victory before July 5. If the remaining differences concerning comparable worth had been the only outstanding issues, a strike would never have occurred. In the absence of an agreement on general wages, however, the demand for still more movement on comparable worth remained on the table.[32] Under those circumstances, comparable worth served as a potent weapon in the public sphere. Without the emphasis on this issue, it is unimaginable that the strikers would have garnered such intense and nationwide media attention.

Given that a voluntary agreement to implement comparable worth adjustments was already in place before the strike, it was, according to management negotiators and city council members, particularly galling to be cast in the role of villains for allegedly refusing to implement such adjustments. As personnel analyst David Armstrong recollected, "The shocker to the city council that really pissed them off was that here the media is crucifying us when here we are being the first to put some money where our mouth is. . . . The people were championing the cause and now they're getting crucified" (interview, Oct. 7, 1986). The rueful words of city negotiator David Turner give us the clearest statement of this dynamic: "The union just came in and beat us over the head with comparable worth" (interview, Oct. 7, 1986).

---

[32]This is a normal bargaining tactic; parties resist movement to their bottom line on nonstrike issues to sustain bargaining leverage for favorable movement on more essential issues.

4 Beyond Industrial Relations: Gender and the City in Silicon Valley

If the urban experience follows the hidden detours of civil society more naturally than the large avenues toward the state, then, at some fundamental level, there is an intimate connection between women and the city, between urban movements and women's liberation.

—Manuel Castells, *The City and the Grassroots*

As I looked out the train window at the Santa Clara Valley on my first day of fieldwork, I began to see it more as a place to investigate and analyze than as a place where I had once lived and then left. As the smaller cities north of San Jose passed by, I was struck by how lush and green the valley was, considering all the changes that had occurred since my birth. Back in the 1950s the valley was still dotted with farms. Our paths to school and friends' houses still ran through fruit orchards that gave the "Garden Valley" its name, and the fields and the canneries still provided us with summer jobs.

All this had changed. The soil now sprouted shrubbery, trees, lawns, city parks, and industrial parks. The farms were gone, and the last of the canneries had moved south to Salinas or across the Diablo Mountains to the big Central Valley. The canneries had been replaced by electronics firms, which spread south from Stanford University in the 1960s. San Jose, at the center of the valley, had exploded in area as a result of annexation and in population as a result of immigration, and the old neighborhoods with their big Italian families had been swept away. Now the valley was wall-to-wall automobile-based suburban tracts and apartment complexes that housed a population of 1.3 million. Nearly everyone was new to the area. Most people now called the place where they lived "Silicon Valley."

I was on my way to San Jose's new civic center, where City Hall and county office buildings now stand, to study the public workers' movements that had surfaced in the city a decade earlier. I did not suspect that tracing the roots of those movements would lead me back to the transformation from Garden Valley to Silicon Valley.

Like much of the rest of the United States, the Santa Clara Valley saw a surge of public worker unionism and militancy two decades ago. Union member-

88

ship leveled off by the late 1970s, at which time a surge occurred in strike activity, which in turn declined by the early 1980s. Only one public workers' strike occurred before 1975—a relatively small walkout by 450 members of the Santa Clara County Employees' Association in 1970—but then, in 1975, a massive strike by five thousand county employees opened the floodgates. At least one public workers' strike occurred in the valley every year thereafter until the San Jose city workers' strike of 1981; then militancy suddenly ceased.

What *triggered* the turn toward adversarial relations in the mid-1970s? Why was the San Jose city workers' strike led by *women* based in human service agencies? Why did the *public works* employees enjoy such favored status in the city and such strength in the union in the earlier period? What, if anything, did all this have to do with the new politics of slower growth and neighborhood services promoted by Mayor Janet Gray Hayes and her successors?

A theory of the goals and resources of public workers' movements is of little use as long as questions about their timing, composition, and fate remain unanswered. The purpose of this chapter is to address these unexplained questions. To answer the core question of this chapter—why the surge of militancy in San Jose and at this time?—we must look beyond the industrial relations system of collective bargaining, labor law, and AFL-CIO affiliation to the broader political universe and to the shifting societal foundations of public life in the Santa Clara Valley.

As we shall see, the turn to adversarial labor relations in San Jose was bound up with a broader struggle between competing political blocs. Variations in the status and behavior of different groups of public workers, employed in different functions and in different agencies, can be explained at least in part by their involvement, through the work they do, in these political blocs. These blocs take shape in political conflict over public policy agendas and organizational power—over the "comparable political worth," so to speak, of the alternative policy agendas of competing political coalitions. These blocs are grounded, in turn, in the basic patterns of urban life—in economic development, in changing neighborhoods and family life, and, increasingly, in public organization itself.

The relationship between the public workplace and the larger social formation within which it emerges and on which it works has been the focus of a great deal of research and debate in state theory (Carnoy 1984; Jessop 1982; Alford and Friedland 1985). Unfortunately, the relationship has been neglected in studies of public sector labor relations. Conceptual tools drawn from state theory serve here, however, with two modifications.

First, among the societal institutions intimately related to public organization—to the state in general, to local government in particular—are not

only the capitalist economy but the gendered family and community structure.[1] The gendered organization of everyday life, of social movement activism
in neighborhoods, and of the welfare state itself all have implications for urban
politics. *Second*, states—and urban regimes—are more than structures of
power. They are also *embodied* in public organization, including the size,
mission, workforce, budget, and programs of public agencies. Participants in
these public organizations—including not only managers but workers and
clients, their organizations, and their social movements—have their own
interests and so, even if movements are launched in response to "external"
influences, state-based participants quickly align with those interests, reinforce them, and may organize and even lead them. The first of these modifications to "the new urban sociology" is necessary to grasp the gendered aspects
of the changes unfolding in San Jose and elsewhere; the second is necessary to
understand the involvement of public workers, their organization, and their
movements in the larger social formation.

Because the purpose of this chapter is to explain the turn toward adversarial
relations in the valley, I turn first to the most conventional explanation for this
trend, in which the focus is the "industrial relations system."

Employee Associations and the Appearance of Union Growth

Industrial relations (IR) scholars conventionally conceive of labor relations—in the public sector as elsewhere—as a distinct system, consisting
mainly of a structure of collective bargaining and influenced heavily by public
policy (Lewin 1986; Sethi, Metzger, and Dimmock 1990), especially collective
bargaining legislation (Saltzman 1985; Freeman 1986). The importance of
legislation is a point of controversy; some scholars have found the effects of
labor law unconvincing (Burton and Thomason 1988), and researchers in this
tradition frequently refer to the effects of "external" or "environmental"
conditions on the industrial relations system.[2]

In the Santa Clara Valley, public sector union membership did indeed
appear to take a dramatic leap forward after the 1969 implementation of the
Meyers-Milias-Brown Act, which mandated that local governments grant
exclusive recognition and "meet and confer" in good faith with employee

[1]The theoretical challenge implicit here, and running through much recent work in state theory as
well as feminist theory, is to specify both the peculiarities of these different domains—institutional ensembles, modes of social reproduction, ways of life—as well as the *interactions* among
them. This would distract us, however, from the tasks of this chapter.
[2]In my view, IR scholars tend to overestimate the importance of these institutions in part because,
in response to labor unrest, people working in the IR tradition have helped shape them. Social
researchers—and others—typically overemphasize the autonomy and causal force of factors
subject to their control, or to the control of those with whom they identify.

organizations. SEIU's Local 715 and AFSCME's Local 101 were both formed within three years of the passage of the act, in 1972; both quickly expanded by chartering chapters in other agencies throughout the valley.

In fact, both had long histories as independent employee associations. Local 101 was the product of the affiliation by MEF—a longtime independent civil service association—with AFSCME, and Local 715 was a product of the affiliation of the Santa Clara County Employees' Association with SEIU. At the time of affiliation, MEF membership was just below seven hundred; five years later, membership had fallen to about five hundred. Local 715 also experienced a drop in membership upon affiliation, although energetic internal organizing enabled that union to rebuild its membership.[3] Until the new labor-management coalitions of the 1980s produced agency shop agreements, the growth of both Local 715 and Local 101 occurred mainly as a result of affiliation or as public employee associations were replaced in cities, schools, and other special districts in the valley. Formal records showing a jump in membership, then, conceal organizational continuity and submerge the unions' earlier histories.[4]

The point is not that employee organization was collapsing but that organizations were adopting a more adversarial stance. Further, affiliation with the AFL-CIO did not necessarily coincide with this transformation. Of the twelve public workers' strikes between 1969 and 1985 in Santa Clara County, seven were conducted by independent associations and only five by AFL-CIO affiliates. In general, before the turn toward adversarial relations, few associations or unions behaved in a unionate manner (Kramer 1962); after this transition, most unions and associations did so. (And after 1980, both would become "associationate" again.)

In some cases, affiliation did coincide with the transformation to a more adversarial stance: Local 715's affiliation with the AFL-CIO reflected the work of a union-minded group that struck in 1970 and won power in an internal election in 1971; four years later, in coalition with SEIU's social workers'

[3]On Local 715's early years, see *CPER* 12:39,71, 14:48, and 15:35 – 38.
[4]In California as a whole, the rate of membership of public workers in employee organizations engaged primarily in collective representation—including, in other words, employee associations—actually *declined*, from 62 percent in 1963 to 48 percent in 1979 (California Department of Industrial Relations 1982:3). Ironically, public workers hired under earlier patronage regimes promoted civil service systems to protect their status during Progressive-era political transitions (Lelchook 1974). Thus this earlier wave of public employee organization-building was also tied to political upheaval and regime transition in local government. These trends paralleled European public workers' movements of the same era, which also demanded administrative justice (Laski 1919). In the same year that he published the words that introduce this book which refer to the public workers' movement in France, Harold Laski was fired by Harvard University for his support of the Boston police strike of 1919: the PATCO of his era (Eastwood 1977).

union, Local 535, Local 715 conducted an eighteen-day countywide strike. In San Jose, however, labor relations were unchanged after affiliation; the public works group remained in power in the local and the chapter for years thereafter. In this case, the shift toward adversarial relations did not take place until the women mobilized, five years *after* the affiliation with AFSCME.

Affiliation with AFSCME produced crucial protection for MEF from SEIU, which had perfected a strategy of carving out smaller units of employees with distinctive interests and offering them an autonomous voice through the creation of their own "legal entity."[5] Local 715, MEF's aggressive "big brother" upstairs,[6] was on the prowl to expand its jurisdiction even before the affiliation with SEIU was finalized; Article 20 of the AFL-CIO Constitution precludes such raids among union affiliates regardless of the desires of bargaining unit members. Far from a turn toward adversarial relations, then, Local 101's affiliation strengthened an entrenched and nonadversarial leadership and protected the local from raids by SEIU organizers.[7] Affiliation with the AFL-CIO gave the *appearance* of union growth in San Jose, but it did not represent an organizational transformation or the rise of a social movement in the city workforce.

In sum, MEF's affiliation with AFSCME *was* at least partly caused by the passage of the 1968 collective bargaining law because the new law promoted increased competition among employee organizations. It is possible, too, that the existence of a bargaining law and union affiliation facilitated the eventual turn toward adversarial relations by underwriting their legitimacy. Given the years of nonadversarial labor relations that followed, however, these developments do not appear to have led to the emergence of adversarial labor relations in the city. And these developments certainly do not explain why Local 715's militancy surfaced so quickly in Santa Clara County[8] whereas a full nine years would pass in the city. Indeed, although the chapter went through the motions of "meeting and conferring," no serious strike threat was made until 1981 —

[5]The use of this tactic—targeting mainly social workers, the most militant local government employees, and then offering the old associations protection from raids through affiliation—is perhaps the main reason SEIU enjoys a stronger position than AFSCME in California's public sector.
[6]Both unions were located at 715 North First Street in San Jose during the 1970s.
[7]The agreement provided that the organization would preserve its existing leadership, maintain control over hiring and the direction of staff (all too rare in AFSCME's regionally centralized "district council" structure), receive and direct the services of two AFSCME-paid full-time staff, and receive a cash subsidy of more than $20,000 over a two-year period (*CPER* 14:48, 67; *CPER* 18:41).
[8]Local 715's base at the county level included health care employees and clerical and paraprofessional social service staff; in San Jose, employees were concentrated in services such as the police, fire, parks, library, and public works departments. The expanding bloc of health and social welfare workers was the prime base for union mobilization in county government and appears to account for 715's earlier militancy.

thirteen years after the passage of the collective bargaining law, nine years after the affiliation with AFSCME, and three years after the women began to mobilize. This *last* development—the mobilization of the women—appears to account for Local 101's eventual turn toward militancy.[9] To explain it, one must look beyond the "industrial relations system" to the changing patterns of life and development in the valley.

Amending Urban Sociology

The story of development in the Santa Clara Valley and how it translated into struggle in the city of San Jose conforms, to a degree, to some widely accepted findings. In the postwar era, explosive growth radically changed the character of Sunbelt cities such as San Jose and the lives of the people who lived in them, creating a new, automobile-based urban form (Abbott 1981). Great waves of migrants settled in new housing tracts, typically built on what had been agricultural land. Development of tract housing fueled this suburblike variation on the urban "growth machine" (Logan and Molotch 1987). The urban regimes (Stone 1989) that governed these cities and drove their development consisted of informal circles of local landowners, banks, real estate developers, construction companies, building trades unions, and city officials who were more or less actively involved in planning, promoting, and implementation; in John Mollenkopf's (1983) term, a "pro-growth coalition."

But neighborhoods are not only real estate markets; they are also places where people seek to live their lives (Logan and Molotch 1987). Nor are cities only growth machines; they also organize collective consumption (Castells 1983; Saunders 1981).[10] In their neighborhoods, people face and must respond to the social costs of urban growth under capitalism (Feagin 1988). Even under conditions of relative affluence, the growth machine is likely to provoke

[9]The insignificance of labor law in California is supported by *parallel* strike trends in the state's schools and other government agencies. The two subsectors are radically distinct legal and organizational environments and are governed by different systems of labor law, adopted at different times. With one exception (San Francisco), these workers never struck together. They produced one and the same strike wave, however (in the *CPER* strike database, r = .79 from 1969 through 1985). Similarly, on the *insignificance of AFL-CIO affiliation*: of 472 local government strikes from 1969 through 1985, associations were involved in 51 percent, unions in only 48 percent. More than half the association strikes—54 percent—were conducted by teachers, but the other 46 percent involved clerks, blue-collar workers, police and firefighters, and miscellaneous professionals. Fully 33 percent of all strikes by noneducational employees were conducted by associations.

[10]By contrast, because John Logan and Harvey Molotch (1987) define "urban" as the spatial dimension of property markets, they conclude that local collective consumption is not urban. Ironically, in writing about the British context, Peter Saunders (1981) arrives at exactly the opposite conclusion. I find *both* urban imperatives at work in local government, while also placing greater emphasis on the spatial dimension of public organization itself.

neighborhood-based movements for participation in planning, social services, environmental protection, and other amenities. Thus, an impressive and growing body of research on cities such as San Jose documents "significant increases in the level of political demand for improved community services, effective growth management and control policies, and a better quality of neighborhood and community life as a result of the mounting social costs of unregulated rapid growth" (Smith 1988:105).

Perversely, the triumph of untrammeled development produces its own opposition. Starting in the 1960s and mounting in the 1970s, neighborhood groups responded, and controlled-growth and "quality of life" agendas emerged to challenge policies organized around untrammeled growth. These neighborhood revolts occurred at different times and with varying degrees of intensity throughout the United States. In San Jose, Janet Gray Hayes was elected mayor on a platform of "controlled growth," promising to "make San Jose better before we make it bigger." Each subsequent mayor has similarly affirmed this agenda.

What was the connection between the competing pro-growth and controlled growth agendas and the eruption of adversarial labor relations in San Jose? How might the revolt of the neighborhoods have contributed to producing the conditions for the women to revolt in the union, and why did the comparable worth agenda achieve such prominence in San Jose, of all places?

First, sprawling urban development, as exemplified in San Jose, had important consequences for neighborhood and family life, and in particular for women. Mass migration away from extended families and ethnic neighborhoods and into the new suburbs of postwar America produced a way of life that, at least in the years immediately following relocation, was socially disorganized and especially difficult for women (Gans 1967).[11] These years also saw the expansion of schools and the rise of public welfare systems to support households headed by women, and, even when they were funded and/or administered by federal agencies, these programs were usually run by local governments.

To a great degree, moreover, the revolt against development was led by women,[12] and the new services for social consumption were both staffed and used by women. The construction companies, real estate developers, public

[11]There is an ambivalence in studies of suburban life, which has been described as both barren (Wekerle 1980) and sociable (Greer 1962). Women appear to be both alienated (Gans 1967; Saegert 1981) and satisfied (Fava 1980; Spain 1988). These findings may reflect the increasingly dangerous character of older urban spaces. They may also reflect the process emphasized here: while relocation cuts off social support systems, it also invites women to rebuild them in ways that reflect new relations between the family, the private sector, and public organization.

[12]This is well documented in the case of the Santa Clara Valley in Flammang 1985 and in Trounstine and Christensen 1982.

works agencies, and building trades unions that formed the core of the
dominant pro-growth coalition, by contrast, were overwhelmingly dominated
by men, based, by and large, in traditional family structures. Thus, conflict
between the growth coalition and the "quality of life" coalition was bound
also to be conflict between men and women. Second, urban regimes are more
than a circle of local elites, more than a collection of private firms that have
strategies for growth and key allies among public officials, and more than the
policy agendas around which these regimes' interests coalesce. The hegemony
of a given property development regime depends in part on a pattern of public
organization responsive to its agenda: the hegemony within city government
of administrators associated with development and public works. This in turn
will be reflected in the missions, powers, and relative budgets of the local
agencies associated with construction and development and also in a special
relationship between workers in those favored functions and the city government as employer. This relationship, in turn, will have drastic effects on
patterns of organization and leadership within the workforce and in and/or
among unions or other employee associations.

Like all formal organizations, these arrangements are recalcitrant or highly
resistant to change—perhaps more than most, because the political context of
public organization permits staff and other interests to defend their stakes in
the budget through political action. Change thus means far more than the
formation of a new circle of elites around a new policy agenda and the election
and consolidation of their representatives in a new governing coalition. It also
requires confronting organizational legacies of the past, redirecting and reshaping recalcitrant public organizations, and changing the shape and operation of local government from top to bottom. This task is so difficult that it is
scarcely ever accomplished, so that older public agencies typically consist of
layers of inconsistent organization, in which the past haunts the present like
some Freudian dream. Public administrators and public workers and their
unions have stakes on these fault lines of endemic tension, of course, and so
their political behavior—including their relations with the workforce—is defined to a great degree by interminable conflict.

It should come as no surprise, then, that the 1974 election of Janet Gray
Hayes did not put an end to the tension between the old and new regimes in
San Jose's city government. Hayes's election was only one step in a longer
struggle in the city—a struggle that involved not only external interests
but participants in city management and in the city workers' union itself.
In the long and difficult process of transition from the old regime to the
new, champions of the new policy agenda sought to remake the city in its
image—not, by any means, to abolish the growth machine in favor of social

consumption but to move toward a new and different balance between these contradictory but ever-present urban imperatives.

In sum, the conflict rooted in the city's suburban model of capital accumulation and the gendered resistance this provoked surfaced in city politics and budget-making and in city administration and city workers' employee organizations, until at last it erupted at the bargaining table. The conflict surfaced in the annual battle of the budget and in conflicts over the size of increases or reductions in city departments, in conflicts, that is, over the relative worth of male- and female-gendered policy agendas—economic development and social consumption. Inside city administration, the same conflict surfaced over the relative power of different city departments and over the relative status and pay of various department heads. Inside the city workers' union, the same conflict surfaced over which employee groups would control the union and over what bargaining demands would be put forward in contract negotiations. In the comparable worth campaign, the same conflict surfaced over the relative worth of male- and female-gendered job classifications.

From "Garden Valley" to "Silicon Valley"

The Santa Clara Valley, a fertile river valley, about fifteen miles across and thirty miles long, runs south from the San Francisco Bay between the Diablo and Santa Cruz mountain ranges. Before the 1950s, the valley had been a backwater to the Bay Area, dedicated as late as that decade to cultivating and processing fruit. Local capital, well integrated around food processing and a compact urban core, dominated the valley's economic life.

During the second half of the twentieth century, an explosion of economic development occurred, fueled by military contracting and revolving around successive revolutions in electronics technology—first the transistor, then the silicon chip. The valley was transformed into a near-mythic locale, one of the fastest-growing and most affluent regions in the United States. New industries spread south from Stanford University, while San Jose's tracts were home to the lower-waged workforce that could not afford the higher housing costs of the Bay Area.

The transformation was sudden and decisive. By 1970, few residents of the region had even heard of the new silicon-coated wafer chips that would revolutionize information processing over the coming decade. In the January 1971 edition of *Electronics News*, Don Hoefler would coin the term "Silicon Valley" to describe the new economic region extending south from Stanford University. Within a decade "Santa Clara Valley" became "Silicon Valley," in the minds of residents as well as increasingly interested observers around the world.

This sudden transformation of regional identity could only occur because these economic developments had profound consequences for the people and neighborhoods of the valley. By the late 1970s, employment was exploding at an annual rate of 8 percent (Trounstine and Christensen 1982). The economic transformation of the valley was accompanied by massive movements of population into its expanding neighborhoods. In the first half of the century, Italian immigrants had come to the valley, and most worked in agriculture and food processing. By mid-century, members of this upwardly mobile group owned most of the small farms that still dotted the region. Immigration expanded to a torrent in the postwar period as the valley emerged as a prime site for settlement by servicemen and their families, by migrant farmworkers leaving rural areas, and by hundreds of thousands of others leaving communities throughout the United States to come to "California," the land of new beginnings. Other arrivals reflected the global history of those years: Palestinians arrived around 1950 and again twenty years later, Cubans in the early 1960s, Portuguese Angolans in the mid-1970s, Southeast Asians starting in the 1970s, Central Americans in the 1980s, and so on.

At any given time in the past half-century, most of the valley's residents were recent arrivals from elsewhere in the United States and the world. Between 1970 and 1990, for example, the proportion of Asian (mostly Southeast Asian) residents in Santa Clara County mushroomed from 1 percent to 23 percent, surpassing the Latino population. As the immigrants arrived, the city's census exploded, from 95,280 to 204,196 in the ten years from 1950 to 1960, and then to 555,707 in 1975; by 1980, San Jose was the fastest-growing city in the United States (U.S. Department of Commerce, various years).

During the 1950s, city officials, working closely with local landowners and developers, pursued an aggressive program of annexation, which resulted in an explosion of city boundaries. This, in turn, began two decades of public works expenditures centered on roads, sewers, the airport, parks, fire departments, libraries, and so on.[13] Investments in public works—especially roads and sewers—supported the new suburban enclaves and fueled the booming construction industry. By 1970, as a result, San Jose became known as

> the archetypal suburb, a sprawling confusion of look-alike houses, shopping centers, and filling stations, criss-crossed by freeways that whiz shoppers and workers away from a once-bustling downtown . . . in a frenzied competition to outgrow neighboring Sunnyvale and Santa Clara,

[13]For accounts of the development frenzy in San Jose, see Trounstine and Christensen 1982 and Stanford Environmental Law Society 1971. See also the vision of city officials in City of San Jose 1957.

the town pushed for annexation that crept along highways and leap-
frogged pockets of empty land, creating an octopus of a city that thrusts
its tentacles into a 340 square mile "sphere of influence." ("Correcting San
Jose's Boomtime Mistake," *Business Week*, Sept. 19, 1970, 74).

Each level of the government played its part in the development explosion.
From 1950 through 1962, 31 percent of all new jobs in the county were in
defense or aerospace industries, and better than one in six civilian jobs
depended directly on military or space programs (Little 1964). Former servicemen with college degrees financed by the GI Bill bought new tract homes with
veterans' home loans. State and federal funds poured in to finance highway,
hospital, and school construction.

Most important for this story, San Jose adopted an aggressive policy of
territorial expansion and housing development, annexing unincorporated
farmland, financing new infrastructures through local bonds, razing older
neighborhoods for freeway construction and central city redevelopment, and
so on. This process was organized by champions of growth in city government. Stanford's Environmental Law Society (ELS), in a 1970 study of San
Jose's development, expected to find that the city's sprawl resulted from a lack
of government influence on growth. To its surprise, the group concluded that
"San Jose . . . is largely the product of policies and practices pursued by city
officials. Rather than the indictment of non-government we had anticipated,
San Jose represents what can happen when a very aggressive city government is
responsible only to a narrow constituency" (1971:16).

An "old-boy" network composed largely of second-generation Italian-
American natives of the valley dominated the city's economic life and political
direction throughout the postwar period of headlong growth. The hegemony
of this circle of businessmen, most schooled by Jesuits at Bellarmine High
School and Santa Clara University, is well documented in Philip J. Trounstine
and Terry Christensen's 1982 study, *Movers and Shakers: The Study of Community Power*.[14]

This "golden circle," as it was popularly called, possessed a powerful public
voice in Joseph Ridder, who as editor-publisher of the morning *Mercury*, the
evening *News*, and the Sunday *Mercury-News* monopolized the valley's newspaper market. Dismissing environmental concerns and nostalgia for the valley's rural identity, Ridder summed up the value of growth with the precision
of a businessman-journalist: "Trees," Ridder declared, "don't read newspapers" (Reinhardt 1965:48).

---

[14]I also attended Bellarmine and, briefly, Santa Clara University.

Inside the city bureaucracy, the city's development interests had their (mostly Italian) representatives. Peter ("Pete") Turtericci, chief of the Department of Public Works, and city manager A. P. ("Dutch") Hamann dominated city government for two decades after the war. Developers and city officials worked in tandem, but the agenda was spearheaded by Hamann, who organized annexations through his own office rather than the city planning department. Hamann was clear about his goals: "They say that San Jose is going to become another Los Angeles. Believe me, I'm going to do everything in my power to make that come true" (Reinhardt 1965:68).

Hamann was true to his word. He sent his staff up and down the main roads leading out of San Jose, knocking on doors and soliciting interest in annexation and development. Developers would purchase farmland beyond city limits, which was both less expensive and more attractive to homeowners seeking idyllic surroundings. City officials would then offer annexation—and infrastructural services—at lower costs than other local cities (ELS 1971:64 – 71). Hamann used the city's regional monopoly on sewage treatment—a legacy of earlier city investments in support of the now-fading cannery industry—to underbid other cities in contests over annexation (Trounstine and Christensen 1982:97). As a result, during Hamann's tenure from 1950 to 1965, the city's land area increased eightfold.

Equally important, the hegemonic residential development agenda of the "golden circle" had an effect *inside* city government. The fiscal and managerial structures of the city—the nature, mission, relative size, and power of city departments—were organized around the "golden circle's" policy agenda. The public works department, for example, dwarfed every other city department in size, influence, and management pay scale through the mid-1970s. Public works officials and their friends in politics and construction companies and building trades unions formed the city's central network of political power. Also important for this story, construction-related workers in the public works department controlled the city's major union—AFSCME Local 101—until 1977.

Recomposing Life and Political Culture in the Valley

In the mid-twentieth century, immigration and the creation of new automobile-based communities transformed social life in the valley. Early in the century, ethnic neighborhoods located near the great canneries that dominated the regional economy enjoyed a thick cultural life and provided a territorial base for class-based politics. City life was personalized and compact, concentrated in neighborhoods grouped around a small but vital urban center and navigable by foot. Politics were polarized between working-class

Italian ethnic wards and more affluent wards dominated by landowners, merchants, and other local business people mostly of northern European ancestry and often also associated with the food-processing industry. The old city supported both a high degree of union militancy and a tangible sense of place and community.[15]

The new population of the postwar period, by contrast, was relatively rootless, socially atomized, and dispersed. The ethnic social ties and political organization of old San Jose were submerged, even swept away, by the flood of immigration. The valley was only sparsely populated with voluntary organizations, and until the rise of new social movements in the late 1960s and thereafter, public corridors were almost totally empty of politically active groups and individuals.

None of this is surprising. Rapid population growth meant that the overwhelming majority of the citizenry were new to their neighborhoods, of diverse origin, and lacking in a common culture and sense of place. Older residents were affected as well, as those features that gave them a sense of place—orchards and fields, riverbeds, rural spaces, big old farmhouses surrounded by watertowers, sheds, and orchards—vanished. Traditional neighborhood institutions—churches, schools—were swamped with unfamiliar new faces. Ethnic neighborhoods and workforces, small to medium-sized family farms, and other traditional support systems were left behind or paved over. Perhaps most important of all, *extended families,* the basic fabric of the more traditional way of life, virtually disappeared.

Increases in the population and economic development meant more than relocation, then, for the people of the valley. As a result of these changes, people were separated from the support systems of their neighborhoods and, especially, their families; inserted into commodified ways of life, making them highly privatized and individualistic; and older, smaller, ethnically bonded institutions were undermined in the process. One can safely assume that this uprooted way of life helped attenuate the patriarchal gender roles associated with these families' communities of origin.[16]

A Feminism of Everyday Life

Starting in the 1960s, the valley's new population repeatedly generated organizational and cultural innovations and social movements. Among the

[15]Twice during the Depression era, city workers voluntarily deferred pay increases to finance a welfare fund for homeless refugees. Glenna Matthews (1977) offers a rich history of life in San Jose during this era.
[16]This direction of thought was suggested in a personal communication by Eli Sagan and encouraged by Therese Johnston's reflections on her psychological practice in the valley.

notable changes was the widespread emergence of women in political leadership. Other students of the valley's recent history have noticed and sought to explain this phenomenon by referring to the entrepreneurial spirit of leaders in the electronics industry—William Hewlett, David Packard, Steven Jobs, and Steve Wozniak (Trounstine and Christensen 1982; Flammang 1985). In fact, the new electronics firms were based in the northern valley, outside San Jose, and oriented toward national and international markets; neither their owners nor their employees participated to a significant degree in local political life or social movements in the early years. It *is* likely, however, that the valley residents' openness to change had to do with the experience of immigration, which had resulted in the "unfixing" of the institutions that had previously oriented their lives, and the aspirations animating the individuals—sometimes self-selected, sometimes driven by local conditions—who left their homes to come to the California of their imaginations.

As Flammang also observes (1985), the emergence of female leaders in the valley's new social and political neighborhood movements and in electoral politics, and the movements' association with gendered human needs, represents a translation of female gender roles from the home into the public sphere. This is consistent with other scholars' observations about women's motivation for community work and grassroots politics (Naples 1992). The surge of women's political action in San Jose was centered on such gendered community needs and was a response, I argue here, to the impact on life in the valley of the economic development and population movement described above.

In the gendered family, women's work of providing care both sustains and depends on interpersonal support networks; women with children are particularly vulnerable to isolation and deprivation. These networks depended, in smaller towns or more ethnically organized communities, not only on extended families but on shared cultural institutions and on a degree of simple stability in what Kai Erikson (1976) calls the material and social "surround." Now women, particularly mothers, cut off from extended webs of relations, many divorced, increasingly employed, and often married to "workaholic" husbands, found themselves thrown into a minimally social suburban setting. They remained responsible for child care and for organizing domestic consumption in general, but the environment in which they lived and worked was more tenuous, less supportive, and more commodified than it had been in the past. Increasingly, they found they had to face their burdens alone, as the valley's rate of divorce nearly matched the rate of marriage and the number of single female parents grew.[17]

---

[17]In 1975, there were 8,079 marriages and 7,540 divorces in the valley; in 1980, 9,190 marriages

These changes affected the valley's women in contradictory ways: they weakened some bonds of domestic patriarchy, while increasing women's burden of care. In a variety of ways, mothers struggled to rebuild the social fabric. Informal networks grew around the sparse collective resources for families—parks, day care centers, churches—and as a result of neighborhood-based efforts to get or protect common resources. The recomposition of the workforce and family also brought issues of gender domination and gendered work into the public sphere (Hernes 1987; Franzway, Court, and Connell 1989). The consequences of these changes were equally ambiguous: strengthening women's citizenship rights, yet subordinating them to bureaucracies.

Judith Stacey's (1990) study of family life in the Santa Clara Valley describes how women became engaged in "reconstructed" community organizations—starting with the "women's re-entry agency" Stacey used as her point of access to the field, and including both feminist political groups and new mutations on Christian life. The proliferation of neighborhood organizations and the emergence of women as their political leaders were deeply rooted in these changes in everyday life, stemming from the move from rural or urban ethnic enclaves to the new urban environment of San Jose.

Neither domestic life nor employment conditions nor public resources changed in pace with the women's extended burden of care; consequently, women were beleaguered and struggles ensued on every front—over new family arrangements, over new ways to work, and over public resources—as new needs were asserted, new social problems were "discovered," and gendered fault lines of conflict widened in homes, neighborhoods, workplaces, and government.

The changes in gender relations made their mark, then, far beyond the walls of the home. The vast expansion of "gendered work," "gendered consumption," and the gendered administration of female clients by female public sector workers was accompanied by the emergence of new "gendered constituencies." Meeting the needs of these constituencies became the focus, of course, of a great battery of new social welfare programs. In combination, the increasingly politicized needs of the valley's families, the growth in politically regulated women's work, and the gendered struggles for family resources and over the worth of women's work became core elements of the neighborhood-based challenge to the "untrammeled development" agenda.[18]

---

and 8,841 divorces. The 1980 census recorded 45,058 households headed by singles, compared with 264,692 couples.
[18]This is yet another variation on the pattern of women's community action described by scholars such as Kathleen McCourt (1977), Linda Gordon (1991), and P. Hill Collins (1990). Nancy A.

Given this set of circumstances, it is not surprising that women emerged as leaders not only in electoral politics but at all levels of social and political life. Starting in the 1960s, women took the lead in a gradually developing series of grassroots neighborhood groups and political action and other social movements: in movements for the extension of public services—libraries, parks, neighborhood centers; in parent groups centered at elementary schools; in a community-based rape crisis center and a battered women's shelter; in movements for the control of growth in the south of the valley; in movements against widening and extending streets and for "neighborhood preservation" in general; in movements against the toxic groundwater pollution that quickly followed the expansion of high-tech industry; and in movements for district-based rather than at-large elections to the San Jose City Council. Women also took the lead in *movement-oriented* activity (as opposed to formal positions in organizations) in the labor movement: as organizers among electronics workers (mainly focusing on occupational health hazards), in health care, and throughout the public sector.

My evidence for this "gendering" of community organization and social movements in the valley is not systematic. It was not a focus of my fieldwork; rather, its importance in urban politics and labor relations emerged retrospectively. This interpretation is strongly supported, however, by other studies of life and politics in the valley.

Flammang (1985) traces the origins of women as political leaders in San Jose to a surge of participation in PTAs and neighborhood associations. Her important study describes, on the one hand, "an association in Santa Clara County between male candidates and the growth machine of a booster political elite which had spearheaded the postwar economic boom that benefited developers." She links female candidates, on the other hand, to "environmental concerns [that] resulted from two decades of rapid, unplanned growth" and to demands for "social services—sewers, parks, schools, libraries, streets, fire protection—[that] could not keep pace with the rapid growth, leapfrog annexation, and increasing traffic congestion and air pollution in the area" (97). Also, though their conceptual framework differs, Trounstine and Christensen (1982) document the same links described here—between development politics, neighborhood organizations, the demand for social needs, and the emergence of women as leaders.

These grassroots movements, based in the gendered sites of women's work with children, in neighborhoods, and in gender-typed ghettos of women's

---

Naples's (1992) study of African-American and Latina women in low-income communities describes the interpenetration of "activist mothering" and welfare state employment.

employment, were not at all identical to the more explicitly radical women's movement that emerged with such strength on the campuses and in big cities in the same period. San Jose's feminism was less self-conscious and less ideological than it was in, say, Berkeley or San Francisco. That movement, self-consciously feminist, only lightly touched San Jose.[19] San Jose's feminism was less "post-feminist" and more a feminism of everyday life, materially rooted in the changing conditions of family life in city neighborhoods and gendered work in human service bureaucracies.

When Blum (1991) seeks to explain the eruption of the comparable worth movement in San Jose, by contrast, she cites the strength of the feminist movement in the city, relying on Flammang's (1985) case study. Although Blum's discussion does follow from Flammang's conclusions, it does not square with Flammang's evidence, or with my knowledge as a participant in progressive politics in the valley during the 1970s. Flammang documents local membership in the National Women's Political Caucus and in more traditional organizations—the League of Women Voters, the American Association of University Women—and public service groups, such as the PTA, neighborhood associations, and social service commissions, none of which were self-consciously feminist. In discussing the new female political leaders in the valley, she persuasively describes the links between these leaders' political agendas and their gendered identities as care-givers, as well as their reliance on the networks of women who organized to defend neighborhood resources. She notes, for example, that Mayor Janet Gray Hayes's first appearance before the city council was as a mother protesting the lack of traffic signs near a neighborhood school. By and large, however, Flammang's informants denied they were feminists.[20] Her findings, in sum, are more consistent with the argument made here, that the changes in women's work, family, and community life in the valley contributed to the emergence of the grassroots feminist impulse.

Challenging the Old Regime

The changing foundations of the economy and residential life provided the context, then, for the new social movements that emerged in the valley. These movements began to fill up the wide-open political spaces around the growing public bureaucracies. New neighborhoods built on old orchards would demand city services, and ultimately impose a new—or at least modified—

[19]Diane Balser's 1987 study of feminism and labor, for example, though centered on the Bay Area, never mentions San Jose or the Santa Clara Valley.
[20]Flammang notes that the women who held political office "belonged to feminist organizations in a larger proportion than the national average of 4 percent" (1985:100)—not exactly a strong claim for the powerful role of feminist political organizations!

political-economic agenda on local government. Among the tangible products demanded were police and fire protection in residential communities, libraries, parks, community centers, health clinics and women's shelters, schools, and other cultural resources. Gathering strength in the 1970s, they forged new networks, built neighborhood organizations, demanded and won new laws, and saw to it that libraries and health clinics were built. Growth also generated demand for less tangible products: chief among them, less growth.

The most powerful social movement of the early 1980s provides an exemplary case of the issues the valley's women confronted and the nature of their response. Through their personal networks, a circle of women became convinced that some environmental cause was responsible for what appeared to be a high rate of miscarriages and birth defects in their small south valley neighborhood. They investigated and eventually discovered toxic pollution in the water table beneath their homes. Further efforts led them to underground chemical tanks stored by the valley's "clean," high-tech industries that were polluting groundwater not only in their neighborhood but in the entire region.

The women galvanized intense media attention, and a series of neighborhood mobilizations swept across the valley in the early 1980s. They produced a powerful coalition for environmental protection, drawing both on neighborhood organizations and on the unions with members whose work touched on the problem—public health nurses, construction workers, firefighters, and so on. By the mid-1980s, the movement had forced industries in the valley to adhere to much stronger environmental regulations (accelerating, perhaps, the relocation of production facilities to other regions) and had spawned an enduring set of environmental action organizations (interview, Peter Cervantes-Gautschi, business agent, South Bay AFL-CIO Central Labor Council, Oct. 17, 1986).[21]

Beginning in the 1960s, the "new immigrants" began to elect their numbers to public office: mostly white professionals, usually associated directly or indirectly with the growing service sector. Usually, though not always, these politicians set the direction for the vague new constellation of interests. Their agenda included controlled growth, environmental protection, safety-related services, and cultural and recreational resources for neighborhoods.

---

[21]This episode is not a focus of this study because it was not centered in the public workplace; however, it is an excellent example of a grassroots movement that produced a labor-community coalition around a public need, informed by a feminism of everyday life. See the San Jose *Mercury-News* special report "Clean Industry, Dirty Water" (July 10, 1983) and, on the same date, "Where It Began"; *Time*, July 25, 1983; and Michael Miller, "Findings of Toxin Leakage in Silicon Valley Hurt Chip Makers' Reputation for Safety," *Wall Street Journal*, Aug. 29, 1984, 25. Starting in 1983, the Silicon Valley Toxics Coalition published the *Silicon Valley Toxics News*, which documents the development of the movement.

After decades in which the remnants of a small-town residential real estate development cabal ran public affairs unencumbered by demands for participation from the valley's new residents, life had become politically contentious again. The new political constituencies that emerged in both the new neighborhoods and the beleaguered old ones were joined, over time, by people who worked inside public organizations in activities that focused on social consumption. Gradually, these developments destabilized previous political arrangements, redefining city politics as a conflict between old and new. These struggles involved not only managers and politicians aligned with various neighborhoods and economic interest groups but also public workers' organizations themselves.

At the same time, community organizing in the East Side produced a growing Mexican-American voice in the valley. Chicano and Mexicano activism ranged from the militant Brown Berets, mobilizing around the need for community self-defense, to a vital Mexican and Mexican-American union reform caucus inside the still-huge Teamsters' cannery union. Divided between the conservative and progressive wings of local politics, Latinos remained marginalized throughout the 1970s. Al Garza, the city's only Latino elected official in these years, looked for support from property developers and construction interests and stood as Hayes's major competitor in the mayoral election of 1978.[22]

Meanwhile, the voice and impact of the labor movement grew in volume and strength with the injection of public sector activism. In the late 1970s, Peter Cervantes-Gautschi, a former SEIU organizer in welfare services, became the business agent for the Central Labor Council. And in 1980, an alliance of public sector activists and neighborhood organizers succeeded in winning the passage of a ballot measure that introduced district elections for seats on the city council.

Also in this period, the *Mercury-News* began to lose some of its enthusiasm for growth at any cost. Joseph Ridder's son, Anthony Ridder, assumed the publisher's role. The younger Ridder had a history of civic involvement, befitting his family's power and prominence. Unlike his father, he favored the valley's new agenda: not "growth," but "quality of life."

Neighborhood activists, antigrowth environmentalists, and others excluded from the old growth coalition thus provided the base for the oppositional

[22]Garza was widely recognized as the developers' candidate, and his political fortunes ultimately fell in a development-related bribery scandal. His political mentor was a powerful east valley school superintendent who built his base on construction and development interests in the process of building district infrastructure. This was a classic extension of pro-growth hegemony into education and into minority political leadership.

politics in the valley. The new political agenda did not by any means represent revolutionary change, however. On the contrary, city officials continued to pursue highway projects and downtown redevelopment, and in 1982 they opened the still-virgin Coyote Valley in the south to developers. The new watchword was "balanced growth," and its champions sought to mediate the demands of what I have been calling the social consumption and development agendas. Achieving this goal required a political battle, however, to unseat the proponents of sprawling residential growth and to overcome a related pattern of managerial power that had become entrenched within the city administration over the years. This battle set the stage and oriented the actors who would appear in the strike for comparable worth.

Confronting the Legacy of the Past

San Jose's bureaucracy was deeply involved in and affected by the policy agendas described above, which, in turn, were strongly shaped by the city's economic development and changing family life. Physical growth was accompanied by employment growth, so that between 1965 and 1978 city employment increased by 219 percent, from 1,965 to 4,303. The city's growth was uneven, however. By the late 1960s, those parts of the city workforce that provided amenities to the new neighborhoods consumed a larger and larger proportion of the city budget. From 1965 through 1975, for example, the city's road maintenance division—the stronghold of employment and union strength for blue-collar craft workers—*declined* by 14 percent. This shift reflected incremental political decisions to reallocate resources each budget year; behind these decisions was a growing tension between interests favoring the newly expanded functions and long-entrenched interests now placed on the defensive.

Although pro-growth, quality-of-life, and other impulses were rooted in institutions outside the city government, these impulses took on a life and form of their own in the government. To be sure, the growth of parks, libraries, health services, community centers, neighborhood preservation programs, and the like occurred in response to externally rooted demands for these services. The public response to demands for these services, however, came in the distinctive form of public organization, and growth in a particular part of public organization—including the agencies, the workforces and their unions, and the clients and constituents organized around them—also increased the political weight of this particular part of the local state.

In short order, groups inside the city—department managers, employees serving particular constituencies, groups within the city workers' union—moved to assert their *own* relative worth within the city's budgetary, political, and managerial domains. They asserted their missions, defended their budgets, and increased the "effective political demand" to which they owed the growth and continuity of their resources and ultimately their collective existence. This mobilization translated directly into a struggle among managers, between departments, and among different groups represented by Local 101. It defined the main fault line of conflict among workers as well as among politicians and within managerial ranks.

Let us look more closely now at this conflict as it surfaced at the upper levels of city administration. Once a new political coalition achieves electoral power, it faces the problem of reshaping a city administration defined by a legacy of the past. Like many city governments in the postprogressive era mold of weak mayors and nonpartisan politics, San Jose was administered by a city manager—an executive hired by the elected city council. In a transitional period, the city manager is a convenient target for disgruntled constituencies on each side of debates over development and fiscal priorities.

The long-simmering struggle over the city's basic direction—and over which groups and individuals would control city government—came to a political head in the mid- to late 1970s. During those years, a succession of city managers was recruited by the new "controlled growth" majority on the city council. From 1975 to 1982, four different men—all but one hired from outside the ranks of city government—held the post of city manager. Each was required to grapple with the challenges of a city administration in transition. Each confronted the power of the old guard in the Department of Public Works.

In 1978, City Manager James Alloway was locked in conflict with "old-line" managers in the Department of Public Works. Those officials' deep but informal connections in the city, particularly to city council members and their key constituents, and their close ties with still-powerful development interests were aligned against those advocating the new controlled growth agenda. Alloway's predecessor, Ted Tedesco, had already fallen victim to their resistance.

Alloway's managerial style leaned toward the use of formal organizational tools: evaluation systems, reorganization, classification studies, incentive systems. Citing reasons of efficiency, he broke up the formerly dominant public works department and created five smaller departments: general services, neighborhood maintenance, traffic operations, water pollution control, and public works. This reorganization was, of course, an assault on his adversaries in public works; that department retained the "leftovers," becoming a shell of its former imperial self.

Also in 1978, Alloway initiated the citywide job analysis and salary study of the city's managerial ranks. This study served, the reader will recall, as a critical opening for the women of the city to demand a comparable study of nonmanagement personnel. The earlier study was, in effect, the first comparable worth study in San Jose, because it cut across managerial ranks in both traditionally male and lower-status predominantly female departments. The ostensible purpose of the study was to justify a special wage increase to secure the city's management staff from the lure of management jobs in the valley's electronics industry. The study would also document, however, the now-diminished scope of responsibility of managers in the recently dismembered Department of Public Works (interviews, Armstrong, Oct. 7, 1986, and Turner, Oct. 14, 1986). Observers in city management, political office, personnel administration, and union leadership all agreed that Alloway used the study to break up what one participant described as "the good-old-boy-club type situation" surrounding the public works department, while strengthening his base among managers in the rest of the city. Behind its technical facade of neutral, scientific rationality and response to labor market conditions, then, the first Hay study was a bureaucratic weapon directed against the pro-growth machine. In their subsequent campaign for comparable worth, Maxine Jenkins and the women of the city—defending equal treatment—would take up the same bureaucratic weapons, building on the same pattern of political change and adding to them the potent political force of a mobilization for gender justice.

This episode served as a key link among the various developments that converged to promote the events described in the previous chapter: the emergence of new political interests in the valley, conflict within city management, reorganization of city government, rationalization of the city's classification system, and mobilization of the women. All reflect the same fissure and upheaval along the same fault line in city politics during this process of political transition.

The identification of city workers' interests with the status of their departments continued to shape the labor relations context in San Jose during the period of fiscal crisis in the late 1970s and early 1980s. As we saw in the previous chapter, the defense of jobs and services became a "real battleground" in labor relations. Conflict on this battleground intensified in the early 1980s as city officials, bitter about the use of the comparable worth weapon in the 1981 strike, targeted the new leadership's base in the libraries and parks for massive layoffs. Armed, however, with new mobilization capacity in the flush of strike success and with labor-community coalitions in city neighborhoods at points of service delivery, Local 101's agile cadre of activists now had the political strength to enter the city's new governing coalition, through their support of Hayes's successor, McEnery.

Local 101's activists were well equipped to prevail in fiscal skirmishes. In response to management pleas of "fiscal crisis" and warnings of layoffs and service cuts, unionists claimed that the shortfall should not be met by paying "unfair" wages; if the public was unprepared to pay for services, it should not expect to receive them. On this basis, the unionists mobilized against service and revenue cuts and for wage increases. Rather than pitting the union against allies in the community, however, this strategy appeared, perversely, to *strengthen* the unionists' position; cutbacks could be attributed to the impact of Proposition 13 and state budget cuts and not to pay increases, comparable worth or otherwise.

In response to budget cuts, for example, union and agency managers in the service-oriented departments took publicly visible steps to implement reductions in services, which they then announced to the community through recorded phone messages and Friends of the Library bulletins. A trivial but typical case in point: in a move calculated by the librarians to create a public commotion, the library stopped stocking a popular line of best-selling novels. The result, of course, was heightened community protest and turnout at budget hearings in defense of the library budget.

Though led by union activists, these mobilizations involved the same managers who benefited from the first Hay study, who had been giving tacit support to the comparable worth principle and whom the strikers ultimately regarded as behind-the-scenes supporters during the 1981 work stoppage. "We all felt beleaguered together," recalled one union member in the library department (interview, Goddard, Oct. 2, 1986). Furthermore, these labor-management-community mobilizations enhanced the power of the comparable worth mobilization, serving as a source of political strength for Local 101. They later provided the resources to achieve union goals without recourse to adversarial bargaining, as the union became a participant in the city's new governing regime.

Joining the New Regime

With the election of Tom McEnery in 1982, the new "limited growth, quality of life" political bloc was now firmly in power. Local 101 was now well ensconced in that bloc, its position reinforced by the reliance of city officials on union "troops" to mobilize in defense of city revenues. In the following period, as described in the previous chapter, the new mayor would continue making comparable worth adjustments, restore lost positions in the libraries, and adopt the modified agency shop provision. Rank-and-file leaders who had emerged in the comparable worth campaign found themselves stranded behind the receding wave of militancy, as the successful comparable worth movement became a proud movement of a different time. Many of the same activists who had successfully challenged gendered inequalities in the city workers' union, in city wage relations, and in budgetary decision-making entered the city's inner circle of power.

These developments might be described as "societal corporatism of the public sector," driven not only by convergent interests in the city's new governing agenda but also in a defensive response to fiscal crisis.[23] The union itself became more hierarchical as the staff's employment status shifted from co-equal employees of AFSCME's regional office, accountable to Local 101's executive board (a status that facilitated Jenkins's earlier support for "revolution in the union"), to subordinates under a regional administrator. Bill Callahan, who had risen from the ranks and followed Jenkins's initiative to staff the comparable worth campaign, left the local in frustration over the new hierarchy; he was replaced by staff with a less combative stance. Collaborative problem-solving prevailed over adversarial relations: for at least the following decade, no serious strike threat was ventured in negotiations. The union acquired new revenue through the modified agency shop rule, which reduced the voluntary nature of union membership by mandating the deduction of contributions to the union from new employees' paychecks. City officials would routinely "check with 101" on personnel matters, and city and union officials would cooperate to manage labor relations problems, including troublesome efforts by the custodians and public works employees to gain control over their own representation.[24]

One Movement on Two Fronts

Based on the account and analyses in this chapter and the previous chapter, it seems clear that the character and course of the city workers' movement in San Jose were closely linked to the politics of growth and austerity. On the one

[23]"Societal corporatism" is a mode of governance identified mainly with state-brokered collaboration by Western Europe's centralized unions and private employers in the postwar period (Schmitter and Lehmbruch 1982). Elite groups controlling major organizations cooperate to manage potential conflict and address common problems while taking on a share of public power and, frequently, public subsidy. Since the mid-1970s, I suggest here, state and local governments in the United States have witnessed a comparable corporatization in response to fiscal crisis.

[24]This history is far from finished. McEnery's administration would perfect a new pro-growth strategy, while protecting the neighborhoods. As the second (and, at this writing, continuing) great fiscal crisis descended on California's local governments in the early 1990s, this new pro-growth regime was confronted by a new round of mobilizations demanding that funds earmarked for downtown development be shifted to neighborhood needs. At this writing, the latest expression of this basic fault line in local politics is an electoral race for the U.S. House of Representatives pitting McEnery against Zoe Lofgren, member of the county board of supervisors and foremost champion of what many now call the "old girls' network" in human services. Now the role of Local 101 and other public sector unions is decidedly ambivalent, however, as they are no longer upstarts but part of the governing regime. These developments must await further analysis, however.

hand, the newfound political strength of San Jose's Local 101 in the early 1980s—garnered in the process of mobilizing against budget cuts and in pivotal elections—provided necessary leverage for the adoption of comparable worth adjustments after the 1981 strike, as well as for the restoration of human service positions in the Reagan era. On the other hand, it would be a gross oversimplification to attribute these gains solely to mobilizations for public services in coalition with neighborhood interests and public officials opposed to Reagan-era cuts. The long-term mobilization of women around the claim to gender justice within the city bureaucracy built the core of the union's leadership, and the 1981 strike established its political strength. At the same time, however, that mobilization proceeded during a time of campaigns against layoffs and service cuts and drew upon relationships and organizational resources mobilized in support of department budgets.

The mobilization by the women of San Jose thus contained two intertwined and ultimately inseparable strands: one asserting the economic value of the women's labor and demanding higher wages; the other asserting the value of the women's work through city politics and grassroots movements at neighborhood-based "points of production." From the point of view of scholars focusing on industrial relations or, perhaps, on comparable worth alone, only the first of these strands merits attention. From the point of view of those involved, these were simultaneous but separate efforts, in which the women confronted different problems in distinct trenches of city politics. From a broader perspective, however, this was one movement on two fronts, each rooted in the changing conditions of public life in the valley, each adding to the force and the resources of the other, and each asserting the worth of the work of the women of the city.[25]

---

[25]Fernando Gapasin's recent 1994 dissertation (grounded in his own work as a public transit unionist) describes similar patterns in a different slice of the valley's public workforce: the valley's transit district. Previously a private company, this organization is an ideal setting to explore the issues covered here while filling an important gap in my account. While the movements described here were sharply gendered, Gapasin's bus drivers' and mechanics' movements were deeply racialized. They paralleled the public service coalition-building of the women of the city, though, revolving around issues of transit safety and service levels.

5 The Nurses of the Valley

Where does one find a private sector workforce similar to the miscellaneous workers of San Jose? How, if one is interested in controlled cross–sectoral comparison—isolating the difference in sector from other factors—is one to find a workplace similar in every respect but its sectoral location?

In this case, the task is impossible. Had we begun with a hospital or perhaps a school, private sector analogues might be available. The diversity of the city or county workplace, however, combining what in the private sector would be multiple industries within a single geographically defined enterprise, is itself part of the peculiarity of public organization.

Yet when I asked people in the Santa Clara Valley labor movement what group I should use for my comparison to the San Jose city workforce, the answer was immediate—the valley's nurses, who had conducted their own comparable worth strike in 1982. Until the 1986 Watsonville, California, cannery workers' strike—also led by women—the city workers' strike and the nurses' strike were by far the most conspicuous episodes of labor militancy in the region in the early Reagan era.[1] Together, they represent a single upsurge of feminist militancy among women workers in Silicon Valley.

Although the comparable worth movement in the Santa Clara Valley began among city workers, it did not end there. Six months after the city workers' strike in San Jose, thirteen hundred private sector nurses walked off their jobs in four Santa Clara Valley hospitals—San Jose, Alexian Brothers, Good Samaritan, and O'Connor—demanding comparable worth. At the time of my fieldwork, in the late 1980s, the memory of the nurses' strike was still fresh in local memory. It was, however, a memory of trauma: an ambitious strike,

[1]On the Watsonville strike of 1986, see Moody 1988:327 – 30.

113

inspired and exuberant, which had ended in demoralized defeat. At the time of my interviews five years after the strike, this sense of trauma remained palpable.

The sense of trauma may explain why, aside from local memories, the event appears to have vanished from history. When I contacted the nurses' union a few years later for help in locating strike photos, for example, I spoke to staffers who were surprised to learn that their union had struck for comparable worth. Of course, the strike was only one of several in the past decade, and union staffers do come and go. This was, however, the first private sector strike for comparable worth anywhere in the country; at the time, it was the longest nurses' strike and involved more nurses than any other such strike in California history.

As I searched the literature on comparable worth, I was further surprised that, although the nurses' strike was much larger, longer, and in some ways stronger and more profoundly feminist than the city workers' movement, the strike had received no mention in that literature. Nor did it appear in the great and growing volume of references to the city workers' strike or in broader discussions of labor relations, comparable worth, gender and the workplace, and so on. It was even missing from discussions focused explicitly on nurses and pay equity.[2] This chapter aims in part to rescue the nurses' experience from oblivion.

Comparisons between the city workers' and nurses' strikes become particularly interesting when we consider the differences: most dramatically, the *success* of the city workers' strike, despite its apparent *weakness,* and the *failure* of the nurses' strike, despite its apparent *strength.* By conventional standards, the city workers' strike—which involved only 25 percent of the workforce, was organizationally weak, and occurred in the middle of a fiscal crisis—should have been a disaster. By the same standards, the nurses' strike should have been a resounding success. The nurses were powerfully organized, 90 percent of the workforce participated, there was a self-consciously feminist culture of solidarity, and the strikers were strong enough to picket their hospitals twenty-four hours a day, seven days a week, and strong enough to remain on strike for three months in steady, drenching rain. Further, despite California's continuing economic slump, the nurses seemed to be facing favorable economic conditions, including a 20 percent vacancy rate at hospitals statewide. Finally, the strike was led by Maxine Jenkins, the gifted

[2]The most accessible source of information on the strike is the *California Nurse,* the official bulletin of the California Nurses' Association, especially "Comparable Pay for Comparable Worth: Massive Strike in Santa Clara," vol. 77 (Feb. 1982) and "Comparable Worth: Issue of the 80's," special section of vol. 77 (March-April 1982).

organizer and charismatic leader who had already blazed a trail through working women's movements in the public sector.

How, then, after the city workers' success, did the nurses suffer such defeat? What were the critical differences between the two movements? These questions offer an opportunity to explore the effects of the sectoral difference—on the claim to comparable worth, on the feminist impulse in the labor movement, and on labor movements in the two sectors.

Grassroots movements and union efforts for comparable worth in the United States overwhelmingly are public sector phenomena (Johansen 1984; Cook 1985; Evans and Nelson 1989; Acker 1989; Blum 1991).[3] I argued in the previous chapters that this is more than coincidence: the claim to comparable worth as we know it has an affinity to the public sector.[4] I also argued that, where the claim to comparable worth has emerged in the private sector, it has almost invariably relied on efforts to use legal or legislative power to regulate wage relations—efforts, in other words, to extend the public sector into the private. The nurses' movement for comparable worth clearly offers a challenge to that argument. Based on my argument, such a movement would be unlikely to emerge in the private sector and would be radically modified and/or fail to achieve its ends if it did emerge. This chapter will show, however, that the comparable worth theme in the nurses' movement was a product not of its own context but of diffusion from the public sector and that this inherited script failed to fit the private sector context.

In the previous two chapters, we found that the demands and resources of the city workers' movement—including the campaign for comparable worth—were deeply shaped by the context within which the movement surfaced. Demands were framed as legitimate and administrable policy, appealing to procedural justice or other politically defined public needs. Further, both the demands and the powers of the city workers' movement reflected the workers' involvement in the broader patterns of coalition-building and conflict in San Jose.

In the nurses' movement, all of these patterns vanished. Instead, the grassroots feminist impulse lent its force to a conventional economic strike. The

[3]Yale University's 1984–85 strike is an exception; there, as in San Jose, "comparable worth" served as a tool and weapon for mobilization, but even more than in San Jose, it was downplayed in bargaining and by the membership (Kautzer 1992); the union used the comparable worth weapon to inflict "embarrassment"—a ruinous condition in Yale's peculiar universe but less menacing to more market-oriented adversaries.

[4]Though this was the first nurses' strike for comparable worth, the demand had been made earlier by other nurses. The best-known comparable worth case involving nurses was (and remains) *Lemons v. City and County of Denver, 1978*—filed on behalf of nurses in the public sector. Strikingly similar to the City of San Jose case, *Lemons* was sparked by a cross-benchmark comparison at the managerial level in local government (Feldberg 1992:195).

movement shifted its attention from the bureaucratic personnel system and the political universe of the single employer to the *occupational labor market.* There was a general disregard for political resources, and the claim to comparable worth mutated from a political indictment of the market standard to a market-oriented appeal to "the laws of supply and demand." Missing, moreover, were the alliance-building—despite the nurses' intense concern for patients' needs—and the public service orientation that characterized the city workers' movement.

Accompanying the diffusion of the language of comparable worth from the public sector to the private, we find a new pattern of organization, new kinds of claims—including a new definition of comparable worth—and new strategic orientations, all reflecting a distinctive market orientation. Beyond such differences in its cultural identity and repertoire of strategies, the movement also confronted the cold, hard consequences of a very different strategic context, including some wicked dilemmas associated with monopsony in the labor market for registered nurses. These dilemmas contributed to a perception among managers of a backward-sloping labor supply curve and among workers and their union to an overestimatation—or what I term "the monopsony illusion"—of their labor market power.

An extraordinary effervescence emerged among the nurses during the strike and an equally extreme demoralization after its defeat.[5] In the analysis that follows, I link this demoralization to a deep and complex sense of injury and anxiety associated with the gendered aspects of nursing work,[6] submerged here beneath the more economistic discourse of comparable worth. My analysis of these dynamics focuses on *the dilemma of autonomy versus care* in these women's developing identities—a dilemma brought to an extraordinary degree of intensity when union nurses "walk away from their patients" in a strike.[7] We shall consider the impact of these occupation-specific gender dynamics as they were played out in a *public sector* nurses' movement in chapter 7.

I shall begin by introducing the nurses and their union and describing the status of California's health care industry in the late 1970s and early 1980s. In the next section, I compare the divergent interpretations of the labor relations situation held by the nurses' union and hospital management officials on the

---

[5]I found similar processes at work in other nurses' strikes, in both the public and private sector.
[6]See Barbara Melosh's study of nurses as "the physician's hand" (1982). The argument developed here supports the substantial body of work (reviewed by Gray 1989) linking RN militancy to the gendered subordination of nurses. It draws attention, however, to effects of the sectoral difference and also to nurses' ambivalence about the assertion of autonomy given their commitment to care.
[7]The roots of this analysis are in Dorothy Dinnerstein's (1976) penetrating and controversial development of Melanie Klein's (1957) work.

eve of the strike. I then describe and analyze the nurses' movement—the emergence of the claim to comparable worth, the character and outcome of the strike, and the experience of the nurses who participated in it. Finally, I focus on some dilemmas associated with nursing work, how they interacted here with the sectoral context and with the strategic choices of the nurses and their union.

The Nurses and Their Union

An affiliate of the American Nurses' Association (ANA), the California Nurses' Association (CNA) is simultaneously a professional association, a political-legislative advocacy group, and a trade union. Though not affiliated with the AFL-CIO, the CNA has been negotiating contracts for nurses in California's private sector hospitals since 1946. In 1949, the ANA adopted a no-strike policy; in 1966, however, facing a wave of strike actions, "sick-outs," mass resignations, and so on by nurses around the state, the CNA formally abandoned this policy for the private sector.[8]

As a professional association, the CNA did not limit itself to collective bargaining. It also used political strategies to influence certification policies for registered nurses (RNs) (and, accordingly, to buttress nurses' occupational status and labor market position). The Economic and General Welfare Division of the organization functioned much like other unions, however: union representatives were assigned to represent members and enforce contracts by bargaining unit and geographical area, and control over staff was centralized in the state office. By 1981, and in 1986 and 1987 when I interviewed them, the nurses of the Santa Clara Valley simply referred to the CNA as "the union."

The CNA contract set the pay scale for the largest RN classification—staff nurse II—at a range of $10.28 to $11.67 per hour. Though relatively low for professionals or semiprofessionals, this represented a significant improvement over nurses' wages in earlier years. One nurse whose career spanned the entire postwar period described her employment history:

> I started in 1951 at St. Mary's in San Francisco. Back then you didn't
> even ask about the pay. I had no benefits. I think I was getting about
> $155 a month and no social security. After I got divorced in 1960, I had
> two kids to take care of and I was making $320 month—only $90 more
> than the nurses' aide. We had no overtime pay and no holiday pay. We'd
> get one weekend out of six or seven off. And we had no respect at all. We
> were there to serve, and we were in the service. I remember getting wrote

[8]As of 1987, the CNA maintained its ban on public sector strikes.

up because I didn't get up to give a doctor my chair. Then we got our first contract in 1965, and that's when things started to change.[9]

As this woman notes, the CNA began to bargain for the nurses in the valley's hospitals in 1965. Historically, four of the five CNA units bargained together, and ultimately they struck together: San Jose Hospital, O'Connor Hospital, Alexian Brothers Hospital, and Good Samaritan Hospital.[10] The agreements governing all four bargaining units shared a common expiration date of January 1, 1982.

Throughout the 1970s, these four hospitals had composed the Association of Hospitals of Santa Clara, an employers' association formed specifically to coordinate collective bargaining. In response to the increasingly competitive health care environment of the late 1970s, O'Connor and Good Samaritan withdrew from the association in 1980 and 1981 respectively. Hospital managers and negotiators closely monitored one another, however, and, in effect, bargained in tandem. Moreover, the CNA still coordinated the bargaining for what were now three separate contracts.

One central difference between the nurses' labor organization and that of the city workforce is so obvious as to be inconspicuous: like most other private sector unions in the United States, the nurses' union had an *occupational jurisdiction*, whereas the city workers' union had an *organizational jurisdiction*. The nurses' bargaining involved a homogeneous workforce facing four private sector employers. The city workers' bargaining involved heterogeneous groups—located, in effect, in different industries—facing the same employer. While the nurses' union represented participants in a single labor market, the city workers' union represented participants in a single public organization.

This difference is reflected in the character and orientation of the labor movements in these two settings. The city workers paid close attention not only to their own status but to that of their dissimilar co-workers while ignoring similar workers in the same labor market. They defined wage demands in terms reflecting this focus: "salary compaction," "internal alignment," "comparable worth." Problems of intergroup conflict were endemic, and alliances across the political-bureaucratic divisions of labor were both

[9]This woman had not participated in the strike because she believed the demands were unrealistic. Like other informants who crossed the picket lines, she spoke only on the assurance of anonymity.
[10]The fifth unit was employed by Kaiser Health Plan, a health maintenance organization. That employer was reimbursed on a monthly per capita basis and therefore did not charge fees for particular services. This new complication in the strategic relationship between labor and management is likely to be very significant for labor relations in health care in coming years, because it undermines the strike's economic leverage, requiring unions to turn to new strategies such as corporate campaigns or public service unionism.

tenuous and strategically important. Different classification groups jockeyed for position in the multilayered classification structure and within the union itself, and on occasion leaders succeeded in framing issues so as to secure alliances that played a key role in successful mobilizations. The private sector nurses and their union, by contrast, paid attention only to nurses; they directed their attention outward toward the RN labor market, rather than inward toward the bureaucratic labor regime.

Not surprisingly, other members of the hospitals' workforce—other professionals, licensed vocational nurses, technicians, clerical, semiskilled and skilled blue-collar workers, virtually all nonunion—did not play active roles in the nurses' movement; nor were they asked to do so. The major northern California health care union—SEIU's Hospital Workers Local 250—had failed to organize in the Santa Clara Valley, although the union had enjoyed a period of dynamic growth elsewhere in northern California in the 1950s and early 1960s. And the registered nurses and their union never considered organizing their co-workers.

This disconnection from the rest of the internal workforce has implications for the claim to comparable worth—a claim based, after all, on internal organizational comparisons. For example, despite their modest wages, RNs enjoyed substantially higher status and approximately 40 percent higher wages than licensed vocational nurses (LVNs, often called licensed practical nurses, or LPNs, in other states), who are below them in the hospital hierarchy and most of whom are black. Although RNs undergo longer and more theoretical training than do LVNs, the pay (and status) gap between the two groups is a source of resentment for many LVNs, who feel it is arbitrary and excessive.[11] In the Santa Clara Valley hospitals, a hospitalwide job classification and salary standardization study might have documented that LVNs were suffering substantial pay inequities. The nurses' union, however, never seriously considered conducting a formal comparable worth study of all the ranks of hospital employees.[12]

The Strike Context

As the reader probably recalls, the City of San Jose experienced a shift toward adversarial labor relations in the wake of its early era of employment

---

[11]During my previous work representing San Francisco's employees, I represented both groups of nurses.
[12]Julianne Malveaux (1992) takes comparable worth advocates to task on such grounds. In the case of the nurses' movement, this disregard appears to have been driven (or at least reinforced) by the nurses' orientation to their own labor market rather than the differentiated internal bureaucracy. Related issues are discussed in chapters 6 and 7.

growth but fiscal and political crises of the Reagan era were accompanied by a new labor-management alliance. The private sector also moved from a period of expansion into economic and political adversity over the same period. These parallel patterns of change had very different consequences for labor relations in the private sector, however: exclusion rather than inclusion and intensified conflict rather than collaboration.

Restructuring in the Health Care Industry

The postwar growth of the hospital industry in the Santa Clara Valley reflected the same demand for human services that drove the political changes traced in previous chapters. In the hospital industry, however, market demand, not political demand, was the force for change. Growth proceeded, in Alan Wolfe's words, in a manner that was careful to "preserve untouched, if slightly expanded, the profit system in medicine" (1982:89). Direct state and federal subsidies, nominal nonprofit status for market-oriented institutions, certification barriers to competition in labor and product markets, and, most important, "fee-for-service" arrangements with state and federal agencies as well as private insurance companies all buttressed the market position of the health care industry but did not undermine its private status. These mechanisms initially insulated the hospital industry from the economic pressures that elsewhere in the private sector began to intensify by the mid-1970s.

Gradually, however, these economic pressures also penetrated the insulating mechanisms in health care. Spiraling private health insurance premiums became the most rapidly increasing costs to private sector employers and passed the major insurers' limits of toleration. Already in the late 1970s, efforts by employers to pass increases in employer-paid health coverage on to their employees were a central issue in most strikes. The similarly spiraling cost of publicly subsidized fee-for-service health care was a central concern of state and federal budget managers. In response, employers formed regional groups to develop and implement health care cost-containment measures.

By 1980, major private employers, insurance companies, public officials, and some unions began efforts to limit hospital costs. The thrust of these efforts was to reduce utilization of the most expensive component of health care—inpatient hospital care—through a veritable alphabet soup of administrative incentives termed "market mechanisms." The policy changes that resulted in California would anticipate national trends by more than a decade.

From the standpoint of private hospital management, the main danger in these developments was unaffordable excess capacity, increased ratios of constant to variable costs, and, ultimately, closure of those hospitals least successful in limiting costs of inpatient care. In part, the hospitals responded by becoming more politically active, through increased administrative, legal, and legislative maneuvering for favorable regulatory policy and for maximum reimbursement of public funds. Thus, whereas in 1970 the California Hospital Association had only one half-time lobbyist in the state capitol, following one hospital bill, by 1980 three staffers were following five hundred such bills in the first six months of the year alone (unpublished report by California Hospital Association to board of O'Connor Hospital, 1981).

At the same time, the hospitals began to compete. They invested in more profitable medical units and market areas, merged with other hospitals, conducted marketing campaigns, made attempts at cost containment, and adopted strategies to attract the most profitable patients—those who were relatively affluent and healthy—while turning away the indigent. The four Santa Clara Valley hospitals that are the focus of this study were all nominally nonprofit (i.e., tax-exempt), but all were dependent on payment by patients and by increasingly cost-conscious insurance carriers and thus oriented toward a market setting.[13]

By 1980, then, the hospitals were operating under new conditions requiring more aggressive, market-oriented management. A financial comptroller for one of the hospitals expressed his rueful evaluation of the situation: "There are too many hospitals for an area like San Jose, and so we are all doing our damndest to stamp each other out—to compete—I think that in the process we have lost what our purpose was and are now there as a business."[14]

For hospital workers, these developments meant tighter wage constraints and heavier and more stressful workloads as hospitals simultaneously attempted to reduce "excess staff," increase patient censuses, and reduce patients' lengths of stay, which also increased the acuity level, or volume of serious health needs requiring nurses' attention at any given time. These changes also led to a flood of poor patients, rejected by cost-conscious private health care providers, into the public sector arena. In private hospitals, the changes also meant greater incentives to attract affluent patients through campaigns to "sell the product" by increasing attention to consumer satisfaction and managerially mandated happy faces. One nurse who had been employed at Good Samaritan Hospital for seventeen years described the developments:

---

[13]The status of these hospitals—quasi-nonprofit and state-regulated, albeit commodity-producing and demand-dependent—strengthens our comparison to public agencies. If anything, their status understates the effects of the public-private difference.
[14]Interviews with nonstriking workers and with representatives of hospital management were secured only with a commitment not to divulge their names or affiliations.

> We don't talk anymore about being "Samaritans" here. It's big bucks
> now. We're competing for the people who can afford to pay. Labor and
> delivery is a big public relations area for the hospital—the idea is we get
> the mother in here and the family will use the hospital from then on. So
> we're remodeling to put a jacuzzi into our alternative birth cen-
> ter . . . and they've got us working to impress the patients. They give us
> little cards to carry around saying "clients not patients" (interview,
> Donna Briones, Oct. 23, 1986).

In sum, in private sector hospitals, economic constraints intensified the
commodity form of health care to capture all-important market share, or
consumer demand. Private hospitals also intensified political action; mainly,
however, to reinforce their market position. By contrast, in the city workplace
of San Jose, fiscal constraints resulted in the political aggregation and articulation of interests, and at times in deliberate *reductions* in the quality and
quantity of services, to generate all-important political demand.

How did the key decision-makers on each side of the nurses' movement
view the situation before the strike? Both CNA officials and hospital bargainers claimed in later interviews that they could see the strike coming. Each
side believed it would gain the upper hand, and both sides prepared for a
strike. Although each side analyzed the conditions they faced very differently,
both framed these conditions, set their own expectations, and charted their
strategy in dealing with the situation based on the logic of labor market
behavior.

Union Leaders' Interpretation of the Strike Context

Three years before the strike, CNA's members at the four hospitals ratified
their contract with grumbling dissatisfaction over the wage and retirement provisions. CNA's state executive director, Myra Snyder, concluded at
the time that a strike in 1982 was likely: "They ratified the last contract, but
they didn't like it. We knew it would be difficult to get them [the nurses] to
accept an offer this time; we would have to come in with something very good"
(interview, Dec. 3, 1986). Snyder's observation was supported in interviews
with nurses and union staff, who reported anger about the previous contract
and frustration with the shortage of staff and heavy workload, increasingly
tense doctor-nurse relations, and intensified conflict with certain supervisors.

Despite the economic constraints on the hospital industry, which by now
were widely felt, the leaders of the CNA, from their central offices in San
Francisco, believed that the Santa Clara Valley nurses were in an ideal position
to achieve a major breakthrough in wages by going out on strike. They were

convinced that the shortage of staff gave the nurses excellent leverage to make wage gains beyond the already substantial rate of inflation.[15] According to the CNA's own data, the labor market in 1981 gave every appearance of such a shortage: statewide, hospitals reported a 50 percent annual turnover rate in the RN workforce and a 20 percent vacancy rate in nursing positions. In the Santa Clara Valley, the pool of registered nurses licensed to practice had dropped from 10,500 in 1979 to 9,129 in 1981, a 13 percent decline in only three years.

CNA officials were also aware of the new fiscal limits and competitive economic pressures for cost containment. In response, however, they claimed, first, that higher wages would mean fewer vacancies and therefore fewer expensive per diem staff. Second, they argued that capital investments—in subsidiary hospitals in new suburban areas such as the southern part of the valley, in new equipment, and in hospital profit centers—should be postponed so that nurses could receive higher wages. Third, the officials recommended that the wages of other hospital employees, which traditionally increased at the same rate as the RNs' wages, should be contained while nurses "caught up."

Hospital Managers' Interpretation of the Strike Context

The hospital managers also expected a strike. They were not unaware of the state of the RNs' morale. Further, personnel officers and nursing administrators had observed the San Jose city workers' strike, including the responsive chord it struck among nurses. They had become convinced that they faced a serious strike threat when Maxine Jenkins arrived as negotiator shortly before the contract was due to expire. According to the chief finance officer at one hospital, "It was known prior to negotiations that we'd have a strike, because of this new lady negotiator. Her history had been in comparable worth. We heard talk about a strike and about her among the nurses. They said she was one tough cookie."[16]

During the period leading up to the strike, key hospital administrators participated in a seminar offered by Mendelson, Fastiff and Tichy, a law firm that specialized in providing aggressive labor relations assistance to employers. In the seminar hospital administrators resolved to prepare to take a

---

[15]The CNA's aspirations on the eve of the strike, as described by Suzanne La Violette, managing editor of *Modern Health Care*, were as follows: "The CNA believes that San Jose nurses with two to three years experience should make $30,000 a year instead of their current $21,500 average" ("Comparable Worth Really Will Spur Lawsuits, Union Demands," *Modern Health Care*, Jan. 1982, 56–58).
[16]This informant spoke on the condition of anonymity.

strike unflinchingly, to hire permanent replacements, and to refuse to restore the seniority of strikers. The Sisters of Charity, owners of O'Connor Hospital, subsequently retained Mendelson, Fastiff and Tichy to manage their negotiations; ultimately, O'Connor—described in the union newspaper as "the pits of the strike zone" ("O'Connor = the Pits of the Strike Zone," *California Nurse*, Feb. 1982)—would succeed in breaking the union.

Nor were the hospitals' administrators oblivious to the nursing shortage. How did they propose to solve it? More generally, how did they explain it?

First, in light of the pressure to contain costs, they preferred to address the shortage by widening the labor market, rather than by raising wages. In their view, the only realistic alternative to hiring expensive per diem nurses was to change state legislation governing nursing practices to permit less trained, less expensive non-RN staff to perform some RN duties. Management negotiators believed, moreover, that granting nurses higher wages would lower, not raise, the supply of labor. According to one senior personnel officer,

> Our last settlement, in 1978, gave them [the nurses] a 12 to 14 percent increase and allowed them to accrue sick leave and vacation on all hours paid and even holidays worked. It's still not creating more nurses. If we raised our pay $300 above the registries next month, they would raise their pay too, and we'd still have trouble recruiting. . . . There was a time when RN wages were low and they worked long hours because they had to. Now the pay is so good the nurse doesn't have to work so long. This job does mentally beat the hell out of people—it's hard work, and it's also my sense that about half of them have kids to take care of too. . . . So when they got lower wages they worked longer hours, and higher wages mean shorter hours.[17]

A senior negotiator at another hospital confirmed this view: higher-paid nurses would be better able to afford to work part time; given the burdens of the work and the pull of their families, the relative utility of escaping from work was so great that the nurses would use their higher wages to purchase more time to escape. In other words, these managers believed they faced a *backward-sloping labor supply curve*.[18]

Second, the managers rejected out of hand proposals to curtail investment and building projects, which they viewed as essential elements of their new competitive strategies. Third, the managers disclosed that resistance to the substantial wage increases that the nurses were demanding was based not

[17]This informant spoke with me on the condition of anonymity.
[18]Linda H. Aiken 1981 presents persuasive historical evidence that vacancies among RNs are negatively correlated with their relative wages. The important point is not whether the curve was indeed backward-sloping but rather the labor market orientation displayed here.

on the cost but on the probable impact on the rest of the workforce. The nurses' wages, after all, were only about 15 percent of each hospital's budget; a large increase for the RNs, several informants noted, would be a minimal cost to the hospital. At the same time, the managers believed that granting higher wage increases to the RNs than to other work groups would have had a demoralizing effect and could perhaps have even led to unionization among the members of the large, nonunionized, lower-level occupational groups. Granting higher wages all around would have been even more problematic; in addition to the higher cost, it would have demonstrated dividends associated with unionization while still not satisfying the RNs' demands for higher relative wages.

In sum, not only were the two sides in adversarial roles, they did not even share a common interpretation of their situation. Each side, however, grasped its interests, opportunities, and strategic position in terms of the labor market. To the nurses' union, the apparent shortage of nurses presented an opportunity to raise wages substantially; to the hospital administrators, a backward-sloping labor supply curve suggested that increasing the nurses' wages would not improve the nurses' recruitment and retention rates, and granting the nurses relatively higher wage increases threatened to encourage other workers to raise their own expectations. None of this augured well for a negotiated settlement.

By contrast, in San Jose, a comparable worth agreement had emerged over a sustained period of time; labor-management conflict was moderated by alliances between union activists and parts of management that reflected the city's new governing coalition; joint efforts to overcome external fiscal constraints dampened the level of conflict and promoted a degree of labor-management solidarity. In the hospitals, neither public policy issues nor common concern with the hospitals' market position generated such collaboration. Each side believed it held the upper ground, and each was prepared to fight.

Emergence—and Mutation—of the Claim to Comparable Worth

As we saw in previous chapters, the claim to comparable worth unfolded in San Jose somewhat "organically" (if that term can be applied to a thing that grows in a political bureaucracy). The nurses' claim to comparable worth, by contrast, emerged suddenly in the short period between the city workers' strike, in July 1981, and before the nurses' strike, in January 1982.

As late as early December 1981—less than a month before the strike deadline—a bargaining survey circulated among the members in attendance at a union meeting for two of the four hospitals did not even mention the claim to comparable worth. Significantly, though—and I will return to this issue—nine of the nineteen questions on the survey focused on problems resulting from the shortage of nurses, or, in the language of the nurses, "short-staffing." Beyond the basic wage demand, according to this survey, the nurses' foremost concerns were that nurses were having to "float" to unfamiliar floors and that hospitals were depending on per diem and registry nurses.

The introduction of the theme of comparable worth occurred when Maxine Jenkins became involved in the bargaining. During the city workers' strike, Jenkins was already employed by the CNA but working elsewhere in the state. As it faced its own strike in late fall 1981, the CNA assigned her to represent the Santa Clara Valley nurses.

According to nurses on the negotiating committee, the nurses were increasingly aware, because of publicity from the city workers' strike, of the claim to comparable worth as a way to justify wage increases. The union did not explicitly assert the claim, however, until Jenkins raised the issue in late 1981 in membership meetings and negotiations, which she coordinated.

There had been, then, no history of job evaluation and salary standardization studies within the workforce by either the union or management before bargaining began, much less a collaborative labor-management exercise, as in the city, yielding recommendations that could be implemented. Rather, both parties focused their attention on the relationship between the nurses' pay in the hospitals and the larger labor market.

To define and justify their claim for comparable worth, Jenkins and the RN negotiators relied on impressionistic data, ad hoc job-for-job comparisons, and patched-together data from other studies. The two main figures they used for comparison were the 35 percent spread between hospital pharmacists and registered nurses and the rough parity in the pay of registered nurses and retail clerks (grocery store checkers). On the basis of the comparison with the pharmacists, the nurses' bargaining team demanded a 37 percent wage increase over eighteen months (29 percent for the first year and 12 percent for the final six months).

One nurse responsible for producing informational material during the strike described the character and purpose of these comparisons: "We did comparative analysis; we had to justify what we did to the nurses—I did comparisons of window washer, fireman, policemen—all the paperwork things people could hold onto—to project [them] to [their] goal" (interview, Donna Peterson, Oct. 23, 1986). Thus, these comparisons were not constructed within a personnel system, structured by legitimate techniques for wage administration. Nor were they deployed as "clubs" for the purpose of gaining publicity. Instead, the comparisons *were* used for political effect: *inside* the strike movement, "to justify what we did to the nurses" and to "project [them] to their goal."

In negotiations and in her language directed at the RNs themselves, Jenkins used some of the rhetoric that she had perfected in earlier public sector campaigns: nurses, as exploited women, must not allow themselves to be victimized by "the market standard," which had "worked against the labor of women for at least 2500 years of recorded history."[19] And although her language met with little sympathy at the bargaining table, it resonated in the workforce. Unlike the city workers' strike, where the leadership was constrained to maintain unity in a diverse workforce, Jenkins and the activists in the nurses' union had no reason to pull verbal punches or to moderate their emphasis on the claim to comparable worth. The claim thus became the battle cry of an explicitly feminist strike.[20]

At the same time, other concerns involving RNs' status, short-staffing, and "nurse burnout"—equally susceptible to feminist interpretation and, potentially, to the assertion of public needs—were subordinated to the claim to comparable worth. Given different leadership, these themes could have unfolded into a discourse and strategic thrust more resonant with the nurses' experience and far more suited to the context within which the nurses were mobilized. In this case, however, the comparable worth claim successfully co-opted them.

Infused with these concerns, the wage claim became more than a wage claim; it resonated with emotionally powerful meanings. The affirmation of "the worth of the nurse" meant much more than its dollar expression. Unlike the city setting, where the struggle for the worth of women's work linked comparable worth to the defense of human services, the nurses' wage demands were linked to their protest over their perpetually frustrated attempts to increase their status, their tenuous professional identity, and their devaluation within the gendered hierarchy of the hospital organization. "If you're going to treat me like a dog," read one popular picket sign, "at least pay me for it."

The gendered basis for and meanings contained in the nurses' grievances are important, and I shall return to them shortly. Here, the important point is the critical *discontinuity* between Jenkins's rhetoric and the discourse of the nurses themselves. The claim to comparable worth as Jenkins articulated it was a powerful rallying cry, but on closer examination the nurses' demand for

[19]See Jenkins's "What Is 'The Market Standard'?" *California Nurse* 77 (1982):10.
[20]On February 19 – 20, in the second month of the strike, the CNA sponsored a comparable worth workshop in Oakland, California. Planned for 200 nurses, attendance was limited to the first 520 applicants. Featured speaker Gloria Steinem toured the picket lines on February 19.

pay equity was founded on precisely opposite attitudes toward the market and the bureaucratic personnel system from the form of that demand in the city.

In San Jose, the claim to comparable worth challenged the reliance on market standards to set pay, calling instead for bureaucratic techniques of position classification and salary standardization across as well as within major occupational groups. In contrast, the CNA's dominant interpretation of why nurses had such low wages focused on distortions in the labor market for nurses. The CNA relied, in this argument, on a widely cited economic study by leading officials of the prestigious Robert Wood Johnson Foundation, published in respected medical journals, that argued that monopsonistic relations among hospitals were restraining the natural operation of the labor market (Aiken 1981; Aiken, Blendon, and Rogers 1981).[21] The study was the functional equivalent of the second Hay study in San Jose, in that both provided scientific legitimation to the comparable worth claims; the role of each was different, however, since the Hay study represented a collaborative effort by both sides. The Aiken, Blendon, and Rogers study, by contrast, was not a product of dialogue and collaboration between the parties.

Aiken's studies built on a widely recognized economic phenomenon: monopsonistic labor markets. In a monopsony, a single employer (or group of employers setting wages together) can hire below the market-clearing rates that would theoretically obtain in a competitive market. To fill remaining vacancies, employers have to offer higher wages.[22] A substantial body of research indicates that monopsonistic practices operate in the RN labor market (Stratton 1985; Link and Landon 1975; Hurd 1973). Ironically, although unionization can serve as a counterweight to monopsonistic wage practices, structures that make possible coordinated bargaining (such as the employers' Association of Hospitals of Santa Clara Valley) also provide a direct mechanism for monopsonistic collaboration in setting prices for labor.

When Jenkins worked in the public sector, she had called upon policy makers not to "crucify women on the market standard"; the Aiken studies, however, refocused the union's critique on employer collusion that did not allow the market to function as it should.[23] Thus, contradictory rhetoric

---

[21]Just as the strike began, the *San Jose Mercury* republished the paper by Linda Aiken, Robert J. Blendon, and David E. Rogers opposite an editorial ("Nurses: Incomparable Worth," Jan. 11, 1982) that supported wage increases for the nurses on the basis of "supply and demand" while rejecting the rationale of comparable worth.

[22]The labor market for nurses in the Santa Clara Valley might be better termed oligopsonistic, although the employer bargaining association, in place throughout the previous decade, and continued informal coordination in wage bargaining approached monopsonistic relations.

[23]Similarly, some advocates of comparable worth argue that, in seeking to eliminate nontask-related, gender-based wage criteria, comparable worth measures move wage relations closer to those in a free labor market (Steinberg 1982).

emerged during the two strikes as the nurses called for comparable worth adjustments not against the market but against monopsonistic distortions of the market, not to overcome the market but to restore "natural" market relations. Jenkins placed her own forceful stamp on this analysis: "Nurses are being driven away from their profession in unbelievable numbers because of basic wage injustice. They are a *captive labor market* whose wages have been fixed at a considerable low level by agreement among hospital managements. In this respect, *hospital administrators are responsible for the nursing shortage*" ("Informational Fact Sheet" circulated during the strike; emphasis in original).

The tension between Jenkins's political claims and the market orientation of the CNA's leadership surfaced in February 1981, six weeks into the strike, after the CNA's statewide officials demoted Jenkins as the strike's chief negotiator and spokesperson.[24] Upon her demotion, the discourse of comparable worth was deemphasized in strike material and public statements. Instead, for example, in a long public position statement issued in February 1982, the new chief negotiator, Ken Absalom, said:

> We are trying to reverse the exodus of nurses from their profession. We know that substantial salary increases will have that effect. But we are receiving no cooperation from the hospital administrators who take the curious view, in contradiction to all their own studies, that money will not solve the nursing shortage. Their attitude is in direct defiance of the laws of supply and demand which are supposed to adjust upward the wages of any group whose services are in short supply.

Absalom's protest against the hospitals' "defiance of the laws of supply and demand" reflects some basic misunderstandings—themselves caused at least in part by the peculiarities of the RN labor market—that misled the CNA leadership. By their very nature, monopsonistic wage relations produce an appearance of a labor shortage, because the rational employer or coalition of employers finds it less expensive to pay wages below the market-clearing rate, while paying higher wages only to those hired to fill the remaining vacancies. For unionists oriented to a relatively competitive labor market, a short supply of workers is properly interpreted as a sign of bargaining power for labor. Monopsonistic markets are not competitive, however, and so the result in this case is only an appearance of a labor shortage. For unionists applying a strategic framework oriented to more competitive labor markets, the result is only an illusion of labor market strength.

---

[24]This episode is discussed further below.

The nursing shortage of the 1980s coincided with a complex of changes—in women's employment opportunities, in women's domestic conditions, in health care finance and organization—that are beyond the scope of analysis here. The low rate of full-time participation in nursing employment—less than half the licensed registered nurses in the United States, according to Aiken (1981)—can be viewed, however, not only as evidence of "labor market behavior" but as an individualized process of *struggle* against the conditions of nurses' employment. Resort to the registry option or to part-time employment reflects one avenue of resistance to unsatisfactory conditions of employment. Nurses who work for the registries exchange stability for independence from the hospital's oppressive authority and often depressing conditions; they lose job security but gain freedom to work when and where they choose. They gain free time—"family time," for many—a particularly valuable utility for women with children.[25]

Another feature of the nurses' movement becomes evident only when we compare it with the city workers' movement: the *absence of a public service orientation.* As we saw in chapter 4, the comparable worth movement was identical in its cast of characters and deeply intertwined in its power with the assertion and defense of gendered public needs. City librarians, for example, fought for the worth of their work in a double sense—their wage value and the value of libraries to the neighborhoods of the city.

To be sure, the nurses were profoundly committed to caring for the well-being of their patients; their personal as well as their occupational identities revolved around this value. And, to be sure, spiraling health care costs increasingly jeopardized the care of lower-income patients, while cost-containment measures introduced new tensions between the quality of care and hospital profits. Nurses found themselves facing this contradiction very directly though its impact on the quality of their work lives. They responded to it in their major grievance, against short-staffing in hospital clinics and wards. Though this grievance played a central role in the nurses' movement, the link to the issue of public service remained undeveloped. In their movement, in their union's activity, and in their dealings with their employers, the nurses never linked their private interests with public needs.

The Nurses' Strike for Comparable Worth

The nurses' strike began when eight hundred nurses walked out of O'Connor and Good Samaritan hospitals on January 5, 1982, and seven hundred

---

[25]Hospital and union officials both estimate that single parents accounted for 50 percent of the nurses on strike. I was unable to confirm this estimate. On the basis of my own experience, I would estimate that approximately 50 percent of all registered nurses with children are single.

more walked out of Alexian Brothers and San Jose hospitals on January 16.[26] At the outset, the union demanded raises of 37 percent over eighteen months, framing that claim as "not merely a raise in pay, but recognition of a basic human right to comparable pay for comparable worth" ("Comparable Pay for Comparable Worth," *California Nurse* 77:8, page 1 – 7). Other demands included improved retirement benefits, improvements in shift and weekend differentials, and the right to twelve-hour rests between shifts. The hospitals' final prestrike offers had ranged from 18 percent to 25 percent over three years, with no improvements in fringe benefits and rights.

During the strike most of the nurses supported themselves, at least in part, on savings and help from family and friends. Most also took temporary or per diem positions at other hospitals, where patient censuses shot up drastically.

The internal organization of the strike was impressive. More than 90 percent of the thirteen-hundred – person workforce participated, and the strikers maintained picket lines twenty-four hours a day, seven days a week, for up to five months in the heaviest rain the valley had seen in two decades. Work teams, organized by hospital unit or ward and by shift, comprised the basic organizational units of the strike force. Representatives of these teams were plugged into a hospitalwide phone tree and mobilization system, and each team was assigned one full shift of picketing per week. Each team also fielded an "assessment team," which monitored staffing and patient needs in the struck unit. Assessment teams were empowered to authorize and dispatch striking nurses to work if patient care conditions became critical; this helped alleviate the nurses' concerns that the strike might jeopardize care and also provided a way to monitor the impact of the strike on hospital units. One nurse explained the importance of this mechanism for her:

> I voted against it [the strike, but] after being informed that patients
> would *not* be neglected and that provisions were built in to guarantee
> that anyone needing emergency care would receive it, including from
> nurses "on the line," I indicated I would support this protest (Diana
> Molarious, *EDNA* [Emergency Department Nurses' Association] *News-
> letter*, April 29, 1982; emphasis in original).

Hospitalwide strike committees also met regularly at each hospital, with representation from various other special committees handling picket coordination, transportation, internal newsletters, food, child care, employment assistance, fund-raising, and so on. Each hospital also contributed volunteers

---

[26]The strike started on two different dates because of confusion by union representatives, who initially failed to file all the advance notices required.

to staff the office of strike headquarters, and each also had "community meetings" for all strikers every other week. Finally, the entire valleywide strikeforce also came together for approximately ten meetings—including one addressed by well-known feminist activist Gloria Steinem.

The organizational know-how behind this impressive structure came in part from Maxine Jenkins. Also, before the strike, a core of women who emerged as strike leaders had participated in a one-day seminar conducted by the labor studies program at a local community college.[27] Both routes led back, however, to expertise developed over the previous decade in the public sector. In Jenkins's words: "Sure, we were well organized. We spent months preparing. I didn't spend all those years in AFSCME for nothing" (interview, Oct. 16, 1986).

The Nurses' Culture of Solidarity

The nurses reported that their motivation and positive morale during the strike stemmed mainly from their time on the picket lines and their interactions with co-workers. The strikers also were pumped up during a series of rallies, parties, benefits, potluck dinners, concerts, meetings, and visits to the picket line by feminist celebrities, including Gloria Steinem, and their own charismatic leader, Maxine Jenkins.

The internal discourse of the strike—expressed in union newspapers, letters to newspapers, strike bulletins, leaflets and open letters, and recorded telephone messages—emphasized the strikers' collective identity as *nurses* and as representatives of *all nurses*. This identity was not tied to their employment at a given hospital but to their shared status with nurses throughout the state and country. According to a strike bulletin, for example: "This nurses' strike over Comparable Worth is the FIRST such strike ever. What happens in San Jose will affect all nurses in the State of California. . . . THE ISSUE OF COMPARABLE WORTH IS AN ISSUE FOR ALL NURSES!" ("San Jose Nurses Strike over Comparable Worth," CNA bulletin, Jan. 25, 1982). The text for a typical hotline recording read: "This struggle for comparable worth is a struggle for all nurses. Here in San Jose we're on the front lines, but we're not alone. Every nurse in the country is watching, and when we win here the victory will be for all."

Repeatedly, the nurses' accounts of their experiences in the strike dwelled on their discovery of solidarity with other nurses. Even the individualistic strategy of taking temporary work in other hospitals became an opportunity to

---

[27]I conducted the first of these community college seminars in "strike strategy and organization" in 1976.

explore this now-powerful collective identity, as nurses encountered other nurses in their new work settings and received moral support from them. Immediately after the strike, one nurse wrote:

> I feel strongly I have just completed a post-graduate course that money never could buy and for which I shall be forever grateful. I majored in community relations and I minored in Turdology. Working through registries and working out on the line and in the message center, I had the opportunity to meet some people that in my former orderly way of life I never would have met. . . . I met NURSES, and I mean NURSES. . . . I know the glory of a bond. That bond exists between nurses, particularly those who are endeavoring to escalate this profession to a more meaningful level. I found it between striking nurses who endured and continue to endure the most difficult days and hours. I found it in the hospitals in which I have recently worked, where so countless many said to me and others, "Thank you for fighting for all of us" (Diana Molarious, *EDNA Newsletter*, April 29, 1982).

Accounts of experiences on picket lines emphasized similar feelings of exhilaration and pride. One striker recalled:

> It was the best three and a half months in my life. We had a real close camaraderie. I don't think I was ever happier in my life than when all us nurses were standing there together, picketing in the rain, hooting and hollering at the scabs. . . . I can still see myself trying to spot the scabs, standing there in the bushes in the rain with a garbage bag over my head.
>
> Every night was *Saturday Night Live* on the picket line. I remember sitting on the picket line with a barbecue grill, cooking and drinking and eating together. . . . One night the police came and asked us, "Did you see who just dumped out the body in the E.R. [emergency room]?" We were so busy yapping we didn't notice. . . . And another night a guy came up to the line and flashed. You know those psych nurses are even worse than us labor and delivery nurses for nastiness. They called us over for a second opinion. Together we laughed him back to his car (interview, Donna Briones, Oct. 28, 1986).

Another nurse had a similar experience:

> It was fun. God, I'll always remember putting posters up on telephone poles in the middle of the night. We made fun out of it because what are you going to do? And the bonfire on the picket line at night. . . . Walking around the hospital in the rain. I really enjoy the rain now. I remember the camper where we stayed. Those were good times, and there was closeness, a lot of jokes—bitching, sure—but a lot of sharing. I learned a lot. I grew a lot. I'm more aware—it's not about power or

> winning—I learned I don't need that to feel whole—it's about being able
> to *do* something (interview, Marilyn Kenefick, Oct. 29, 1986).

The same nurse recalled her final days on the picket line, after demoralization
had set in: "Early on, the picket line was large. . . . In the end there was only
me. My husband would come and sit with me. It was raining so hard."

Defeat and Surrender

Despite the politically charged culture associated with the claim to comparable worth, the nurses' strike was in effect an economic action, aimed at
forcing the hospitals to raise wages by disrupting revenue-generating production. And despite the market-mediated illusion that the nurses had a strong
bargaining position, the decisive economic force at work in the industry
remained the pressure to contain costs. Because it occurred precisely as the
hospitals were turning toward more market-oriented and competitive strategies, the strike provided a perfect opportunity for restructuring the hospital
organization. According to hospital administrators, it was a blessing in dis-
guise, producing a "leaner, meaner" hospital organization. "The physicians
learned there were some things they could do for themselves," chuckled one
informant.

Inside the hospitals, the nonstriking nurses, other staff, managers and
supervisors, and replacement workers flown in from all over the West Coast
worked under siege to sustain patient care. According to one hospital administrator,

> We functioned pretty well. It was no burden on me. We had the nurse
> managers back in patient care. There was a lot of camaraderie. People
> rallied around the head nurses and supervisors. We had real tight staff
> utilization review. The nurse instructors went to work. There was a de-
> liberate effort to get the maximum out of each unit. We hired more
> LVNs, and the pharmacy took on staff.
> We got our census way down. Each patient was reviewed each day, and
> we canceled all elective surgery, and had a much more active outpatient
> operation. Our profits were real good during this time even though the
> census was down.[28]

A nonstriking nurse described changes in her hospital's organization and
her perception of the administrators' priorities:

[28]Name withheld by request. See similar comments by Richard Peryam, spokesman for San Jose
Hospital, in Jack Sirica and Cathy Calvert, "Nurses' Strike: Fight for Equal Pay Undone by
Miscalculations," San Jose *Mercury-News,* April 11, 1981.

Now there's higher acuity—and they got rid of some support staff. Before the strike, we had 420 patients. . . . A year later we were down to about 250—even though we were licensed for 535 beds. After the strike, we lost the children's psych unit, adolescent and adult alcohol and rehab unit. All they talk about now is "competition"—remodeling the lobby and grounds, spiffing up the cafeteria.

Given their belief that they faced a backward-sloping labor supply curve, hospital administrators judged that wage increases would only perpetuate or increase their need to hire more expensive registry nurses. They also believed that giving the nurses disproportionate wage increases would stimulate unionization among the other nonunionized hospital personnel. Under these conditions, the hospitals had little incentive to meet the nurses' ambitious demands. Thus, O'Connor Hospital hired permanent replacements within the first month of the strike; ten weeks into the strike, the other three hospitals followed suit.

By now Jenkins and some of her inner circle were getting pessimistic. Seeking to negotiate a settlement that would preserve seniority rights and ward and shift assignments in exchange for lower wage increases, they met with bargainers for the hospitals. The CNA's state leaders were so confident of their strong bargaining position, however, that they scuttled this effort, removed Jenkins from the role of chief negotiator, and prevailed upon the nurses to remain on strike to the bitter end.[29]

A settlement of sorts—although more a surrender—was reached at three of the four hospitals on April 9, three months after the strike began. The fourth hospital—O'Connor—refused to settle and subsequently decertified the union. The wage terms at the other three hospitals were 25 percent over three years—a substantial raise but a far cry from the 37 percent the nurses had hoped to achieve in eighteen months. The back-to-work agreement also left in place the permanent replacements hired during the strike; these and other nonstrikers kept their shift and work assignments. Strikers would not return to work en masse but as needed, to less desirable assignments. Losing their rights to the assignments they had before the strike was a particularly bitter pill, given the variety of nursing assignments and the prevalence of night and weekend work. In an interview conducted four years later, one personnel officer disclosed that the last striker had been rehired only several months earlier.

[29]Nevertheless, Jenkins was blamed for the eventual defeat of the strike. See for example, Jack Sirica and Cathy Calvert, "Nurses' Strike: Fight for Equal Pay Undone by Miscalculations," San Jose *Mercury-News*, April 11, 1981. Several former strike leaders believed that the CNA's leadership "forced [them] to stay out to teach us a lesson." Both interviews and archival data, however, support the sincerity of the officials' belief that they held the upper hand.

Nurses continued to be among the most assertive workers in California throughout the 1980s. But because of the debacle of 1982, the very term "comparable worth" remained anathema among nurses throughout the decade,[30] and the charismatic labor organizer who inspired the movement subsequently retired from union organizing.

Autopsy of Defeat

The entire thrust of the nurses' campaign was aimed at mobilizing RNs for collective action to wield bargaining power in the labor market. The nurses' "good bargaining position" proved to be a chimera, however. And while the claim to comparable worth evidently did help sustain the strength of the mobilization, it was inadequate to produce strike success. Rather, economic conditions (and market-oriented strategic orientations by both union and management decision makers) doomed the nurses to defeat.

In chapter 2, I noted that the early surge of public sector unionism was influenced by private sector strategies and other institutions. The experience of the Santa Clara Valley nurses carries a similar warning about reversing the direction of diffusion—more likely in the current period, as beleaguered private sector unionists look to relatively successful public sector unions for new strategic models.[31] The nurses' experience reinforces a more general lesson: if social movements are to succeed, strategies must respond to the particular conditions they face.

How could the outcome have been different? On the one hand, given the economic conditions, the demand for a 37 percent pay increase was probably unrealistic. On the other hand, the union never took advantage of the high degree of public regulation of health care and hospitals; nor did it seek to exert political pressure on these nominally nonprofit organizations. Despite the intrinsically political character of the claim to comparable worth and despite the CNA's long tradition of advocating for the favorable regulation of nursing work, the nurses never exercised *political* power. Political action would have required attention to the process of alliance-building, both in the workforce and in the wider political universe. Rather, the nurses relied on the traditional

[30]Though the term "comparable worth" was used among the nurses, some media reports referred to "pay parity." The switch to the use of the term "pay equity" among California nurses occurred immediately after the nurses' strike in Santa Clara County. When I visited the picket lines during two later private sector nurses' strikes—in Santa Rosa in 1986 and in San Francisco in 1987—RN activists explained that the term "comparable worth" was not to be used because of its association with the Santa Clara Valley nurses' strike.

[31]Starting in the mid-1980s, for example, the AFL-CIO launched an organizing effort aimed at building employee associations in the private sector, with the aim that, like civil service associations in the 1960s and 1970s, these associations eventually would become unions. See Leo Troy's trenchant (1986) comments on the prospects for this effort.

economic exercise of market power through the withdrawal of labor power. Jenkins's powerful discursive resources were employed, in effect, to mobilize organizational resources within the workforce in order to exercise market power. Jenkins herself acknowledged this in retrospect:

> With a bit of arrogance like PATCO, we thought our strong organization—you can't keep those nursing units open without us because by law nurses are licensed to perform certain practices no one else can perform—nurses thought they could carry it on their own. It became clear as the strike dragged on that community support and support in the hospital was needed, but that was not part of the strategy and could not be now (interview, Oct. 16, 1986).

Though the quasi-nonprofit hospitals were nominally governed by nascent public spheres—boards of directors that included representatives of "the community," middle-class volunteers, church and business representatives—no effort was made to activate, challenge, or reform those spheres of influence. Nor did the nurses and their union attempt to develop crucial political alliances with others in the hospitals, most notably their co-workers. Rather, they elected to "go it alone."[32]

One former strike leader emphasized this issue. She recalled the one-day class in strike organization she had taken at San Jose City College and compared what had been covered there (drawn from lessons learned in the public sector) to the actual strike situation:

> Let's see, we had a telephone tree, picket committees, strike headquarters, posters, food, office, transportation, survival, job placement, emergency services, public relations. But you know, we had no community groups. We went to the [governing] boards toward the end of the strike—that was too late. We should have done that from the beginning (interview, Kenefick, Oct. 29, 1986).

Had the unions sought to make these tax-exempt, commodity-producing, "quasi-private" hospitals into "quasi-public" agencies by activating and participating in the nascent public spheres of their community-based boards of directors, or by attempting to pass laws or regulations governing them, then the outcome might have been different. Had the nurses built alliances in the community they served around the need for improvements in the quality of

---

[32]The strike did stimulate valleywide support among other unionists and led to the formation of a regional strike support committee that later served to channel essential resources to Watsonville during the cannery workers' strike.

care and linked this issue to better staffing levels, the outcome of the strike might have been different.

Further, had the union addressed the sources of problems such as burnout directly, it might have been able to draw nurses into the debate over the structure and financing of the health care industry in the United States. Among the leaders of the strike, as we shall see in the next section, there was a profound critique of gender relations on the job; in principle, at least, this critique was not inconsistent with the claim to comparable worth. Had this critique been articulated and pursued to the point of producing an agenda for job redesign, and had the need for this job redesign been linked to agendas for restructuring the health care system, again, the outcome might have been different. Reflecting, however, U.S. trade unionists' characteristically economistic orientation, the nurses' claim to comparable worth was not only stripped of its appeal to public sector norms of salary standardization but ultimately reduced to an appeal to "the laws of supply and demand."

A departure from conventional economic bargaining certainly could not have been adopted and implemented suddenly, on the eve of the strike; like the mobilization that occurred among the city workers, nonconventional tactics would have required a long process of development. At the same time, had the nurses' movement identified the nurses' needs with public needs and drawn on the levers of public power, the strike might have been more successful. But then, the nurses' movement would have *been* a public workers' movement.

Nurse Burnout and Comparable Worth

Underneath the market-oriented language that came to define the demand for comparable worth were powerful tensions, deeply rooted in the gendered occupational identity of the nurses. The strongest theme, in the intense "culture of solidarity" (Fantasia 1988) that erupted during the strike, was the abuse of nurses as women. As a result, although the claim to comparable worth was framed as a demand for higher wages, "comparable worth" took on an emotional resonance referring less to pay comparisons with predominately male jobs than to other implicitly feminist grievances.

Described in the code words "stress" and "nurse burnout," these issues arose in various ways, especially in discussions of the long working hours, the emotional burden of the nurse-patient relationship, and the arbitrariness of authority. Jenkins discerned this current among the women she was trying to mobilize:

It wasn't just the pay. It was the way they were treated. There were grievances, hostilities stored up. Absolutely the bitterest grievances I ever saw
were among RNs. The director of nurses was usually the villain of the
piece. One liked by the nursing staff would really be an exception. The
physicians—I would not abide rudeness to RNs. . . . physicians yelling
at the nurses. Things they wouldn't say at home to their wives. It was the
demeaning way they were treated (interview, Oct. 16, 1986).

One nurse with twenty-one years' experience talked about her feelings:

There's a lot of anger . . . and there has to be a scapegoat. And it's you.
It all came out when the feminist stuff was verbalized—our real emotions
go back to these frustrations—and the strike was an opportunity to let it
all out. We were feeling suppressed, demeaned. The strike was going to
redeem us. I felt in my gut it was fighting for autonomy we didn't have
from a nursing point of view. Money wasn't the real issue, the real issue
was . . . recognition for work that I do, in the form of money. You're
damn tired (interview, Donna Peterson, Oct. 23, 1986).

Jenkins acknowledged that she honed her discourse to "articulate this
humiliation": "I articulated this humiliation in my speeches. I gave it a feminist
twist: nurses, I said, are not handmaidens of the physicians nor of the administration but they are professionals in their own right" (interview, Oct. 16,
1986). In other words, Jenkins linked frustrations built into the nurses'
semiprofessional status with their abuse as women. This was her "feminist
twist" on the assertion of professional identity.

The experience of burnout was connected to and compounded by anxiety
over the burden of responsibility for patient care in the context of short-
staffing. As Jenkins skillfully articulated it, however, the discourse of comparable worth contained a simple *economic* formula for resolving the short-
staffing. Stress, she said, was caused by the shortage of nurses. Higher wages
would increase the supply of labor, which, in turn, would increase the staffing
levels; higher wages would also permit women to work fewer hours and to
escape the hospital wards to their families and other personal commitments.
Higher wages, in other words, became the solution to "nurse burnout."

Autonomy, Ambivalence, and the Burden of Care

Like nurses everywhere, the nurses in the valley labored under pressure even
before economic pressures forced an intensification of the work. The irregular
hours required to staff twenty-four-hour institutions, including the need to
work weekends, nights, and "back-to-back" sixteen-hour shifts, produced
tension, as did the proximity to disease and death in an impersonal factory

setting. But a particularly powerful force in the development of the nurses' movement was the conflict between their tenuously secured and frequently devalued professional identity, on the one hand, and their regimented working conditions, on the other. These occupational dynamics are deeply intertwined, moreover, with contradictions surrounding the changing gender identities of nurses.

In a penetrating and problematic turn of phrase, nurses have been termed "the physician's hand" (Melosh 1982). This term reflects the division at the heart of the hospital model of medical care and the doctor-nurse relationship. That division also coincides with the division in gender roles in the hospital organization (Lowery-Palmer 1982).

To grasp the dilemmas confronting nurses, one might consider the interplay between their gender-based occupational identity and the emergent feminist movement. During the 1970s, the feminist movement had a strong influence on a cadre of students in nursing schools, as well as on nurses who were already employed. This intensified contradictions deeply rooted in the nurses' identity. Strands of that identity—including one version of the claim to professional identity and also the more traditional "Florence Nightingale" identity— define RNs as care-givers and emphasize the value of a holistic approach to patients and also of personal commitment and even self-sacrifice (Melosh 1982; Game and Pringle 1983). These themes are deeply resonant, of course, with "female" gender roles of service provider and nurturer, rooted in the domestic organization of women's work as care.[33] Thus, the very professional identity on which nurses rely for status and self-esteem is grounded in part in a traditional gender role.

Feminist self-assertion, however, implies turning away from the "Florence Nightingale" attitude and demanding respect, fair pay, and the right "to take care of myself." Whether framed in feminist terms or not, this shift implies a potentially wrenching self-assertion; it requires emphatic self-assurance that it is, indeed, legitimate to care for oneself as well as (and sometimes instead of) one's patients. When such an assertion is voiced in strike action—"abandoning the patient"—the turn away from this deeply inculcated identity is even more wrenching.

This dynamic is overlaid with equally ambivalent attitudes toward the weakening bonds of patriarchal authority embodied in the doctor-nurse relationship, as well as in the increasingly tenuous traditional family structure. Thanks to these gender dynamics, then, unionization among nurses can be a

---

[33]Rooted as well, arguably, in the gendered personalities produced by matrifocal childrearing (Dinnerstein 1976).

deeply contradictory process. On some level, it is liable to generate a reservoir of anxiety, which will be directed either painfully inward or angrily outward.[34]

In combination with the extraordinary stress associated with the work, it is not surprising that feminist anger was articulated during the nurses' strike in a profoundly emotional manner and contributed substantially to the shared identity infusing the nurses' movement. The intensity of the movement was certainly amplified as well because the participants shared the same occupational identity. Strikes are frequently effervescent occasions, drawing upon solidarity against a common adversary, the break in the taken-for-grantedness of organizational reality, and the exuberance of the sudden self-organization. Here, this effervescence was certainly magnified by the ambivalence and anxiety, by the primal solidarity of the homogeneous workforce, and by the vertiginous sense of being pioneers to produce a powerful charge of charismatic potential.[35]

Maxine Jenkins served—to her own ultimate bad fortune—as a lightning rod for these powerful forces. Her career had now become a crusade for comparable worth, and she wore this charisma with skill and passion. Hers was the strongest voice speaking *to* the nurses as well as *for* the nurses, "articulating this humiliation" and giving it her "feminist twist." Perhaps even more powerful than her voice was the image conveyed by her stance as leader of more than a thousand women in their challenge to the hospitals' administrators.

One nurse who had been a long-time union leader chose not to support the strike because she considered the demands unrealistic. She described her reaction to Jenkins and her charisma: "Maxine Jenkins got them to strike. She didn't understand our problems, she wasn't a nurse. She came over from the city. . . . We never got along too well. . . . She reminded me of Hitler, all these people going 'Heil Hitler! Heil Hitler!' " (name withheld at request of informant).

In the exhilarating early days of the strike, at any event, Jenkins was a symbol of self-assertion for many nurses: the strong woman who "wore boots" and could face down hospital administrators and directors of nursing. Several informants reported feeling hero worship for her. The same nurses also described how, as the exhilarating strike turned into a demoralizing defeat,

---

[34]This is not to dismiss more straightforward grounds for pain and anger but to suggest that these may be intensified by this dilemma of autonomy versus care.

[35]The "mechanical solidarity" of relatively homogeneous mobilizations in the private sector makes such movements particularly conducive to such eruptions. Chapter 7 turns to a public sector case involving nurses; there, these anxieties appear to have had a different and more ominous effect.

this attitude was reversed. Now Jenkins carried the burden of hubris, the blame for failure. At the time of my interviews four and five years after the strike, participants still expressed powerfully ambivalent feelings about Jenkins and the strike experience. Some expressed a sense of betrayal and disillusionment with her even as they affirmed that she was a scapegoat and a victim of political maneuvering by higher-ups in the union.

Jenkins herself was personally wounded by the strike. Four years later she described the painful experience, six weeks into the strike, when she realized that it would not succeed and sought to assemble a face-saving settlement, only to be displaced by the CNA leadership:

> From that point I just cracked up. . . . There'd been a lot of hero worship. . . . I was the one who was saying all the things they wanted to say. Then my leadership began to be called into question. And it was like the walking dead. I felt like I was moving through time and space on an alien planet—totally alone. One nurse I was personally close to, I expressed some of this to her—she jumped on me (interview, Oct. 16, 1986).

If my analysis is correct, these nurses' attachment to Jenkins, and their sense of rage and abandonment at her failure, were intensified by the wrenching ambivalence associated with their assertion of autonomy despite their commitment to care. This is, to be sure, highly speculative. In interactions and interviews with nurses in comparable situations, they have often expressed anxiety about "abandoning their patients," but I have seldom heard this concern articulated among strike leaders. In other nurses' strikes, however, I have observed similar behavior, suggesting such anxiety and a near-manic energy, "intensifying the moment," even compared with the effervescent culture of many strike mobilizations.[36]

I interviewed the same woman whom Jenkins said "jumped on" her. In the midst of describing the strike, she talked about the tension between nurturance and autonomy in the nurses' relationships with their patients:

> [This tension's] all wrapped up in this professionalism stuff. The overlapping of this autonomy [in both patients and nurses] creates this conflict. No matter how much we struggle under the guise of women's rights, comparable worth, we're always the mother, the proverbial tit to society, the surrogate whore. . . . When I was in nursing in the '60s, if you told the patient what their temperature was you got written up for being unprofessional—now the patient is supposed to be autonomous, the patient is dictating to us. They're ill, and they're like infants, and they

---

[36]The interpretation given here is based on observations of many strike movements—seven involving nurses—including a mobilization reported in chapter 7.

want Mama to take care of them. But [patients] want autonomy too. "You will give me the Demerol *now* or I will get the physician." There's this conflict in the patient between regression and autonomy. The nurse helps, and then the patient casts the Mommy aside. We are used, and cast aside (name withheld by request).

Although she speaks of a conflict within the patients, this nurse is clearly voicing a protest about her own condition: "We are used, and cast aside." Given the context of our conversation, her grievance may apply not only to the treatment of nurses by patients but by hospital employers and union leaders. We have seen, however, how the rubric of comparable worth—now interpreted as wages at the market-clearing rate—redefined a whole category of such grievances—burnout, short-staffing, the abuse of nurses as women—in a manner reflecting the institutional logic of the private sector setting in which the movement occurred.

The Feminist Impulse and the Sectoral Difference

I do not evaluate here the hospital administrators' judgment that a pay raise would not have eliminated the short-staffing. Their judgment certainly was not inconsistent, however, with Jenkins's promise that higher wages would have permitted the nurses to work fewer hours and therefore spend more time with their families. In any event, it is likely that changes in the occupational options for educated women, the intensification of hospital work, and the growth of the feminist movement did result in an upward shift in the slope of the labor supply curve for nurses, which diminished effects of wage increases on the labor supply and increased the nurses' willingness to strike against lower-than-market-clearing wages. More significant for my conclusion in this case is the pervasive importance of market relations in the perceptions, demands, and strategic orientation of both labor and management, in contrast to the political-bureaucratic logic of the public workplace.

This account shows that the emergence of the claim to comparable worth in the nurses' strike was an effect of the recent, controversial, and successful strike in the public sector and that the claim followed Jenkins from the public sector to the private. In that process, the claim to comparable worth was radically redefined to *appeal to* rather than *challenge* the market standard.[37]

[37]It might well be argued that gender disparities revealed in San Jose's broader labor market surveys reflected other distortions in the labor market so that both movements appealed—in effect—to a market standard. The differences, though, remain considerable: in the character of the social movements—their demands and resources—and in the self-understandings and institutionalized practices of other actors in each sector.

Further, like most other private sector unions in the United States, the occupational inclusivity of the California Nurses' Association contrasted sharply with the inclusivity of such major public sector unions as AFSCME.

Moreover, none of the labor market or other economic dynamics that had such a decisive effect on the nurses' strike had a comparable impact on the city workers. The city workers' movement was led by librarians, who mobilized mainly by building a broad coalition with other occupational groups in the city workforce, library users, community groups, and participants in the political universe of city government; they disregarded librarians in other agencies. The nurses, by contrast, mobilized with other nurses and disregarded other workers in the diverse hospital workforce. While the city workers' union built a coalition within and against a political bureaucracy, the nurses' union built a coalition within and against a labor market.

Again in contrast to the city workers' movement, the nurses' strike lacked a public service orientation. Although the nurses directly confronted human needs in their work, public needs were never given voice in their strike, and the political coalitions that could have been built around these public needs never materialized. Instead, the nurses were constrained by labor market dynamics and by their own operating assumptions, which were built on a private sector framework. Participating in that institutional universe, they were further constrained by the monopsony illusion of labor market power.

On the one hand, taken alone, none of these differences conclusively demonstrates the effects of the sectoral context on labor movements. Taken together, however, they reveal a pattern of differences clearly related to one another and to the sectoral distinction. On the other hand, Maxine Jenkins argues that the nurses' strike was "the same as the city," even as she acknowledges the diffusion of the claim to comparable worth from the public sector to the private:

> [The nurses' strike] was women demanding feminist representation. Peo
> ple in San Jose made a specific demand for comparable worth on their
> own, and RNs didn't say that, but at membership meetings they re
> sponded to the idea that "we are underpaid because we are women."
> They had seen what happened in San Jose (interview, Oct. 16, 1986).

And, to be sure, the feminist impulse was not transplanted from the public sector but rooted in these nurses' everyday lives. As the discourse of their strike reveals, not only gendered wage inequality but also deeply felt and shared dilemmas associated with changing gender roles—asserting both the worth and the trauma of women's work of care—played a powerful role in their mobilization and its aftermath. The feminist critique of gender inequality does have a particular affinity to the formal equality and administrative justice native to the public workplace. But though the form of its expression and the fate of its efforts vary, the feminist impulse is no more native to the public sector than to the private.

6 The Custodians of the Valley

San Jose's janitors were the unsung heroes of the women's campaign for comparable worth in that city. Without the support of these mostly Mexican-American city employees, the women probably would not have won and held the union leadership role that enabled them to launch and win their campaign for comparable worth. Regrettably, the janitors' critical contribution has been obscured in accounts of this episode. This pivotal alliance merits particular attention because it was no random event but reflects a broader pattern of coalition-building in similar workforces.[1]

Being neglected by scholars was the least of the janitors' problems, however. Ironically, during the same years that the women of the city received a series of comparable worth adjustments, the janitors saw their jobs disappear as the city contracted out more than 70 percent of its custodial work. By the time I visited with the janitors in 1986, most of San Jose's custodial work was being performed at or near minimum wage, without union protection or civil service rights.

This chapter compares the experiences in this period of the city custodians and the private sector custodians of the valley. By the 1980s, it was apparent that labor unions in the private sector had begun a period of accelerated decline. It was also evident that the new strength of labor in the public sector contrasted sharply with this trend (Troy 1986; Kochan, Katz, and McKersie 1986). By the late 1980s, however, these patterns appear to have been reversed

---

[1]The same pattern appeared in Santa Clara County, where public works employees sought to decertify SEIU Local 715 in favor of "a real man's union." As in the city, the county's custodians served as a critical counterweight against the mostly white and female human service unionists' adversaries in public works. Women in *both* of the major local government agencies of the Santa Clara Valley won and held leadership in their unions, thanks in part to the custodians' solidarity.

among the custodians studied here. Those in the public sector lost ground, while those in the private sector revitalized their union and reorganized their industry. The achievements of the "Justice for Janitors" campaign among the private sector custodians support the observation by industrial sociologist Dan Cornfield (1993) that "the conditions of labor movement decline may also be the conditions of labor movement revitalization."

These two cases, along with the two comparable worth movements studied in previous chapters, invite comparison both within and between sectors: between the very different occupational groups in each sector and between similar groups across sectors. In each sector, moreover, one more or less successful case may be compared with one more or less unsuccessful one. Figure 6.1 illustrates these patterns of comparison. When we eventually turn to the public sector nurses of San Francisco, the pattern of comparison will become fully symmetrical: by sector, by success and failure, and (indicated by the diagonal arrows) by occupational group.

The first two sections of this chapter present and analyze the cases of the two custodial workforces. The final section compares social movement unionism in the public and private sectors, based on all the cases considered so far. This section draws *parallels* between the kinds of claims and types of resources deployed in "public service unionism," on the one hand, and private sector "organizing unionism," on the other. It concludes by focusing on the decisive difference that appears to distinguish public workers' movements: their involvement in the perpetual contest over the definition of the public needs that orient civil service work.

The Custodians of the City

During the 1970s the ranks of San Jose's custodians grew with the expansion of facilities in city neighborhoods in the wake of the explosive population growth of the postwar period. By 1979, the city's 104 custodians were the largest mostly Latino group in the city workforce and in the membership of the Municipal Employees Federation of AFSCME, Local 101.

Before the late 1970s, when the women of the city challenged the hegemony of the public works employees in their union, the city's custodians did not play an active role in union life. The custodians also were outside the old public works power base in the city and in the union and so were natural allies for the women against the hegemony of the men in public works. Though they would serve as key partners in the comparable worth campaign and the strike of 1981, the custodians did not initiate this relationship. Rather, the women turned to the custodians because they constituted a major bloc of union votes.

Figure 6.1. Strategies of Comparison within and across Sectors, Occupational Groups, and Outcomes

	Sector	
	Public	Private
Outcome		
Success	Women of San Jose (public sector nurses)	Private sector custodians
Failure	Custodians of the city	Private sector nurses

Note: Diagonal arrows indicate comparison within occupational groups.

The city custodians had a problem of their own, however: contracting out. Immediately after the 1978 passage of Proposition 13, city officials began to enter into contracts with private sector building maintenance contractors for larger and larger portions of the city's custodial work. After the initial layoff of CETA employees (described in chapter 3), layoffs were accomplished by attrition, in a deliberate and effective strategy to sidestep union resistance. By 1986, only thirty-one city custodial positions remained; these were concentrated in the larger facilities with higher visibility, such as City Hall and the main library.[2]

Concurrent with these events, the Asian population of the valley mushroomed: from 1 percent in 1970 to 8 percent in 1980 to 23 percent in 1990. One result was the emergence of a new low-wage labor market of new immigrants, mostly from Vietnam and other Southeast Asian countries. Many of these immigrants were willing to accept hours, wages, and working conditions unacceptable to the Mexican-American workers who composed much of the valley's secondary labor market. These recent immigrants would perform most of the city's contracted-out custodial work at less than half the city's already modest pay scale.[3]

During the period leading up to and including the 1981 strike, the custodians brought the issue of contracting out to Local 101, and the matter

[2]In 1978, in-house positions were used in seventy locations; by 1986, in-house positions covered four locations and contracted services covered eighty-seven (memorandum, James Daniels, building maintenance supervisor, to Susan George, deputy city manager, April 11, 1986).
[3]The hourly wage rate for city custodians was $7.85 in 1981; with fringe benefits, the dollar cost to the city was $10.36. Estimates by custodial supervisors and other city officials of wages in the private sector ranged from $4.00 to $4.50. I encountered substantial resistance—from employers as well as employees—to providing me with access to the predominately Vietnamese workers on the contracted-out jobs.

appeared on the bargaining table in 1980 and 1981. Operating under continuous threat—occasionally implemented—of layoffs, union leaders reasoned that contracting out was a lesser harm and its reversal a lower priority.[4] Accordingly, the union dropped the issue early in the negotiations that led to the strike of July 1981 (interviews, Estruth, Nov. 4, 1986; Turner, Oct. 14, 1986; and Callahan, Nov. 12, 1986). "We got cheated in that strike," argued one custodian. "They [union officials] told us if we supported equal rights we would get support against the contract. Then they wouldn't back the custodians against the contract" (interview, Steve Lopez, custodial foreman, Sept. 12, 1982).

In the aftermath of the strike, alarmed by the steady erosion of their numbers as a result of the contracting out, the custodians finally began to mobilize on their own behalf. In 1983, Glenn Heath—a white man who had served as shop steward and a member of the negotiating team for the custodians through the strike—was promoted to foreman. Gilbert Villalobos, an outspoken young Chicano, was elected in his place. A circle of custodians working with Villalobos began a campaign of protest.

In a tactic directed as much against the union as against the city, Villalobos and his supporters began filing as many grievances as possible. "Can you believe it, he was actually *soliciting* grievances!" recounted one scandalized manager (interview, James Daniels, Nov. 4, 1986). Bud Griffith, the union business agent who had replaced the more assertive organizer Bill Callahan, described Villalobos's tactics in similar terms: "He was actually going around and *asking* people to file grievances!" (interview, July 22, 1986).

Unfortunately, the custodians lacked allies in their revolt. Had they been a majority in their union and workplace, they might have had less need for allies; in the diverse city workforce, however, they were a relatively small part of the membership of their chapter in Local 101.

Also in 1983, the frustrated custodians attempted to decertify Local 101, hoping to obtain more forceful representation from the Operating Engineers, which already represented skilled blue-collar workers in the city. Again Villalobos, along with a small core of Mexican-American men, spearheaded the campaign. More than enough signatures were obtained on a petition to require an election, and had an election been permitted, it is likely the attempt at decertification would have succeeded.

The custodians were undone, however, by legal hurdles and organizational power. Under the collective bargaining law governing labor relations in

---

[4]The same logic, of course, could have persuaded union officials to deemphasize the claim to comparable worth; it did not.

California's local governments, the public employer effectively serves as its own regulatory agency—ruling, among other things, on the validity of petitions and the appropriateness of bargaining units.[5] The city ruled the custodians' decertification petition invalid because it proposed forming a separate bargaining unit for the custodians.

The only valid petition, according to the city, would have added the custodians to the existing blue-collar unit represented by Local 3 of the Operating Engineers. Without Local 101's permission, however, Local 3 would have been constrained from representing the custodians by Article 20 of the AFL-CIO Constitution—the provision designed to prevent raiding between unions.[6] In other words, the custodians were surrounded by a legal and organizational prison that effectively precluded independent decision-making and representation.

Losing patience with the troublesome custodians, the leadership of Local 101 then amended the union's bylaws to allow the appointment rather than the election of shop stewards and then removed Villalobos from office. Simultaneously, city officials offered him another job at a higher wage in the Operating Engineers' jurisdiction. Villalobos accepted the offer, landing in a lower-level road maintenance position in the public works department—also a predominately Latino work group.[7]

Contracting Out and Custodial Morale

When I arrived in San Jose to conduct fieldwork in late 1986, the custodians' organized resistance to contracting out had subsided, although they remained disgruntled. In my initial interviews, both union and city officials characterized the custodians as having the lowest morale and highest rate of personnel problems of any work group in the city. Managers said the custodians' relations with their supervisors were troublesome and that they had difficulty recruiting and retaining "good workers." They also said that in this part—and this part alone—of the Local 101 jurisdiction, excessive and unreasonable recourse to civil service complaints, discrimination charges, and union grievances was a vexing problem. Their perception was that many of the custodians

[5]One might infer that this law biased labor relations entirely toward management. Like everything else of interest here, however, regulatory decisions are the product of political processes within which employee organizations and their allies participate.

[6]It is unlikely that the custodians would have fared any better with Local 3, which was dominated by relatively high-wage public works employees.

[7]Ironically, the Operating Engineers proceeded in 1986 to negotiate one of the few two-tier wage plans in California's public sector, which lowered their starting wage in order to "free up" money for an extra pay adjustment for the higher-paid—and predominately white—maintenance workers.

were childlike—poorly educated, socially inept, frequently afflicted with personality problems—and had a tendency to "act out."

In the post–Proposition 13 era, the opportunity for cost savings was an obvious factor in the city officials' decision to contract out custodial services.[8] During the same period that contracting out was sharply *decreasing* the costs of custodial services, however, comparable worth adjustments were being implemented that *increased* the relative pay of city workers in predominately female classifications. By 1986, for example, savings from the contracting out amounted to less than half the costs of the comparable worth adjustments. This strongly suggests that although cost may have been a consideration, other motivations—including the custodians' relative political weakness—influenced the decision to contract out.

And, in fact, when asked to explain the decision to contract out, both upper- and lower-level managers said that in addition to cost considerations, it was also an effort to deal with disciplinary and other personnel problems that plagued the custodial workforce: to put it bluntly, to make it easier to discipline and fire these workers and thus motivate satisfactory performance. An upper-level executive cited cost savings as the first consideration and "personnel problems" as the second (interview, Ellis Jones, July 28, 1986); at lower levels of management, the custodians' "excessive" civil service rights and unionized status were given as the *primary* motives for contracting out the work (interview, James Daniels, Oct. 22, 1986).

In my interviews with the custodians, they too repeatedly mentioned their low morale. They complained that their supervisors did not respect them and that their union did not represent them. One seventeen-year veteran voiced his protest as a claim to dignity and fair treatment intrinsic, in his view, to his civil service status: "I'm a public servant. I got rights, I work for the city, and I deserve respect, just like the city manager" (interview, Bob Elder, Oct. 2, 1986).

According to the custodians, the main cause of their low morale was "the contract" and their union's inability or unwillingness to oppose it. In part, this was due to continued threats to job security. In 1986, after the custodians' workforce had been reduced by more than 70 percent, city officials assured them (and affirmed to me) that there would be no more contracting out. Over the following year, however, custodians reported that supervisors frequently suggested—while admonishing custodians to behave and work harder—that management might change its mind.

[8]According to a 1986 internal study, the city saved $975,908 annually by using contract custodial services (memorandum, James Daniels, building maintenance supervisor, to Susan George, deputy city manager, April 11, 1986).

In addition, the custodians complained that those hired through contract-ing out were paid substantially less than the city custodians and that their performance was allegedly slipshod. As a result, the city custodians felt the worth of their jobs was demeaned. One custodian described the situation as follows: "The main thing is you don't know what the future holds. Next week or next month they could turn around and give your job to someone for a minimum wage. After working seventeen years, you feel like you're nothing" (interview, Elder, Oct. 22, 1986).

One long-term employee bitterly compared the custodians' conditions with the gains made by the women of the city: "Look what the union did for the women, and look what they done for us. They got together and they took it out of our skin, that's what they did, and then they got together and fixed it so we couldn't do nothing about it" (name withheld by request).

The custodians' recourse to discrimination complaints and union griev-ances, and city officials' desire to eliminate these resources for this workforce, point to a tension that existed between their status and the norms of public personnel administration. There was a discrepancy, that is, between the custodians' unequal treatment, low status, and offended dignity and the promise of equal treatment and due process rights implicit in civil service employment and union representation. This discrepancy is also evident in city officials' description of the custodians' "childlike" need for close supervision, in contrast to the lax and friendly style of employee relations observed else-where in the city.

Supervisors' concerns about control were compounded by the organization of the custodians' work. Although some assignments were clustered in large buildings, many others covered sites in outlying locations. The administrator of building maintenance in San Jose had come up from the ranks of building trades employees in the city. He had little experience supervising custodians and expressed frustration at the challenge of monitoring workers on such "roving" assignments.

The new regime of contracted-out custodial work certainly relieved city officials' concerns about the custodians' excessive civil service rights, as the new custodians were excluded from the system of administrative justice. In the absence of civil service rights and union representation, a simple new person-nel policy was in effect: one complaint and a worker was given a warning; two or three complaints and the worker was terminated (interviews, Jones, July 28, 1986; Daniels, Oct. 22, 1986; Heath, Oct. 22, 1986; and Lopez, Sept. 12, 1986).

Both lower- and upper-level city officials responsible for administering the contract were aware—as were the city custodians—of reports of "unconventional" employment practices at contracted-out worksites: children working with their parents at night; allegations of "favors" provided to city-employed inspectors by the owner of the custodial firm; allegations of cash payment for part or all the contract workers' wages (permitting continued receipt of welfare stipends), and so on.[9] Further, the contractor persistently failed to file required reports with the city demonstrating compliance with affirmative action provisions and other terms of the contract. Among these provisions— evidently in error and never enforced—was a requirement that the employer pay the wages that prevailed in local union contracts. There was no investigative action on these matters by city officials, however (interview, Juan Pifarre, City of San Jose Affirmative Action Compliance Officer, Oct. 22, 1986).

Despite the formal separation of the new custodians from public employment, contracted-out positions remained linked to the city's authority system because the city supervised the majority of the contracted work. Thus, whereas the contractor assigned only one employee to supervise the entire operation, the city assigned two senior custodians and a senior construction inspector as "roving inspectors." In effect, then, the contracting-out mechanism created a new class of quasi-public workers with sharply lower pay and status.

City Custodians' Resources for Resistance

A private sector union might have responded to such an episode by seeking to take wages out of competition: by organizing, that is, the lower-wage, unorganized workers on the contract. The response of public sector unions to privatization, however, is typically limited to political opposition—a result, according to the argument of this book, of their general lack of orientation toward the labor market. In San Jose, organizing never arose as an option. Instead, the custodians attempted to pursue their interests within the political process of bargaining, backed by lobbying and occasional collective action. Unlike the men in the public works group, however, the custodians lacked natural allies in the city's pro-growth coalition. And unlike the women in "social consumption" functions, the custodians lacked strong natural allies in San Jose's neighborhoods, among client groups, and in the emergent "controlled-growth" governing coalition.[10]

[9]Local advocates for Southeast Asian immigrants and welfare department staffers explained that fear of retaliation and informal work arrangements involving low and unreported wages and "double-dipping" into welfare income were widespread (interview, Allette Lundberg, Santa Clara County Targeted Assistance Program, Nov. 6, 1986). Contracted-out custodial employees uniformly refused interviews, as did the owner of the company that hired them.

[10]Latino community organization was as yet too weak to play a strong role. The one Latina city

The leaders of the custodians also lacked the coalition-building skills that helped the librarians assert their leadership in the city workforce. Nor did the custodians (or their union) possess the capacity for research necessary to assemble information on mismanagement, labor practices, hidden costs, and other issues that might have helped the campaign. Finally, they lacked the discursive resources—or power of voice—wielded by people like Maxine Jenkins and the highly articulate librarians. The custodians were unable to articulate their claim either as a public interest or as a matter of administrative justice.

When I secured access to the city workforce through both union and city officials in 1986, each asked specifically for informal feedback on my findings regarding the custodians. In reports provided to union and city officials in 1987, I sketched the analysis presented above. I attributed the custodians' low morale to their low occupational status, to their authoritarian-style supervision, to their weak union representation, and to the threat of contracting out. I recommended training and employee-involvement programs that would emphasize the "professionalization" of these workers. I argued that the central factor in the custodians' demoralization was "the contract" and, consequently, urged union and city officials to bring the work back in-house.

I had concluded that the difference in the fates of the custodians and the women of the city stemmed at least in part from the custodians' inability to fashion and wield effective political weapons. I had a faint hope that framing contracting out as an issue of racial justice might put this conclusion to a test (and also be of some use to the custodians). So, I also suggested that the contracting-out policy had a disparate racial impact and could be challenged on the same potent grounds of basic fairness—in this case, racial rather than gender based—that had armored the claim to comparable worth.[11] I suggested that an examination of the wage effects of contracting out would reveal that the wages for the work performed by predominately white personnel—mostly professional and technical work—were markedly increased through contracting-out, while wages for the work performed by predominately nonwhite employees—such as the city custodians and the food service employees—were decreased.

The city officials were not receptive to my comments. The president of Local 101, Mike Ferraro—a city librarian who had been an activist in CLAW—listened politely. Nearly four years later, then a union business agent, he

---

council member during the 1980s—Blanca Alvarado—would emerge as the janitors' main champion in city government, but her base was among the more conservative interests associated with the Mexican-American Chamber of Commerce.

[11] Julianne Malveaux (1992) also notes that comparable worth does not address the disparate racial impact of mechanisms such as contracting out.

recalled our conversation: "I remember you telling me that the union had the clout to bring the contracts back in if we made it an issue like comparable worth. I was skeptical" (interview, Oct. 24, 1990).

More receptive to my report were the custodians' shop steward, David Alday, and the president of the MEF chapter, Joan Goddard. By the time I interviewed Ferraro, most of the custodians who had opposed the outside contract had left city service or abandoned the struggle to prevent the layoffs. Alday, however, had been part of that original circle of insurgents. A soft-spoken man, he was appointed shop steward after the leaders of the local withdrew the right to elect stewards. Alday was also stubborn, however, and he never changed his position on the contract.

Joan Goddard, a librarian and a thoughtful, principled unionist, had been drawn into union life through the comparable worth campaign. She knew and sympathized with Dave Alday, whose worksite was at the city's main library. In 1987, she joined with Alday and several other union members to form a new union committee against contracting out.

Alday and Goddard's campaign was by no means comparable in scale to that conducted by the women of the city a decade earlier.[12] Nonetheless, Alday and Goddard addressed the issue at union meetings, formed a union committee, and made the rounds of city council members, seeking to sensitize them to the issue. They called upon council members to bring custodial work back "in-house" and suggested that preference in hiring could be given to those in contracted-out jobs. They found support for their position inside the union, especially among public works employees who opposed the practice of contracting at *higher* than city wages for construction inspection and other services.

On the city council, the most responsive member was Blanca Alvarado, whose base was among the more conservative parts of the Mexican-American community. Union staffer Mike Ferraro later recalled:

> Blanca Alvarado was the linchpin. She framed [the issue] as a Justice for Janitors issue. She said, "These are mostly minorities, and they are the lowest-paid people in the city. By going out to use contractors, we were paying them sub-sub-minimum wages, and this was a very negative social statement" (interview, Oct. 24, 1990).

Union activists were surprised and troubled when the contract for custodial services was awarded to a firm owned by Alvarado's brother. According to Ferraro, he subsequently lost the contract, and Blanca Alvarado again advocated that the positions be returned to city workers.

[12]This account is based on a series of interviews with David Alday, Joan Goddard, and Mike Ferraro between 1986 and 1991.

Although in my reports to union and city officials I had suggested that the contracting out of custodial work could be framed as an issue of racial justice, Goddard and Alday emphasized public service issues. They focused on the quality of the work since the contracting out, having enlisted city employees to help gather data on the volume of complaints about cleanliness and other shortcomings. In retrospect, their approach fits nicely with the argument made here that public sector workers are constrained to articulate their demands as in the public interest. And although administrators in the city bureaucracy were generally not impressed with Goddard and Alday's argument, one key city official, Susan Hammer, was. Her support was enlisted in a manner very similar to that of mayoral candidate McEnery's a decade earlier during the comparable worth campaign.

With prodding from Goddard and Alday, Local 101 made the contracting-out problem an "endorsement issue," and candidates for the city council and for mayor were asked to take a position on it. Susan Hammer had been a city council member in the late 1980s and in 1990 was elected with the union's support to succeed Mayor Tom McEnery. Before the 1990 election, she attended a candidates' forum conducted by the Friends of the Library at the branch where Joan Goddard worked. On a visit to the ladies' room, Hammer was most disturbed by the condition of the facilities. Goddard and her fellow union members took advantage of her reaction to emphasize the effects of contracting out on the quality of custodial services in city buildings. Like McEnery nearly ten years earlier, Hammer promised to help the union if she was elected.

Later that year, as the mayoral election moved into gear, the contract for custodial services came before the city council for renewal. A representative of SEIU Local 1877, representing private sector custodians, was on hand to make a pitch for using a union contractor. Alvarado spoke against the contract, as she had for several years, on the grounds of racial justice. Ferraro recounts what happened next: "We went in to say [the contract] should be in-house, but we never thought this would go anywhere. Alvarado supported us, as we knew she would. Then Susan Hammer stood up and spoke against [the outside contract] and suddenly we had a majority" (interview, Oct. 24, 1990).

Building maintenance managers at the meeting protested the city council's decision, citing the burden of increased cost. The council dismissed their objections and directed staff to phase out the contracting over a two-year period starting at the end of 1991.[13]

---

[13]As I prepared this manuscript in the summer of 1993, I learned that Hammer's administration put execution of this decision "on hold" in the face of the fiscal crisis of the early 1990s. At this writing, it still remains to be seen whether the custodians and their union have the political capacity to enforce the city council's decision. It is likely that progressives in the city's Latino

In 1991, however, Mayor Hammer's administration placed the plan to bring custodial work back in-house on hold, in response to the renewed fiscal crisis in that period. In the same year, the local AFL-CIO central labor council (CLC) secured the passage of a city ordinance creating a review and enforcement process to ensure that compensation for contracted-out city work meets prevailing union standards. By 1994, all contracted custodial services were unionized (interview, Amy Dean, CLC business agent, June 8, 1994). Also in that year, the city finally began to bring the work back in-house, starting with the police administration building—by far the largest single contracted site (interview, Ferraro, May 19, 1994).

Throughout the fifteen-year process of response to privatization described here, there was no link or coalition between city workers' efforts to stop the contracting out and private sector custodians or their union. The city custodians never turned to their private sector counterparts for help; nor did their union seek to organize the contract employees. Similarly (and unlike the private sector Local 1877), Local 101 did not participate in legislative efforts to set union standards for contracted work; nor did the labor council seek to involve Local 101 in that effort. "AFSCME wasn't involved," according to the CLC business agent, "because it didn't involve them. Their people are all in-house" (interview, Dean, June 8, 1994).

In sum, in response to private competition, the city custodians and their union sought neither to organize workers in the larger labor market nor to impose public regulation over the terms of contracts. Those initiatives came, when they came, exclusively from the private sector. Rather, the city custodians responded to the privatization of their work with efforts focused entirely on the political universe of the agency itself.

In 1991, both Goddard and Ferraro—reflecting on the reversal of the city's policies of contracting out—suggested that the city custodians' recent progress was due, at least in part, to developments in the private sector. "We tried to talk to them [city officials] for a long time," Goddard recounted, "but its really sinking in might have been the effect of the Justice for Janitors efforts. I mean, they [the private sector janitors] were the ones out there demonstrating and we were not."

What were these private sector developments, and why did they help to stem the tide of privatization? This question brings us to the second case study of this chapter. I describe first the crises plaguing the private sector custodians and their union in the mid-1970s.

---

community will achieve a new measure of political power because of the new strength of the now-Latino-identified private sector janitors' union and as a result of the probable election of long-time progressive contender Tony Estremera to the city council in the mid-1990s, which may strengthen the custodians' hand.

The Private Sector Custodians of the Valley

Custodians are the only segment of the workforce employed by Silicon Valley's electronics industry who are unionized in significant numbers. Through aggressive organizing, SEIU Local 77 established a foothold in the building maintenance industry in the 1960s.[14] The rapid economic growth of the late 1960s and early 1970s proved hospitable for union growth—in part because profits were high, in part because building maintenance was a small part of production costs, in part because of the "protection" from competition that the union provided unionized firms by picketing companies employing nonunion contractors, and in part because employers' operating assumptions regarding union versus nonunion janitorial labor promoted the use of unionized services. In thriving times, paying union scale was considered an acceptable price for a relatively stable, trustworthy, trained, and disciplined custodial workforce. Major employers considered nonunion firms in the building maintenance industry unreliable, referring to them as "mop and bucket operators," and commonly they were not even allowed to bid on major contracts. A maintenance firm executive explained:

> You got security concerns in these fancy plants; you don't want a lot of turnover; you got a job to do and a product to get out; you don't need a lot on headaches with these fly-by-night kind of guys; you don't mind going with the union and paying a little more.[15]

Facing an expansive yet insulated market, unionized contractors formed the Associated Building Maintenance Contractors of Santa Clara Valley to avoid price competition among themselves by pursuing joint collective bargaining.[16] By the early 1970s, all the larger building maintenance contractors were unionized.

As the economy of the valley grew, the union grew, but soon the impetus to organize declined. One management official actively involved in the contractors' association recalled:

[14]During most of the period covered in this case, the local involved was SEIU Local 77, whose jurisdiction covered Santa Clara County and its northern neighbor, San Mateo County. In 1987, the local merged with Local 18; the new local, 1877, included Alameda and Contra Costa counties as well.

[15]Maintenance firm representatives agreed to interviews on the condition of confidentiality.

[16]This coalition directly parallels the Association of Hospitals of Santa Clara Valley, described in chapter 5. By contrast, *public sector* employers may agree to share wage data to facilitate compliance with salary standardization procedures, but no such bargaining coalition exists among agencies.

The union got lazy. Instead of organizing two hundred little buildings, all they had to do was stay in with five big companies. They
wouldn't have to organize. They grew in the early '70s because of that,
but by the late '70s they were losing members. When the GM plant went
out of business, there were two hundred new bucket operators in the
market. When the union can't protect the union employers from compet-
itors by strikes and organizing, then you know they're gonna be in
trouble.[17]

Restructuring in the Building Maintenance Industry

In the expansive years of the 1960s and early 1970s, Local 77's leadership
was Italian-American, as was most of its core membership—a few hundred
high-seniority men with years of continuous employment who were personally known by union officials, reliable supporters in union elections, and
occasional visitors to union meetings. By the mid-1970s, however, former
farmworkers from the southwest United States, Mexican-Americans, and
recent immigrants from Mexico and Central America formed the majority of
the membership.[18]

By the mid-1970s, the local had become the private franchise of its leader,
who attempted to bequeath the local to his son on his retirement. Combined
with other grievances, this process of succession provided an opening for a
challenge to the local's established structure of leadership. A series of internal
struggles followed around both the terms of contracts and the process of
succession and union democracy. By 1977, the local's unruly membership had
become ungovernable and in that year the local was placed into trusteeship by
the president of the international union.[19] During the subsequent decade,
the union experienced two disastrous strikes and was taken out of trusteeship
and then returned to it again; by the mid-1980s, the local was virtually
nonfunctional.

The internal conflict that erupted in the mid-1970s reflected not only a crisis
over succession in Local 77 but *new economic conditions* in the Santa Clara
Valley. The recession of 1975, combined with growing global competition in
the electronics industry, had a sobering effect in the valley, and the contractual
arrangements that pervaded the building maintenance industry made it highly

[17]It would be unimaginable for someone in the public sector to make the last comment.
[18]I draw here on my personal knowledge of SEIU Local 77 in those years, though I was not directly
involved in the union. My responsibilities as a field representative for SEIU Local 715 in the early
1970s included Santa Clara County's large custodial workforce.
[19]Presidents of internationals have the authority to suspend local union bylaws and disband
elected leadership if the union is unable to represent its members or to manage its finances. This
procedure permits the international to preempt internal rebellions and appoint satisfactory
successors to retiring or discredited leaders.

vulnerable to this reversal. In the office complexes and the new business parks that house Silicon Valley's namesake industry, custodians were typically employed by building maintenance contractors; these contractors were retained by client companies, or by building owners or management companies that in turn leased facilities and services to private companies. Custodial employees were typically one or two steps removed, then—through their employers' contracts with building management companies and through those companies' leases to tenant companies—from their co-workers in the facility they "serviced." And though custodial wages were a small share of corporate costs, they were a large share of the costs for building managers.

By the mid-1970s, many local companies and buildings were purchased by national corporations. After comparing the valley's high costs of building maintenance with the lower rates in other regions, many of these corporations demanded reductions. New, nationally managed, nonunion building maintenance companies offered stability and security at a sharp discount. Other participants in the building maintenance labor market also brought increased competition: immigrants from Latin America and Southeast Asia, blue-collar workers laid off by local plants, and so on.

Unlike the hospital industry, building maintenance had little or no market power or political or fiscal "buffer" to cushion or delay the impact of austerity: competition cut like a knife, early and deep. Firms facing tighter markets began to examine the bottom line on plant and office space more closely; building managers facing stiffer competition for tenants were forced to reduce their costs or risk economic disaster.

This difference between the building maintenance and health care industries' vulnerability to economic pressure had a very direct effect on labor relations. Unionized building maintenance contractors were able to contain wages—they declined sharply in real terms after 1975—but had less control over health care costs. According to a management consultant for the industry, the increase amounted to 50 percent during the two-year term of the 1979 contract; during the subsequent three-year agreement, health insurance costs increased again, this time by 100 percent (name withheld by request).

As a result, by the mid-1970s unionized contractors were losing contracts to nonunion employers; as union members lost their jobs, the union began to lose its dues base. Also by this time, the union had lost its capacity to organize the unorganized. Now union officials faced a single choice: agree to a pay cut or lose a significant part of their jurisdiction (and dues base). The interests of union officials and unionized building maintenance contractors were aligned here: On the one hand, the loss of contracts by employers meant the loss of union dues, which directly affected the union budget. On the other hand, wage cuts would sustain the dues base and could be rationalized as being in the members' interests.[20] All this ultimately led to new strains within the union and, ultimately, to the collapse of unionism among the custodians of the valley.

Accordingly, the two-tier wage arrangements that surfaced in many industries in the early 1980s were adopted much earlier in the valley's building maintenance industry: first on a plant-by-plant and company-by-company basis, then in the entire workforce. As early as 1974, the SEIU's sister local, 18, in nearby Alameda and Contra Costa counties, began to negotiate supplemental agreements amending contracts to lower pay where contractors faced competing bids from nonunion firms. On a case-by-case basis, Local 77 began to do the same. These agreements threatened to cause political embarrassment within the locals and so were adopted in private, without the knowledge of the membership. When this practice ultimately came to light, however, the political damage to incumbent officials was significant.

In 1977, a caucus of Spanish-speaking custodians mounted a strong challenge to the official union leadership. They demanded union democracy, asked for Spanish translation at membership meetings, protested the concessions to employers, and in that year succeeded in electing a majority to the executive board, the union's policy-making body. Their leader—a non-English-speaking custodian who had been an attorney in Central America and who was running for the union's top leadership position—was removed by his opponent from the ballot, however, because he allegedly did not have the qualifications needed to run for office. The insurgent executive board majority was refused admission to the union office by the incumbent administration, so they picketed the offices of the custodians' union, which happened to be located in the same building as the valley's central labor council office. The international president then placed the local into trusteeship, dissolved the offending executive board, and appointed an international vice president as trustee.[21]

In 1978, without ratification by the membership, the union's trustee and the contractors' association formalized the two-tier arrangements in a side letter to the contract. Under this "modified two-tier" plan, contractors competing against bids by a nonunion contractor could hire workers at 70 percent of the regular rate, with similar reductions in health benefits, vacation, and sick leave. After five years, these new lower-paid workers would receive standard

[20]When a new nonunion contractor takes over a job, the existing custodial workforce may be employed at the employer's discretion.
[21]I was offered the job of running Local 77 on behalf of the international's trustee. After interviewing members of the insurgent group, I declined the offer.

wages. Because of the high turnover rate among custodians, there was a rapid accumulation of custodial workers paid at the lower rate.

When the trusteeship renegotiated Local 77's three-year agreement in 1981, the agreement was extended to cover *all* newly hired union members or members with less than one year of seniority. The wages of this group were set at $5.31 per hour. It would remain at this rate for the term of this agreement and the next—through 1987. Union and management negotiators agreed to call this the "New Member Advancement Program."

The 1981 agreement would expire on August 1, 1984. In the meantime, the union had been removed from trusteeship under the leadership of Charles Perkel. Hired from outside the local, Perkel was white and a college graduate. He had been selected by the international to assume the leadership of the local while it was under trusteeship and had subsequently won election when the trusteeship was lifted. His position was insecure, however, since two caucuses were angling for leadership. Further, one of the business agents, Mike Garcia, had developed a reputation as an effective advocate for the custodians. Though affiliated with neither caucus, Garcia had attracted support for his defense of the union's undocumented immigrant workers; he was widely perceived as a strong threat in the upcoming elections.

The Custodians' Strike of 1984

By 1984, 30 percent of Local 77's membership was in the New Member Advancement Program; eliminating the program was the prime issue on the members' agenda in the negotiations that year, according to business agent Mike Garcia (interviews, Jan. 13, 1987) and caucus leader John Serminio (interview, Nov. 6, 1986). The issue never surfaced in negotiations, however. Negotiations on wages dragged on for two months past the August 1 expiration date, as the members grew increasingly impatient. Three times, in October, November, and December, Perkel submitted a settlement proposal to the membership, recommending ratification; three times it was rejected. Finally, on December 13, 1984, with the reluctant cooperation of the union leadership, fewer than five hundred of the fifteen hundred custodians in the unit went out on strike, with Garcia providing the major leadership in the field.

The strike might best be described as *disciplinary*; it was less a weapon used by the union than a mechanism for employers to chastise their employees, or to force them to accept the management offer. Trade unionists consider December a very difficult—even suicidal—time for a strike. Union members are particularly hurt by the loss of income, and the emphasis at this time of year on enjoyment of family life leaves members disinclined to participate in collective action. Typically, in fact, unions cancel membership meetings for the month of December.

The critical test of resolve and organizational strength in a strike usually comes in the second or third week. The December 13 strike date, then, was probably the worst possible day of the entire year on which to take such an action. A management negotiator, speaking on the condition of confidentiality, recalled: "They were going out two weeks before Christmas; they couldn't win and we all knew it. Perkel felt he had to gel his unit, though, and we figured we might as well put them out, let them smarten up."

Among the major sites of strike action were IBM and National Semiconductor, two firms that had played leading roles in ensuring that—aside from the custodial workforce—the electronics industry remained a union-free environment. But although the firms were major employers in the region, the strike generated surprisingly little public attention; between its morning and evening editions, the San Jose *Mercury-News* published only three small articles on back pages.

As the strike began, management negotiators retracted their previous offer to make raises retroactive to the August 1 contract expiration date. Retroactive payment of those raises—which the custodians had earlier rejected as inadequate—thus became the key issue in negotiations and in Perkel's statements to union members and the press.

At the same time, Mike Garcia was articulating a less tangible theme among the striking janitors: the need for respect. "There never would have been a strike if there was respect on the job. Supervisors tell our people to do this and do that, and if they don't like it, they'll bring in other people from Mexico. They're trying to pit vulnerable people against each other" (Jack Sirica, "Striking Janitors Demand Respect," San Jose *Mercury-News*, Dec. 15, 1984). Garcia's rhetoric of respect struck a chord among the custodians, many of whom felt the low status of their work was a personal indignity. "Janitors demand respect!" became the main slogan on the picket lines.

Management negotiators, however, dismissed the issue, saying simply that the supervisors' behavior had never been brought up in negotiations. Privately, one management negotiator was contemptuous of—and bewildered by—the custodians' claim: "Respect! That was Garcia's big deal. When you don't have economic issues, how do you make a deal? How do you negotiate respect?"

On December 20, after eight days on strike, the custodians ratified a settlement on management's earlier terms. The agreement also required that workers pay for increases in the cost of health premiums and continued the New Member Advancement Program. Further, the raise that was put through did not apply to the starting rates established under the New Member Advancement Program; that rate was frozen for yet another three years.

The face-saver for the union was a "ratification bonus" of $100, in lieu of retroactivity. (Those working under the New Member Advancement Program were excluded from this provision as well.) And this solution facilitated another change: the implementation dates for all the wage increases were moved back four months, saving the employers substantially more than the cost of the ratification bonus and reducing the cost of the settlement to less than the original offer the workers had rejected. As one management negotiator chortled, "We sure snookered them on that one."

Perkel borrowed Garcia's language on respect to put the best face on his interpretation of the settlement: "Our members knew that a strike was going to cost them more in wages than they'd earn in back pay. But those custodians were willing to make a sacrifice in pay during the week before Christmas. Now they've gained the ear and the respect of management" (Michael Rezendes, "Janitors Win Back Pay, End Strike," San Jose *Mercury-News*, Dec. 22, 1984).

After the strike—despite gaining "the ear and the respect of management"— the caucuses in the union circulated a petition asking the international to use its power of trusteeship to remove Perkel and conduct new elections. The international complied with half the petition: the union was put back into trusteeship and Perkel was ousted, but new elections were deferred. Garcia was transferred to yet another building maintenance local, in southern California, also in trusteeship. When I visited Local 77 in 1987, the international was preparing to merge it with Local 18, in nearby Alameda County—also now in trusteeship because of similar developments.

"Justice for Janitors!"

During the mid-1980s, the national leadership of SEIU, however, adopted a new, aggressive organizing stance. The elderly Charles Hardy had retired from the international presidency. Some of the more conservative international vice presidents who had ruled regions of the country in a baronial manner lost office or retired, while younger leaders had a stronger voice in determining the national union's direction. Starting in 1987, successful strikes and organizing drives by SEIU janitors were carried out under the slogan "Justice for Janitors" (in the movement's shorthand, "JfJ"). Across the country, among the most effective of these mobilizations would be Local 1877's campaign in Silicon Valley. Among the other areas where mobilization occurred were St. Louis (Bill Smith, "Area Janitors Plan to Rally for Pay Raises," *St. Louis Post-Dispatch*, Dec. 4, 1986), Denver (Bureau of National Affairs, "Denver Janitors Are Target of SEIU Organizing Drive," *Retail/Services*

Labor Report, June 2, 1986), Philadelphia (Douglas Dabney, "Janitors Win Union Rights," *Philadelphia Tribune*, March 18, 1988), San Diego (Diane Lindquist, "Union Starts 'Justice for Janitors' Drive," *San Diego Union*, May 3, 1987), Hartford (Helen Machado, "300 Janitors Hold Rally," *Hartford Courant*, May 24, 1993), and Los Angeles (Sonia Nazario, "For This Union, It's War," *Los Angeles Times*, Aug. 19, 1993). In Los Angeles, for example, union membership would increase from 30 to 90 percent among those who cleaned highrises in downtown Los Angeles and in Century City. Over the next five years, SEIU's membership in the building maintenance industry would stabilize and then increase by 35,000—from 165,000 to 200,000 members—an astonishing record, given organized labor's general pattern of decline (Sonia Nazario, "For This Union, It's War," Aug. 19, 1993).

How has the Justice for Janitors campaign been able to bring about such an impressive reversal in union membership rates? The first essential factor is the internal regeneration of the union's organizational capacity. Santa Clara County Central Labor Council business agent Amy Dean describes this in terms that echo efforts to improve productivity in other organizations challenged by economic pressures: "You need to build a team that's real focused around a challenge, and that's what Justice for Janitors did. They gave themselves a performance goal—to organize the industry in the valley—and they held themselves accountable for it" (interview, June 8, 1994). In the case of Local 77, the union members' insurgence created the context for this regeneration by driving out a regime that had lost this organizational capacity and then by driving out another regime, imposed through the Perkel trusteeship, which proved unable to regain it.

Second, JfJ leaders frame the claim to union representation, wages, benefits, and rights as a civil right, in a manner reminiscent of movements by black public sector sanitation workers in the 1960s. This enables organizers to excite the imagination and commitment of custodians and thereby generate and sustain "mini-movements." This approach also promotes alliances with civil rights, religious, and women's organizations and other community institutions, helps convince local public officials to take a stand on behalf of justice for janitors (Howley 1990; Banks 1991; Blackwell 1993), and embarrasses private employers. In California, the Justice for Janitors campaign also draws on the social movement traditions of Central American immigrants (Goldin 1989) and on the legacy of Cesar Chavez's farmworkers' movement—another effort to counteract overwhelming employer power and brutal labor market conditions through grassroots political mobilization. In short, the discourse of the campaign resonates powerfully with the demands for "respect" that Mike Garcia articulated during the 1984 custodians' strike.

This redefinition of unionism as social justice mobilizes solidarity more effectively than the economic self-interests emphasized by business unionism: not only within the union and among community organizations, but also with other labor organizations. The hard times of the 1980s and 1990s are conducive to a revival of social movement unionism not only among custodians, of course, but elsewhere as well. JfJ's brand of social movement unionism allows the campaign to tap—and to encourage—social movement unionism and interunion support in local labor councils and other quarters of the labor movement.

Third, the JfJ campaign is based on a strategic analysis of the organizing context. JfJ strategists recognize, first, that the National Labor Relations Board's union certification procedures do not protect collective bargaining rights.[22] Accordingly, they demand recognition based on union membership as proven by card counts and rely on direct action—including recognition strikes—and corporate campaign techniques to enforce that demand. Their aim is to avoid extended strikes; when strikes are necessary, they are to be used as disruptive guerilla tactics or protest actions.

At least as important as the failure of the NLRB, however, is the "outsourced" status of the custodial workforce, which insulates these workers from the building owners and from larger firms that purchase their services. All U.S. industrial relations institutions—collective bargaining procedures, labor laws, conventional strategic repertoires for union power—presume that important decisions affecting workers' conditions of employment are made by their employers. Mike Garcia describes the incongruous results for "outsourced" workers, like the members of his union:

> It is lawful . . . for a building owner to fire a cleaning contractor who pays $6.90 an hour, insisting on a new contractor who pays $5.00 an hour. But if the janitors who lose their jobs picket to protest the actions of this building owner, it is a violation of 8(b)(4) and the NLRB will go to court to get an injunction to stop our picketing within forty-six hours. The building owner who willingly and directly causes wages to drop and workers to lose their jobs is a protected "neutral third party," and workers are told it is illegal to picket the company that is responsible for eliminating their jobs (statement before the U.S. Commission on the Future of Worker-Management Relations, Jan. 27, 1994).

JfJ campaigns seek to overcome this disadvantage by conceptualizing their organizing targets as *regional networks of contractors* arranged around one or

---

[22]For an argument reflecting the consensus of industrial relations researchers in support of this judgment, see Kochan, Katz, and McKersie 1986.

a few larger client corporations or core firms. Although these contractors are likely to operate on a small profit margin and to be highly vulnerable to competition from lower-cost producers, the custodians' wages affect only a small part of the costs of the larger core firms. The larger firms are also more likely to be involved in relationships or activities that would make them vulnerable to corporate campaign tactics: shareholder meetings, consumer markets, government contracts or other regulations, and so on. JfJ campaigns treat the contractors as "cut-outs," or devices that allow the core firms to evade responsibility for the wages and working conditions of their employees. Accordingly, JfJ campaigns target the core firm as the "real" employer in an effort to produce a three-way agreement.[23] To (1), the agreement between the contractor and the core firm, they seek to add (2), an agreement between the union and the core firm or its association on wage and benefit standards, and (3), an agreement with the contractor or its association on job security, worker rights, portability of benefits, rehiring rights, and other issues of more narrow concern.[24]

Rebuilding Local 1877

In 1987, responsibility for directing Local 77—still in trusteeship—was assigned to a group of SEIU organizers using the JfJ strategy. The local's new trustee was Susan Sachen, a former organizer for the United Farm Workers. Sachen hired former custodians and others with community organizing experience, relied heavily on mass picketing and political action, and built up an infrastructure of rank-and-file shop stewards.

By late 1989, the Justice for Janitors campaign had stopped the loss of union jobs to nonunion contractors. Also in 1989, Mike Garcia returned to the local—now merged with Local 18 and called Local 1877. In May 1990, the trusteeship was lifted as Garcia was elected to lead the union. In 1990 and

[23]JfJ organizers call these "tripartite agreements"; to avoid confusion with the common usage of that term (referring to agreements among labor, business, and government on national or regional industrial policy), I use the term "three-way agreements." JfJ's effort to organize the industry's product markets echoes the achievements of the United Mine Workers of America in coal a century earlier (Commons 1905; Brody 1991).

[24]The architect of the JfJ strategy is Stephen Lerner, former organizing director for SEIU's building maintenance division. His emphasis on periphery-based three-way strategies derives from six years of organizing in subcontracted apparel shops for the Amalgamated Clothing and Textile Workers' Union. Lerner was trained by Cesar Chavez's mentor, Fred Ross, Sr., when Ross left retirement in the early 1970s to train boycott organizers for the United Farm Workers of America (interview, Lerner, Jan. 29, 1993). The strategy of targeting core firms to organize peripheral employers was developed and effectively employed in the 1970s by the Ohio-based Farm Labor Organizing Committee, headed by Baldemar Velasquez. Corporate campaign techniques were fully developed and effectively employed by the United Farm Workers by 1970. For a blueprint of the JfJ strategy, see Howley 1990 and Banks 1991; for Lerner's more general prescription for union organizing in the 1990s, see Lerner 1991.

1991, the local's membership grew from forty-five hundred to fifty-five hundred (interview, Garcia, Oct. 17, 1990).

Public agencies, publicly owned buildings leased to private firms, private buildings leased by public agencies, and other sites affected by public policy or subsidy proved particularly vulnerable to the campaign. In the summer of 1990, for example, the laboratories of the National Aeronautics and Space Administration (NASA) in Mountain View, California, threatened to pull their contracts with a unionized custodial firm and hire a nonunion replacement. According to Garcia, he subsequently called NASA administrators but received no response; nor did the administrators even acknowledge receipt of a petition signed by the workers. "So we pulled our people off the job. But they stayed there on the base and marched around. We put out calls and had a few hundred people marching with them. Within a few hours NASA called down and ordered the nonunion contractor to sign the [union] contract" (interview, Oct. 17, 1990).

City-owned buildings leased to private firms through the downtown Redevelopment Agency and city government's more general efforts at downtown redevelopment also provided a target for JfJ's politicizing tactics. In the spring of 1988, for example, hundreds of janitors had marched through San Jose's redevelopment area, protesting the use of public funds to subsidize employers using low-wage, nonunion custodial labor (Michael Medina, "Janitors Protest against Low Wages," *El Observador*, March 9, 1988; Delia Rios, "They Say They're Tired of Being Swept Aside," San Jose *Mercury-News*, April 1, 1988). Not surprisingly, then, the theme of "justice for janitors" began to appear in city officials' deliberations over the fate of their own custodial workforce. The appeal to "justice for janitors"—with its implicit charge of racial injustice— had the impact of a political hammer in the city's political universe, as had the claim to comparable worth ten years earlier.

The main thrust of the JfJ campaign, however, was directed at private employers. In 1990, for example, the management firm for a bank building owned by an old San Jose family elected to "go nonunion." In response, "eighty or ninety janitors" from the local surrounded the building, vociferously exercising their freedom of speech. When the workers' compensation department of a law firm owned by the same family began to receive calls from unions threatening to boycott its services, dialogue began and a settlement was reached (interview, Garcia, Oct. 17, 1990).

Another successful campaign—to organize Shine Building Maintenance— drew national attention in 1991 and 1992. Shine's largest client was Apple Computer, which prided itself on its progressive personnel practices. Accordingly, Local 1877 used corporate campaign tactics to assert Apple's responsibility for the wages and working conditions of the custodians hired through its contract with Shine:

> Protesters disrupted an international computer show and unfurled a union banner in the middle of a speech by President and CEO John Sculley before an audience of thousands. They held a hunger strike on Apple's front lawn and declared an international boycott of Apple Products (Michelle Levander, "Apple's Janitors Go Union: Victory Is First Step in Broader Campaign," San Jose *Mercury-News*, March 3, 1992).

The Apple campaign also ended in success for the union. By 1993, the building maintenance industry in the valley was effectively organized again, as only a few major employers continued to retain nonunion firms. In that year, Local 1877 expanded its "campaign for justice," now targeting the valley's landscaping and grounds maintenance industry. That industry is also composed of relatively small firms operating on small profit margins, dependent on contracts with large building owners or corporations, and that workforce too is composed mainly of low-wage recent immigrants and so may prove vulnerable to the same campaign tactics.

Despite the new organizational strength of the union and its success in stemming and reversing the loss of membership, by 1994 the local had still failed to recoup the economic losses of the 1980s. In 1981, unionized janitors outside the New Member Advancement Program were paid $6.41 an hour; the 1994 agreement raised wages to between $6.90 and $7.20 an hour—at the higher rate, a 26 percent loss in real wages—and the New Member Advancement Program remained in place. (Information on wages is from Garcia's statement before the U.S. Commission on the Future of Worker-Management Relations, Jan. 27, 1994.)

Nonetheless, having secured new resources for mobilizing its members, new bonds with its members through its cultural identity with its Spanish-speaking majority, new legitimacy through internal democracy, new respect through a string of organizing victories over powerful corporate adversaries, new allies in the neighborhoods of the valley, and new recognition as a pioneer in strategies that appear effective in the new corporate economy, Local 1877's leadership is now secure. Because of their own expanded engagement in the union's activity, members are less likely to perceive the leadership as complicit in their misfortunes and more likely to view the union as the structure of their own collective action.

Garcia explained the implications of these changes for the internal life of the union:

We use an organizing approach rather than a service approach. In
the old days the reps didn't have to go out in the field; they just sat in
the office and waited for somebody with a grievance to come to
them. The people saw the union like an insurance company where
you pay your dues and then you go if you have a problem, not like a
union. Now the reps have to go out in the field every night and come
back and talk about it in the morning. And instead of taking care of
problems for people, they have to organize and develop leaders and
train them to handle the problems themselves. That doesn't mean
we always win. We still have a long ways to go. But at least they
don't blame us, like they used to. If they blame anybody they blame
themselves, for not coming out and fighting harder. And that's the
way it should be (interview, Oct. 17, 1990).

The Future of Private Sector Unionism

Influential scholars have argued that the future of private sector unionism
depends on a shift away from adversarial relations to a "high-wage" strategy of
productivity enhancement through worker involvement and skill training
(e.g., Kochan, Katz, and McKersie 1986). It is particularly important, some
emphasize, "to develop an organizing agenda that does not rely on deep-seated
job dissatisfaction as the primary (or sole) rallying cry for worker mobilization" (Kochan and Wever 1991:378). Others confidently pronounce that
adversarial unionism and collective bargaining are obsolete and will be replaced with "facilitated consensus" and lawsuits by individuals and protected
groups (Heckscher 1988).

Worker involvement and skill training are worthy aims. But such agendas
do not provide a power base that will induce employers to abandon their
preference for union-free environments in favor of even the most collaborative
union. Moreover, these arguments focus on labor-management relations in
the narrowing core of relatively high-wage, high-skill jobs, while directing
attention away from the growing numbers of workers who inhabit the world
of low-wage, low-security jobs in the firms surrounding that core. Custodians
in the building maintenance industry, among those hit hardest and earliest by
the intensified competition of recent decades, have honed a periphery-based
strategy that could strengthen labor unions in the neglected portion of the
private sector.

The janitors' story is by no means representative of recent developments in
all private sector workplaces; their case was selected to permit controlled
cross-sectoral comparison with the city custodians. The case *does* suggest,
however, that a union thrown into disarray though economic restructuring
can serve as an arena for the emergence of a social movement, which can,

in turn, fuel a rebirth of social movement unionism in the private sector and, in the process, result in increased organization among low-wage, semi-skilled workers, including immigrant workers in the expanding service sector. This is a more likely path to labor movement revitalization for many lower-wage private sector workers than the "high productivity/high wage, labor-management cooperation" strategy urged by some scholars and union officials.[25]

Case Comparisons: Two Logics of Change

Clearly, not all cases in the public sector will follow one path nor all cases in the private sector follow another. Nor should we expect social movement activity, innovations in labor relations, or successful outcomes to be concentrated in one sector. Institutionalized labor relations, imitation of strategies from other times and places, labor-management collaboration, social movement activity, innovations that imply radical social change, and successes and failures have occurred in both sectors, at different times and under different conditions. Further, "success" and "failure" may mean different things according to different models of unionism. What is important for our purposes is that, within each sector, distinctive structural conditions define what is possible; distinctive logics of change influence variations over time and among cases; distinctive sets of factors are associated with success and failure.

A single set of factors, for example, appears to account for the sharp differences in the experiences of the city's custodians and employees in its predominately female classifications over the same period. Both groups were initially marginalized within their unions and neither enjoyed strong labor market position, yet the women were able to move steadily closer to pay equity during the same period that the custodians were being replaced by low-wage, "privatized" workers. If the arguments developed here are sound, these two patterns of change stem from variations in each group's access to the power of voice—so potent in the public sphere—and to strategic coalitions. The latter difference stems, in turn, from their different positions in the shifting patterns of political inclusion and exclusion in the city's governing regime. The human service workers, as we have seen, were associated with a neighborhood-based, "limited-growth" coalition, ascendant against the residential development-

[25]Readers may be interested in the more assertive approaches to issues beyond the conventional scope of representation within the firm that have matured over the past decade and in the important and widespread efforts by labor-community coalitions to build new public and quasi-public economic development planning bodies in response to plant closings. The best source on these trends is the *Labor Research Review*, especially issues 9, 10, 14, and 19, published by the Midwest Center for Labor Research.

oriented coalition that had benefited their predecessors in union leadership, the public works employees. The custodians lost ground in the 1980s because they lacked such political resources. They made marginal gains late in the decade, however, when they turned to political action that emphasized the public service issues associated with their work and when the potent political appeal to "justice for janitors" found its way into the halls of government.[26]

The janitors in the private sector were just as vulnerable as the janitors in the city to their employers' cost-saving measures, and just as aggrieved by their union's inability (or unwillingness) to challenge them. Like those in the public sector, the janitors in the private sector rebelled against their union in the early 1980s. Also like those in the public sector, they faced a union bureaucracy that was out of their control and so made little headway. Why, then, did the organizing model of unionism—Justice for Janitors—surface in the private sector and not in the public?

The answer is that these two cases reflect different structural conditions, different logics of change, and so different factors leading to success or failure. The public sector custodians were isolated and outnumbered within the diverse union organization and the still more complex political universe of the public bureaucracy, while the private custodians, for all their problems, mobilized across a large labor movement of custodians who shared similar problems. Though the custodians in both jurisdictions were offended by the low status accorded their work, only the homogeneity of Local 1877 permitted solidarity to be achieved around the shared demand for "respect" and later "justice for janitors"—just as the homogeneity of the private sector nurses permitted them to achieve an intense, even effervescent collective identity during their strike. As the sole occupational group in their homogeneous, labor market – based union, the private sector custodians were able to make their union ungovernable. The public sector custodians, by contrast, remained isolated in the city's political-bureaucratic universe, unable to mobilize coalitions of the sort that empowered the city's librarians. Though they displayed, in response to the mobilization of the women, a strong capacity for solidarity, they were unable to tap the powers of solidarity that, in different ways, served the women of the city and the private sector custodians of the valley so well.

How does one account for the differences within the *private* sector, between the nurses and the janitors? Both engaged in social movement unionism, and both deployed what might be termed new political resources. The nurses launched the first private sector strike for comparable worth, asserting gen-

[26]The predominately Mexican-American parts of the valley's public workforce are unlikely to make significant gains unless the more progressive organization and political leaders in the Latino community gain in strength.

dered claims that had proven potent in the city of San Jose; the custodians wielded a similarly evocative (if less specific) claim to justice, using an array of innovative tactics for mobilizing, building alliances, and putting pressure on their adversaries.

Why did the custodians succeed in renewing their union, whereas the nurses were demoralized by defeat? Again, these two different patterns appear to stem from the same set of factors: each group's ability (or lack thereof) to reshape its union's strategic repertoire—including its political resources—to gain economic leverage against private employers, who were themselves restructuring in response to intensified competition.

Until 1987, the experiences of the private sector nurses and custodians were directly parallel in an important way: both were undone by the marketplace. As they lost market position, however, the custodians and their union assembled new political-organizational resources. Indeed, there were some similarities between the janitors' new organizing unionism in the Santa Clara Valley and the successful earlier surges of public service unionism in the city of San Jose and elsewhere: (1) both wielded claims appealing to universalistic standards of justice; (2) both relied on creative and flexible mobilization tactics, rather than simply economic action or the withdrawal of labor power; and (3) aiming to influence public opinion, both depended on alliances that extended beyond the labor market.

On closer examination, distinctions remain, however. First, the call for "justice for janitors" serves as a resource for mobilizing custodians and their allies, for building and strengthening coalitions, and for influencing public officials. It is not, however, a "club" that, like comparable worth in the public sector, can be wielded directly against the private sector employer.[27] "Voice," in other words, builds and influences political organization but has limited direct impact on private employers' decision-making. The fate of the nurses' movement provides an excellent example. It too asserted the worth of nurses' work, deploying a discourse that had served as a club in the city, to build a powerful movement in the private sector.[28] Unlike the women's campaign in the city, however, the powerful rhetoric that joined the protest against "nurse burnout" with the claim to comparable worth fell on deaf ears in management circles. It was wielded mainly *within* the nurses' workforce, to "project them to their goal."

---

[27]It is worth noting again that "justice for janitors" lacks the rigorous technocratic logic that informs the claim to comparable worth in the public sector; it lacks the stamp of political bureaucracy.

[28]That particular discourse also served, I have suggested, to submerge a more profound critique of the gendered organization of nursing work beneath its economistic formula.

Second, the main strategic thrust of the flexible new tactics deployed by public service unionism is to wield political power. The main strategic thrust of the flexible new tactics of organizing unionism in the private sector is to inflict or threaten *economic damage* on the adversary, in the absence of an effective economic strike. This objective is less common, and at times even counterproductive, in the public sector.

Third, whereas coalitions of public workers must extend across the political-bureaucratic division of labor to generate political strength, the main strategic coalition of private sector workers remains within the wider private sector labor market. To be sure, the Justice for Janitors campaign relies on community coalitions and aims to influence public opinion on behalf of the workers. This produces political leverage, which can be useful, especially where employers do business with the public sector. But this leverage is just that: leverage. When the corporations of Silicon Valley and the Justice for Janitors campaign meet in combat, management decisions are made not in city council meetings but in corporate suites, on the basis of power relations, economic constraints, and operating assumptions that revolve around economic strategies. In the public sector, by contrast, the terms and conditions of employment are themselves public policy.

7 *The Nurses of the City*

Our process of comparison has taken us from the strike among the city workers of San Jose to its nonidentical twin, the strike among the private sector nurses for comparable worth, and then to the histories of the public and private sector custodians. Now, it takes us to a movement by nurses in the public sector. With this case, our cycle of comparison—by sector, by occupation, by success, and by failure—will be symmetrical and complete.

We return in this chapter to the setting where this book began: the city and county of San Francisco. Chapter 2 framed events there as questions; this chapter seeks to answer those questions, using conceptual tools developed in the previous cases.

The return to San Francisco also completes my own path from native participant to outside observer and back, retrospectively at least, to participant observer. Given the depth of my own involvement, this is the most difficult and delicate case but also, for me, the most meaningful case for comparison.

In the spring of 1981—months before the San Jose city workers' strike and nearly a year before the private sector nurses' strike in the Santa Clara Valley—the nurses of the city and county of San Francisco voted and mobilized to strike. Unlike the nurses in San Jose or the city workers, the leadership of the nurses' union in San Francisco did not champion the claim to comparable worth, although the issue surfaced spontaneously among the nurses themselves. Further, the nurses did not ultimately strike, although they prepared to do so. They did, however, carry out a prestrike mobilization: they voted to authorize a strike, built a strike organization, engaged in mass picketing, then settled with the city on the brink of the strike deadline. Like the San Jose city workers and unlike the private sector nurses of the valley, the city nurses' movement was successful.

So far, this book's argument regarding the character and course of public workers' movements stands on the single case of San Jose. There, we observed a labor movement rooted less in the labor market than in the political-bureaucratic universe of the public agency, itself shaped by the politics of urban growth and fiscal crisis. The demands and resources of that movement took shape, I argued, within this peculiar context for mobilization. This chapter seeks to demonstrate the relevance, in a different setting, of the same conceptual framework. That framework, the reader will recall, has two parts: the first, developed in chapter 3, concerns the peculiar demands and resources of the public workers' movement; the second, developed in chapter 4, locates this movement in the historical context of local government in the postwar era.

Nurses are a small part of a city workforce. The argument developed here requires that we locate the larger public workforce in the changing conditions of urban life and politics. The analysis, then, again traces a pattern of related developments beginning, in this case, with the city's political regime and arriving, eventually, at the mobilization of the nurses of San Francisco.

San Jose is an archetypal Sunbelt city. It was powerfully shaped by postwar shifts in population, by public policies favoring suburban development, and by its location in the now-near-mythic Silicon Valley. These features were closely tied to certain social and political changes that were decisive in our analysis of the case of San Jose. What, if any, parallels exist in the older city of San Francisco? This question requires that we examine the connections, traced in chapter 4 for San Jose, among the public workplace, the urban political economy, and the governing political regime.

We have also followed throughout this book a trail of controlled cross-sectoral comparison. Whereas chapters 3 and 5 made possible the comparison between the first strikes for comparable worth in each sector, chapter 6 contrasted the experiences of a single occupational group—custodians—in the two sectors. Taken together, these chapters also contrasted the experiences of custodians in each sector with members of *different* occupations within the *same* sector—nurses in the private sector and other city workers in the public. Now the same questions arise for the nurses as for the custodians: How do the experiences of the city nurses in San Francisco compare with those of the private sector nurses of the valley—whom they resemble in every respect except their sectoral location? Are public sector nurses in San Francisco more similar to the private sector nurses or to other occupational groups in San Jose?

It should come as no surprise that, as in the case of the custodians, there are deep and clear commonalities, associated with the nurses' labor process and the gendered character of nursing work, that extend *across sectors* within the RN occupational group. For our purposes here, however, the important factors are those that determine *the trajectory of change in labor relations over time*. In this respect, both public and private sector nurses resemble members of other occupational groups in their own sectors more than they do one another.[1]

This chapter will show that the dynamics of labor relations in San Francisco were similar—and in some ways identical—to the patterns that surfaced in the city of San Jose and the county of Santa Clara. In each setting, the public workers' movement mobilized in defense of jobs and services. In each case, public employee organization and demands followed the logic of bureaucratic personnel administration rather than market relations. In each setting, coalitions within the workforce and among the larger constellation of interests in the agency's political universe were decisive bases of union power. In each setting, the histories of different groups of workers employed in functions associated with different policy agendas followed different trajectories, and these trajectories were affected, at least in part, by the tension between the two urban imperatives: the drive for development, and neighborhood-based demands for social consumption. In each case, revolts by workers in female-dominated job classifications drove much of the militancy of the era and, to a degree, shifted the center of union power in local government away from male-dominated police and construction trades and toward the female-dominated human service workforce. In each case, moreover, the realignment of labor relations under Reagan was followed by the emergence of new labor-management coalitions that set the tone for labor relations throughout the 1980s.

Regime and Antiregime in San Francisco

City life and politics in San Francisco—California's only "old city"—and San Jose—California's archetypal "new city"—differ in important ways. San Francisco is a classic central city, recently restructured as it took its place as a second-tier "world city" for banking and producer services; San Jose, by contrast, is a residential city for many employees of the globally oriented electronics, defense, and related industries on its northern and, increasingly, its southern flanks. Each city in its own way is a crucible of cultural change: San Francisco, fed by the ferment of Pacific Rim and Latin American populations and by its taproot into some of the most creative impulses in American

---

[1] I have argued, however, that—given the extent of public funding and regulation of the health sector—many private sector nurses actually work on the cusp of the two sectors. Depending on the learning processes of participants, the increasing politicization of health care can trigger a variant of public service unionism on this soil.

culture; San Jose, constructing a new way of urban life under conditions created by massive migration to its new automobile-based neighborhoods.

San Jose's growth machine was fueled by annexation and the development of tract homes; San Francisco's, by downtown redevelopment. While San Jose's neighborhood revolt occurred mainly in its new neighborhoods, San Francisco's neighborhood movements have encompassed more diverse and lively urban enclaves, such as the African-American Western Addition (Mollenkopf 1983), the Latino Mission District, the gay Castro District (Castells 1983), and the funky Haight (DeLeon 1992).

But despite these differences, the two cities share patterns of urban politics — the politics of growth and fiscal crisis — that I have associated in San Jose with the turn toward and then away from public militancy. The rise of adversarial unionism in the late 1970s in that city was spearheaded by human service workers and linked to a "social consumption" or "quality of life" response to the untrammeled residential growth frenzy that remade the city in the postwar decades. The reversion to nonadversarial, "associationlike" labor relations in the 1980s reflected both the new union leaders' participation in the city's new political regime and a defensive aggregation of interests against external threats in the era of Reaganism. Comparable patterns hold, we shall see, in San Francisco.

San Francisco's pro-growth coalition and the vigorous neighborhood revolts that it provoked are well documented. John Mollenkopf used the city as a central example in his seminal study (1983) of urban pro-growth coalitions and neighborhood resistance to redevelopment; also, the city's vital Castro and Mission neighborhoods are the scene of two of Manuel Castells's (1983) case studies of urban social movements.

More recently, Richard Edward DeLeon's (1992) study of San Francisco politics since 1975 describes the achievements of the city's growth-control movement, the collapse of San Francisco's growth-oriented political regime, and the dilemmas of the progressive "antiregime" that succeeded it. DeLeon summarizes a story told by all these scholars, "the rise and fall of the pro-growth regime in San Francisco":

> Taking root around 1960, this urban regime dominated the city's development strategy and land-use planning for a quarter of a century. The dominant image of the city under this regime was that of a command and communications center providing advanced corporate services to Bay Area businesses and multinational firms pursuing commerce and trade with Pacific Rim nations. That became its strategic function within a developing global hierarchy of cities. A local growth machine emerged to convert strategies into plans and plans into organized action backed by

government authority and popular support. Neighborhoods were leveled, populations displaced, and corporate cockpits installed in the
skyscrapers that were built to give form to the function of the city as a
capital machine. The "transformation of San Francisco," to use the title
of Chester Hartman's (1984) excellent book, was rapid and complete in
the downtown financial district. Waves of development soon began hit-
ting neighborhoods in the North Beach district, South of Market, and
other areas of the city. It was around this time—the late 1970s—that the
slow-growth movement emerged to do battle with the downtown business elite and its city hall allies. At the same time, the progrowth regime
began crumbling. Weakened by local slow-growth opposition, it collapsed completely in 1986 under the weight of national crises in finance
capital and commercial real estate markets (1992:10).

To be sure, the politics of growth took their own course in San Francisco.
San Jose's pro-growth coalition was supplanted by a new political regime
defined in part by a slow-growth, quality of life agenda for the neighborhoods
but embracing in the 1980s a new drive for downtown development. Castells
and DeLeon describe, in contrast, the virtual collapse of San Francisco's pro-
growth coalition, producing not a new political regime but an "absence of
central urban policy" (Castells 1983:105) or, in DeLeon's term, "antiregime."

Nonetheless, the parallels between the two cities reinforce the conclusion of
Carl Abbott's (1981) major study of Sunbelt cities: in what many have come to
see as two polar types of American cities, *convergent trends* have occurred—
deindustrialization, middle-class neighborhood movements, continued immigration from Latin American and Pacific Rim countries, growing ethnic
political organization, deepening inequalities, and the emergence of a range of
urban problems. "Special circumstances of growth," Abbott concludes, gave
Sunbelt cities "a postponement but not an exemption" from the political
fragmentation accompanying the breakdown of what had been hegemonic
growth agendas in America's older cities (1982:261). In both kinds of cities,
untrammeled growth agendas met opposition provoked by their own success,
based both in neighborhoods and in public sector interests organized around
social consumption.

These studies document a process of urban development and political
change in San Francisco related but by no means identical to that described in
studies of San Jose and sketched in chapter 4. All these scholars would agree
that San Francisco's postwar regime was rooted in a classic pro-growth
coalition, at least until the election of George Moscone in 1976. After that year
the progressive countercoalition, composed of public service workers, residents of neighborhoods dominated by minorities, and other neighborhood
activists, proved unable to form a viable alternative governing coalition. First,

they lost power with the assassination of Moscone and Harvey Milk in 1978, and then they collapsed in disarray during the Agnos years a decade later. My purpose here is not to repeat this analysis but to add an as-yet-neglected dimension to it: the impact of this shifting political context on the character and course of the public workers' movement, on the one hand, and the role and significance of the public workers' movement in this political history, on the other.

Public Workers and the Politics of Growth and Austerity

As in San Jose, the turn toward adversarial labor relations in San Francisco was preceded by a spurt in public sector employment. After only a 7 percent increase in the first half of the 1960s, city employment jumped by 23 percent from 1965 to 1970; it would increase by only 5.5 percent over the next five years and decline by 2.2 percent from 1975 through 1980. Growth was not uniform, however, across all city functions. Employment in road maintenance—a base for the construction trades unions—declined, for example, from 390 in 1965 to a mere 219 in 1985, while total city employment spiraled from 16,657 to 24,804 in the same years (U.S. Department of Commerce, Bureau of the Census, *City Employment*).

These figures reflect highly politicized annual decisions concerning the city budget: to allocate or to reduce new resources, among competing interests, in periods of growth and constraint. These decisions are the result, on the one hand, of a local calculus of power; they gradually *reshape*, on the other hand, the organizational base for future conflict. In short, by 1970, this growth reflected sharply increased political demand for human services; equally sharply, it enlarged the organizational base of public employees interested in the provision of those services. Thus, the stage was set for a confrontation between the public workers and the growth machine's political regime.

Curiously, despite the notoriety of San Francisco's labor wars in the 1970s and their prominence in the politics of that period, they are neglected in most studies of the city's politics of those years.[2] Electoral politics, development policy, and neighborhood movements all command attention, but the city as an organization, much less its workforce, scarcely appears.[3]

[2]Boehm and Heldman (1982:44, 66), by contrast, amply document the tensions between the building trades unions and the city's pro-growth elites, which climaxed in a conflict over the status of public workers that dominated public life in the city in the mid-1970s. They document the importance of this conflict in the rise of important political figures such as Dianne Feinstein and Quentin Kopp.

[3]Curiously too, despite Castells's focus on politically organized collective consumption in city life, neither the state *production* of these collective resources nor the social movement of those producers ever attracts his attention.

The involvement of various parts of the city workforce in San Francisco's politics is visible in this work, however, if only barely. Mollenkopf, for example, describes the strong support by building trades unions for pro-development regimes (1983:190) while noting later that Moscone was backed by "the liberal wing of the labor movement (particularly the public employees)" (207).[4] And DeLeon describes "a pattern of labor union support for pro-growth proposals that would persist into the 1980s" (1992:68); he notes in passing, however, that the city's human service employee unions appeared on the opposing, slow-growth side of these confrontations (73) and he also notes the latter's "multi-issue agenda and substantial clout" (25). Reading between the lines of these accounts, it is possible to trace the opposing roles of the city's powerful Building Trades Council—which represented construction trades workers and laborers in city public works operations as well as in private firms—and its human service unions, especially the largest, most politically active city union, SEIU Local 790 (the name assumed after 1982 by Local 400, discussed in chapter 2).[5]

SEIU Local 400, the miscellaneous city employees' union, by contrast, was both a major progressive force in the city's labor movement and the main ally of the city's diverse and easily fragmented neighborhood movements. Because of its internal diversity, the union penetrated almost every neighborhood and public policy arena. Present in its diverse—and predominately female—membership were neighborhood leaders based in the city's mostly white counter-cultural enclaves and its African-American, Latino, and Asian communities.

These ties placed Local 400 in a central position in the networks that formed the basis for progressive political coalitions in the city. Along with the participation of antigrowth employees of the city's planning department on the local's executive board, these ties also bound the union to the antigrowth movement. The union's own internal unity required, moreover, that this diversity be fashioned into a coalition.

Potentially, then, Local 400 was an organizational linchpin for challenges to the city's entrenched governing coalition. Meanwhile, of course, construction trades unions retained their alliances with developers and pro-growth political entrepreneurs. These opposing patterns of involvement in this core urban

---

[4]Mollenkopf (1983) also notes the transformative potential of public workers' movements. Mollenkopf himself served as a consultant to Local 400 in 1980, while I was employed as a business agent for that union.

[5]The political involvement of the building trades unions was grounded in their alliance with unionized contractors involved in publicly funded, subsidized, or regulated construction, from school repairs to downtown office tower construction. This, more than their interest in the relatively small number of public sector trades workers, was what joined these unions and their growth-machine allies in a common political project.

political contest—over growth versus neighborhood needs—precisely fit those described in chapter 4 for San Jose and Santa Clara County.[6]

Though quite contentious in the San Francisco of the 1970s, the politics of public sector labor relations were decidedly muted during the decade that followed. These turns—toward and then away from adversarial labor relations—are evident in table 7.1, which shows the number of city workers' strikes from 1970 through 1990. After a decade of intense strike activity—in which at least one strike occurred in every year but 1977, and unabated by the passage of antistrike legislation in 1975—strike activity suddenly ceased in 1980. The calm of the following decade was broken by only two strikes late in the decade, both unauthorized or wildcat actions.

The *absence* of civil service militancy in the 1980s may be just as significant as its *presence* in the 1970s, leaving, as it did, progressive and oppositional politics for the slow-growth movement alone. Of particular interest was the coalition established between SEIU's Local 790 and Mayor Dianne Feinstein. After all, until then, Feinstein's political career had been a crusade against public worker unionism. And Local 790, after all, had been the city's most strike-prone union during the 1970s, a central part of Moscone's progressive coalition in 1975, and, until the early 1980s, the main labor movement ally for slow-growth advocates. The new alignment of Local 790 with Dianne Feinstein, which coincided with the collapse of public worker militancy in the Reagan years, surely had a significant effect on the subsequent history of San Francisco city politics.

Might this trajectory have followed a different path? On the one hand, the similarity of these trends with those observed in the very different context of San Jose suggests that the structural force of fiscal politics in the 1980s was quite strong. On the other hand, as Maxine Jenkins's powerful role in sparking the first comparable worth strikes in San Jose attests, individuals and small groups can have an important impact on the direction of events. In the account that follows, moreover, we shall observe *two trends* in response to fiscal crisis. One group—like many labor leaders in local government—did indeed enter into a pragmatic coalition with city management; the other—not limited to one agency, one occupational group, or one union—relied mainly on grassroots mobilizations and labor-community coalitions. After a period of conflict, the former group gained the upper hand.

---

[6]This central cleavage in city politics, emphasized by all the scholars cited above, was overdetermined in San Francisco as elsewhere by conflict over law and order. In San Francisco by the late 1970s, this mainly meant conflicts between the city's vibrant gay community and yet another social movement of public workers: cultural reactionaries in the police department and police union. (See note 11 on page 185.)

Table 7.1. City Worker Strikes per Year in San Francisco, 1970.1990

1970	0	1980	1
1971	2	1981	0
1972	2	1982	0
1973	2	1983	0
1974	3	1984	0
1975	1	1985	0
1976	2	1986	1
1977	0	1987	0
1978	1	1988	0
1979	2	1989	1
		1990	0

The $17,000 Streetsweeper Era

By the mid-1970s, strikes by city workers had become annual events in San Francisco. As I noted in chapter 2, these strikes were disturbing to public sector unionists—partly because they were accompanied by antagonism among different parts of the city workforce, partly because they repeatedly ended in debacles for the unions. It was during this period that city officials discovered how to turn a city workers' strike into a political asset, using what I termed the "$17,000 streetsweeper" strategy. A cadre of local politicians rose to prominence in this period by "taking on the unions"; prominent among them was Dianne Feinstein.[7]

Chapter 2 described, for example, how during a strike in March 1974 by locals affiliated with SEIU, city officials and the local newspapers capitalized on the interruption of sewage treatment operations—which caused a stream of raw sewage to flow into San Francisco Bay—to mobilize public opinion against city workers. City officials also made much of the high wages earned by blue-collar craft workers, though craft workers were not involved in this strike.

As a legacy of the pro-growth coalition in San Francisco, construction-related craft workers in city employment and their unions had long enjoyed a special relationship with the city's power structure (Kazin 1987). Members of private sector craft unions enjoyed preference for city jobs—blocking the mobility of the mostly nonwhite and female lower-wage city workers. Further, the wages and benefits of craft workers, along with those of the city's well-organized uni-formed employees, were governed by special sections of the city charter. And, unlike those of other "miscellaneous" city employees, the wages of craft workers routinely matched the rates set through union contracts in the private sector.

[7]In a conversation seven years later, a hospital employee recalled the first time he saw Feinstein. In a well-staged maneuver, then-county supervisor Feinstein donned a candystriper's uniform and, before the eye of a television camera, pushed a cart through a picket line.

By the 1970s, the political position of the craft unions had decidedly weakened, however. Democratic party officials, threatened by the city's increasingly unruly human service workers' unions (who were closely allied, by the mid-1970s, with community-based groups) found the craft unionists' perks a most inviting issue for defining the terms of a new antiunion offensive.

In 1974, the laborers' union persuaded civil service officials to classify streetsweepers as "laborers"—and thus as entitled to the private sector union scale for semiskilled construction workers. Through the efforts of Dianne Feinstein, then a member of the board of supervisors, public officials, the press, and ultimately the public fastened upon these workers as a symbol of the allegedly excessive pay of city employees. Wielding this message, in November 1974, Feinstein advanced Proposition L as an amendment to the city charter. Although her rhetoric on behalf of the measure targeted craft unionists' pay, the measure would have eliminated collective bargaining for all city workers, in favor of a prevailing wage formula.

Proposition L narrowly failed to win passage, however. Leading the opposition was none other than Maxine Jenkins, then on the payroll of SEIU Local 400. The reader will not be surprised to learn that Jenkins redefined the measure in feminist terms: prevailing wages would tie women's wages to the unequal "market standard" and prevent comparable worth adjustments.[8]

In 1975, San Francisco's police struck, further influencing public opinion against city workers and their union. The officers showed little reserve in their picket line behavior. Weapon-toting picketers clashed with members of the public, leading the American Civil Liberties Union to file a suit against police officers who carried their service revolvers while picketing. Finally, a wave of vandalism against nonstriking officers was punctuated by the explosion of a pipe bomb at the mayor's home (*CPER* 27:20).

By the next elections, anti-public worker sentiment in the city was strong enough for Feinstein and other anti-public union politicians to win passage of a string of antiunion ballot measures, including a new version of Proposition L. One measure effectively banned strikes by requiring the termination of strikers[9]; another banned wage bargaining by requiring that wages be set through rigid salary surveys.[10]

By the mid-1970s, San Francisco's antilabor politicians had a sure grasp of their new strategy. It attracted attention among public officials around the

[8]See, for example, Jenkins and Feinstein's opposing columns in the *San Francisco Chronicle and Examiner*, Oct. 13 and Oct. 24, 1974.
[9]Except in the case of the nurses' strike vote, described below, SEIU refused to acknowledge the legality of the sanctions against strikers, which were in fact never implemented.
[10]Ironically, when she served as mayor during subsequent years of fiscal crisis, Feinstein condemned these pay formulas because they prevented the imposition of still lower wages.

state and the nation, to whom it was transmitted through conventions and associations of elected officials. As Katz (1984), Lewin et al. (1988), and numerous other observers have reported, local government officials began to view strikes as useful political and fiscal events.

In retrospect, it seems evident that the grievances and strikes by different groups of city workers drew upon very different sources. On the one hand, the "miscellaneous workers" in the city's human service departments assumed an active, assertive role. They struck repeatedly (if not always successfully) and clerical workers mobilized within their union, against their second-class status and continued marginalization. The craft workers, on the other hand, struck defensively in 1976 (and would do so again in the housing authority in 1979) against the loss of their favored pay status. Police and firefighters remained aloof from the rest of the workforce; their 1976 strike, however, reflected their working-class, ethnic organizational culture, infused with resentment against the minorities and gays who were taking over working-class neighborhoods.[11]

The same two trajectories were evident in San Jose when public works and police employees also sought to defend their threatened status, power, and pay, while the women of the city sought—successfully—to improve their conditions of employment.[12] Both patterns are intelligible, however, only when seen as part of the changing political balance between the politics of growth and social consumption in San Jose and in San Francisco.

The Miscellaneous Workers' Union

As in San Jose, a single union represents the majority of San Francisco's workforce—more precisely, a joint council of SEIU locals. After bargaining units were defined and representational rights settled in the mid-1970s, a total of 15,500 San Francisco city workers were represented by the SEIU joint council, which included Local 535 (social workers), Local 250 (hospital workers), Local 66A (custodians), and Local 400. Local 400 was the largest of these locals, with a jurisdiction of approximately 11,500 city workers,

[11]It was no accident that a former police office and firefighter, Dan White, cut short the progressive Moscone regime. As DeLeon (1992:50) notes, and as I can attest, the murders of Moscone and Milk received strong support from personnel in the city's police department. Moscone's successor, Feinstein, reversed his attempts to liberalize the police department.

On the night White received a sentence of seven years and eight months for the double murder, outraged citizens and police fought in the city's civic center. That night, in the basement of the Hall of Justice, I was conducting a class in strike strategy for unionists in the city's police department. We had just agreed that the police lost their 1976 strike partly because of their adversarial relationship with many San Franciscans, when they were called to "White Night" riot duty. Class was adjourned.

[12]Compare, for example, the simultaneous strikes on April 6, 1979 by the comparable worth activists and by the city police in San Jose (p. 61).

including clerical workers, registered nurses, and other professional, para-professional, and technical employees. (Local 400 represented a similar slice of the much smaller workforces in the quasi-autonomous Housing Authority and Redevelopment Agency, and comparable classified or nonteaching employees in the city's school districts.) In 1981, Local 66A was merged into Local 400; then, in 1983, after the episode of internal conflict described below, Local 400 was merged into the Alameda County – based Local 390 to form Local 790.

Though much larger, SEIU's jurisdiction was comparable to Local 101's jurisdiction in San Jose; because California's counties also provide public health and social services, however, SEIU's also included a unit of nurses comparable to those represented by the California Nurses' Association in the Santa Clara Valley's private sector. Unlike either San Jose's Local 101 or Santa Clara County's Local 715, however, no major skilled blue-collar or public works engineering groups were included in the Local 400 bargaining units. Rather, reflecting the strength of craft unionism in San Francisco, the public works groups were all in building trades unions, overwhelmingly private sector organizations. In San Jose, by contrast, the special status of the public works groups was reflected in their long domination of the internal life of Local 101 until the mid-1970s, when both union leaders and their pro-development allies faced challenges to their rule. There was no such favored group in Local 400. By the mid-1970s, then, Local 400 was in a position analogous to that of the women of San Jose: its members were second-class city employees, weakly represented (if at all) in labor relations, and the union was marginalized in city politics.

As in San Jose, San Francisco's union membership appeared to grow sharply in the early 1970s. Local 400, for example, had only one thousand members in 1973, spread throughout the entire twenty-five-thousand – person city work-force. That year, the local benefited from a merger with the seventy-year-old, eight-thousand – member Civil Service Association, as employee organizations positioned themselves to secure representational rights under the new collective bargaining law. Membership in the new combined organization quickly sagged, however, to around three thousand—a pitifully low proportion of the local's jurisdiction. Thus, as in San Jose and in Santa Clara County, the appearance of sudden union growth in San Francisco conceals a more complex and continuous history.

The largest occupational groups in Local 400's jurisdiction were the clerical workers and nurses. Neither group, however, participated actively in the union's leadership during the 1970s. Rather, the active membership was concentrated among other smaller administrative and professional groups:

librarians, city planners, and management assistants. California's local government bargaining law permitted supervisory and nonsupervisory workers to be represented together in the same union. In 1982, at the time of my own involuntary departure from the union staff, more than half the members of the executive board—many of whom had held leadership posts in the old Civil Service Association—were supervisory employees.[13] In this respect too, the appearance of union growth cloaked continuity.

The administration of Local 400 was subordinate during the 1970s to Tim Twomey, the head of the SEIU's hospital workers' Local 250 and an SEIU vice president (also the son-in-law of the SEIU's aging president, Charles Hardy). Twomey's own local covered northern California's health sector. He dominated SEIU locals throughout northern California by assuming control of locals placed in trusteeship and then placing his own operatives in leadership positions.[14] In response to the revolt by Local 400's clerical workers in 1974, for example, and also at other pivotal moments in the local's history, Twomey installed his own operatives in top staff positions in that union.

In the mid-1970s, Local 400 passed through difficult straits. In 1974, the SEIU Joint Council was compelled by a restive membership—spearheaded by social workers—to embark on a strike. The strikers demanded across-the-board, rather than percentage, pay increases—intended to narrow the gap between low-paid and higher-wage workers. City officials complied, and the settlement gave lower-paid employees 10 percent raises and higher-paid workers 1.5 percent (*CPER* 21). Political heat from the "sewage in the bay" incident, dissatisfaction with the settlement among administrative and professional employees, and general conflict in the union left the local in disarray.

Then came the 1975 revolt by the women of the city, based in the four-thousand – person clerical workers unit and led by Maxine Jenkins and her partner, Louise Statzer. Immediately after the strike, Jenkins gained public prominence as the most vocal and effective opponent of Proposition L. Along with Statzer, she turned the anti-L campaign into a grassroots feminist campaign against gender-biased pay and gendered working conditions.

[13]Each of these groups—and the supervisory groups associated with each of the nonprofessional groups—had its own bargaining unit in San Francisco. On the one hand, this formula gave small professional, administrative, and supervisory groups disproportionate representation on the local's executive board. On the other hand, the local's bylaws also gave strong powers to the general membership meeting. These powers were curtailed through trusteeship when the clerks revolted in 1975, and through a reinterpretation of the union bylaws and merger into Local 390 across the bay when conflict broke out over the new coalition with Feinstein in 1981 and 1982.
[14]My old local, Local 715 in Santa Clara County, was an exception; it was militantly independent of Twomey since its affiliation in 1972. Also, trusteeship of Local 77, in San Jose, described in chapter 5, was assigned to another SEIU vice president, from southern California, because of conflicts within the Hardy / Twomey family.

Statzer and Jenkins's activities brought them into conflict with the SEIU hierarchy, and their activities quickly unfolded into a campaign for union democracy. The awakening of the massive clerical unit threatened the hegemony of the smaller professional groups in the local and Jenkins and Statzer's popularity threatened the positions of the union's officers. After a dramatic few months, they were fired; the action was vetoed by a majority vote in the union's membership meetings; the local was placed in trusteeship, dispensing with such democratic encumbrances, and they were fired again.

Gerry Hipps, the local's executive secretary, suffered a nervous breakdown during this period. After convalescing, he returned to his former employment on Local 250's staff. Hipps was replaced by Vince Courtney—another Twomey operative—who ran the union during its trusteeship and was subsequently elected to office when the trusteeship was lifted in 1977.[15]

Had the international union tolerated democratic processes in the local, it is likely that the rate of clerical membership in Local 400 would have increased and that the local would have acquired a more assertive leadership based among the women of the city, as occurred in San Jose. The international effectively suppressed the challenge by the clericals, however, and the local was left with a narrow base concentrated in supervisory, professional, and managerial ranks.

Despite its low rate of membership, Local 400 remained the largest city union because of the sheer size of its miscellaneous jurisdiction, and, despite its internal difficulties, Local 400 was a visible and important presence on San Francisco's political scene during the 1970s. Most union officials, including Twomey, Hipps, Courtney, and Courtney's successor, Pat Jackson—another Twomey operative—took liberal positions: supporting the election of George Moscone, siding with neighborhood activists on growth controls and district elections, and so on. Moreover, the day-to-day interests of the union's members—in libraries, schools, social service offices, and health centers—were closely bound up with neighborhood needs. Staff from the city planning agency, some of whom who were on the local's executive board, were also participants in the city's slow-growth movement; they ensured that the union would align itself against the development agenda throughout the decade.

Before the 1975 $17,000 streetsweeper campaign secured the passage of charter amendments abolishing city workers' bargaining rights, Local 400 had not established itself as an effective bargaining agent—or, perhaps more to the point, as an inside player in city politics. Miscellaneous city workers in the

---

[15]This account is based on the recollections of participants and articles in the *San Francisco Examiner* (June 5 and June 10, 1975), the *San Francisco Progress* (April 2, April 20, June 6, June 13, and June 20, 1975) and the *Union W.A.G.E.* (Women's Alliance to Gain Equality) *Newsletter* (May-June 1975), graciously provided to me by Denise D'Anne.

SEIU's jurisdiction remained excluded from special salary formulas, which granted police, firefighters, municipal bus drivers, and—until the mid-1970s—craft workers relatively high wages. Rather, the miscellaneous workers were governed by another wage formula that left them earning less than prevailing wages.[16]

Despite Local 400's internal weakness and the strike debacles of the mid-1970s, prospects for the union appeared to brighten in late 1976 when the local joined with neighborhood organizations to elect George Moscone as mayor. The progressive Moscone was opposed by the city's growth coalition—the Chamber of Commerce, development and construction interests concentrated in the city's downtown, and the building trades unions associated with that bloc. His support was centered in a broad labor-community coalition in which Local 400 occupied a central position; his administration promoted racial inclusion, neighborhood empowerment, and controlled growth. The union's prospects faded, however, when the mayor and Milk, the city workers' staunchest advocate on the board of supervisors, were gunned down in 1978.

Moscone was automatically succeeded, under the terms of the city charter, by the president of the board of supervisors, Dianne Feinstein—principal sponsor of the devastating "$17,000 streetsweeper" antiunion strategy. The last years of the decade, then, found Local 400 reeling from further setbacks after years of political assault, at odds with the most powerful players in city government, facing a growing tax rebellion and rising Republican power in California politics. The future seemed dark indeed.

Confronting Austerity in the Aftermath of Proposition 13

Given the difficult conditions of the post – Proposition 13 era, coming on the heels of a disastrous decade for city worker unionism, the final years of the 1970s witnessed a surge of surprisingly effective militancy in San Francisco's city workforce. The political force of public service unionism surfaced in labor-community mobilizations in defense of public services and against mismanagement. The successful San Francisco Housing Authority strike of 1979 was one dramatic case in point.

[16]The high pay rates among craft workers were sustained after 1975 by adjusting salary survey procedures to translate hourly rates in private sector construction—where workers are paid only on the basis of hours worked in a seasonal industry—into annual rates for city employees. The salaries of police, fire, and transit workers were pegged to "highest-wage" comparisons and included retroactive adjustments to ensure parity with current-year raises in other areas. By comparison, the miscellaneous workers' wages were based on standard labor market comparisons for benchmark classes (see appendix). July 1 raises were set, moreover, based on salary surveys conducted late in the prior calendar year; later updates were discretionary but could not include raises granted after March. Also, fringe benefit increases, such as dental coverage, required a vote of the electorate; in the anti – public worker climate of the period, these were regularly rejected.

In this case, a labor-community coalition of workers and tenants struck immediately before the mayoral election, jeopardizing Feinstein's efforts to woo black support as the moderate alternative to her conservative rival. Rather than simply withdrawing their labor power, the strikers mobilized as actors in city politics—thanks largely to the initiative of housing authority workers with roots in African-American neighborhood movements against development. As described in chapter 2, the dramatic strike produced an unqualified union victory. It would be difficult to imagine a more drastic departure from the history of public service unionism in San Francisco, and difficult as well to imagine a more hopeful episode from the standpoint of public worker unionists. Nor was this an isolated event. The same brand of unionism reappeared immediately in a very different context: the city's five-thousand – employee health department, to which we turn below.

The surge of public service unionism was not the only new trend in labor relations in this period, however. The new fiscal politics and political realignments of the post – Proposition 13 era had created the conditions, in San Francisco as in San Jose, for a new labor-management coalition. The conflicts that unfolded inside Local 400 and in the health department were as much contests between two responses to the austerity of the post – Proposition 13 era within the union as they were internal union and labor-management conflicts.

By late 1980, labor relations in the city in general and in the health department in particular were in a state of great turmoil. As in San Jose, revenue cuts as a result of Proposition 13 in 1978 had been followed by a partial bailout from state coffers, a wage freeze in fiscal year 1978 – 79, and renewed tax-cutting amendments on the 1980 and 1981 state ballots. The dominant theme of the period was austerity: layoffs, service cuts, positions left vacant, and the threat of further layoffs and service cuts.

The alternative responses to the fiscal crisis that took shape inside Local 400 eventually led to intense political conflict within the union. One response was to undertake grassroots campaigns, such as occurred in the housing authority, described in chapter 2, and in the health department, described below; the other strategy was to form a new political coalition with Mayor Feinstein, now angling for the second spot on the 1984 Democratic presidential ticket.

By 1979, the health department—the largest city agency—was hard hit by a combination of escalating health care costs, new constraints on revenue, and new caps on state reimbursements for care of the medically indigent. As noted in discussion of the health care industry in chapter 5, these developments drove economic and fiscal crises, related but different, in California's public and private sector hospitals. In brief, the private hospitals, subject to intensified market pressures, turned poor patients away while scrambling after more lucrative, privately insured patients, leaving the indigent to crowd fiscally strapped public agencies. San Francisco officials responded by slashing resources in neighborhood-based health centers and community clinics while concentrating resources in the city's general hospital.[17]

Meanwhile, Proposition 9, another voter initiative to cut taxes, was due to appear on the ballot in June 1980. As in San Jose, San Francisco officials sounded the alarm and proposed drastic cuts. As early as fall 1979—just before the crucial runoff election between Feinstein and conservative challenger Quentin Kopp—Feinstein's office projected that the deficit for the coming fiscal year would be so large that by January 1, 1980, the city should lay off one thousand workers in the health department, to "soften" anticipated layoffs of three to four thousand by the start of the new fiscal year on July 1. In a measure calculated to provoke a response from both neighborhood groups and Local 400's library-based leadership, she also proposed closing some branches of the library and reducing hours in others.

Feinstein's maneuvers in this period reflected a widely embraced strategy for managing austerity in the post – Proposition 13 era. Assuming the stance of defenders of the local budget, officials projected worst-case fiscal scenarios, took early steps to enact drastic cuts, encouraged public sector unions and community groups to campaign against budget constraints—ballot propositions or state legislative agendas—and in the end cemented their political positions by enacting less severe cuts. This strategy helped catalyze new labor-management coalitions in cities and school districts throughout California. In San Francisco, this strategy served Dianne Feinstein particularly well: the political space to her left having been cleared in a hail of gunfire, it paved the way for her makeover from "conservative" to "centrist."

As the largest city union, and given its links to a great variety of neighborhood and other interests, Local 400 now was in a strategic position to convene and set the direction for a labor-community coalition aimed at stopping Feinstein's proposed cuts. The local's history of involvement in the campaigns and coalitions of the neighborhood movements of the 1970s put Local 400's leaders in a particularly well-suited position to build such a coalition. The coalition they assembled was composed of the leaders of a broad cross-section of city workers' unions and community organizations. Further, Feinstein's position as mayor was insecure; having lost earlier mayoral elections and now in office only as successor to the assassinated Moscone, she desperately needed

[17]After my departure from the Local 400 staff in 1982, I served as director of San Francisco's consortium of community-based health clinics in the early 1980s.

support against her still more conservative opponent. This gave the coalition definite political leverage.

During the same period, the housing authority employees moved toward their strike. The course the citywide coalition followed would be very different from that of the housing authority workers. It was, however, virtually identical to that of the San Jose city workers during the fiscal crisis of 1982.

Leaders of the labor organizations—the central labor council, representatives of big international unions, top officers of Local 400—met with Feinstein and reached an agreement to support her election campaign and to support an increase in the municipal bus fare. In exchange, Feinstein was to withdraw her proposals for the mass layoffs due to occur on January 1. Privately, she also agreed to include a provision in the upcoming contract for Local 400 that would automatically grant the union "agency shop" when enabling legislation, then in the pipeline, was adopted in Sacramento.[18] Local officials (and, through them, SEIU's international union leadership) also privately agreed to support Feinstein in her bid for vice president of the United States.

The citywide coalition in defense of public services now focused its efforts on Feinstein's election and on the adoption of the Muni (municipal bus) fare increase. These things accomplished, the coalition was dissolved. Feinstein emerged as a leading candidate for vice president in 1984—touted mainly by SEIU. Despite occasional tensions, the political coalition between Feinstein and SEIU officials remained in place through her subsequent two terms in office.

In short, under the pressure of Republican ascendance and fiscal austerity, a new labor-management coalition in San Francisco emerged between Local 400 and the union's old nemesis—Dianne Feinstein—in city politics. This new arrangement ended an era of labor mobilization and management countermobilization while producing unprecedented organizational, political, and fiscal stability and security for Local 400.

Parallel events were unfolding in the city's large unified school district, where school superintendent Robert Alioto orchestrated his own version of the $17,000 streetsweeper strategy.[19] The teachers' union, an American Federation of Teachers (AFT) affiliate, had been drawn into an intensely bitter strike in 1979. Like most other city strikes in the mid-1970s, the union conducted a

---

[18]At the time, voluntary membership in Local 400 stood at only 35 percent of the employees in the bargaining units affected. According to provisions of the law, once an agency shop was in place, workers could rescind it only if, following a petition for an election, a majority of those *in the unit* (rather than a majority of those voting) voted against it. An alternative approach, promoted by the group purged from Local 400 in 1982 (and implemented in the city's school district, where I served as business agent), required an election open to the entire bargaining unit prior to the adoption of agency shop.

[19]I observed developments in the school district in my capacity as business agent for nonteaching school district employees during this period.

conventional private sector – style strike, disregarding public opinion and public service issues. The strike resulted in a debacle for the union, and the demoralized workforce would subsequently vote to decertify the AFT local in favor of an employee association allied with district management. Then in the spring of 1980, the district mailed layoff notices to every teacher. Motivated by the threat of layoffs, the teachers and their unions, parent groups, and other school-based interest groups supported the district administration in a frantic campaign over subsequent months to increase state "bailout" funding for the district.

In contrast to these labor-management coalitions, another response to the fiscal and political crises of the period was to form labor-community coalitions against mismanagement and in defense of public services. Both the labor-management coalitions and the labor-community coalitions promoted their own approaches to revenue generation in the face of Proposition 13 (the former supported higher bus fares, for example, while the latter pressed for new fees on development), to union power (one emphasized labor-management coalitions, the other labor-community coalitions), and to internal union democracy (inside Local 400, battle lines formed over the election of union representatives and also over voting on agency shop). Through their new relationship with city officials, the union officials brokering the labor-management coalition acquired new political and fiscal resources to manage the union's internal life. By contrast, the labor-community coalitions maintained a more adversarial relationship with management, relying instead on rank-and-file mobilization, coalitions with client groups, and targeting bureaucratic authority in grassroots campaigns for reform of city government.

Not surprisingly, these competing responses gave rise to political combat inside Local 400. By mid-1980, union staffers associated with the housing authority strike and the public health campaigns would be removed from responsibility for these volatile parts of the workforce; by mid-1982, they would be purged from the union.[20]

Public Service Unionism in the Health Department

In the years after the passage of Proposition 13, members of Local 400 in the health department formed alliances in defense of public health ser-

[20]Under the bylaws of Local 400, a vote of the membership was required to hire and fire staff; this protected business agents, myself included, who opposed the union's alliance with Feinstein. In 1982, just before a union election, we were fired—charged, among other offenses, with supporting a proposed amendment to the union bylaws that would have permitted the election of union representatives. When union members sought to overturn the firing at the membership meeting, they were ruled out of order, and the meeting turned into a brawl. Five years later, a jury in California Civil Court found the firings illegal; by that time, however, Local 400 had been merged into Local 390. On the merger, see *CPER* 56:40.

vices with other labor and community-based health care advocates, including the union of interns and resident doctors at the county hospital and neighborhood and minority group activists. Like the housing authority strike of the same period, these campaigns targeted mismanagement and top-heavy administration, demanded increased service-level staffing and more responsive services, and proposed service-level worker involvement in management decision-making in response to short-staffing and funding cutbacks. These campaigns featured petition drives, media exposure, and mass picketing in front of City Hall. Among the demands of the picketers was that city officials rescind both service-level layoffs and increases in management staffing planned for mid-year 1980. Inside the hospital, Local 400 organizer Nancy Elliott installed a "patient care documentation system," modeled on the grievance system, through which union members documented, analyzed, reported, and requested corrective action on shortcomings in patient care.

Also during this period, a citywide labor-community coalition, centered in the health department, mobilized against Proposition 9. As a counter to the proposed hike in Muni bus fares, this coalition demanded and won passage of a "Muni Transit Impact Fee" through City Hall, in effect creating new taxes on downtown development to supplement the budget for municipal transit.

Then, in October 1980, the interns' and resident doctors' union launched an extraordinary strike, in which the central demand was that the city end short-staffing and improve patient care at the hospital by filling vacant positions, especially among the nurses but also among other technical, blue-collar, and clerical ranks. The interns and residents continued to work but picketed between shifts, refused to fill out billing forms that were vital for hospital revenue, and conducted a political campaign in the media and at City Hall. The strike had a powerful impact; within four days, negotiations produced an agreement with the mayor and public health officials to fill the vacant positions.

In San Francisco's public sector, as in San Jose's private sector, the problem of RN short-staffing now surfaced in labor relations. In San Francisco, however, the issue was framed differently and pursued by a different constellation of workers, relying on a very different set of strategic resources. In San Francisco, the issue first surfaced as a public health issue, not as a wage problem and not even as a problem of nurses' own conditions of employment. Interns, not nurses, took the leading role in the strike, although many nurses picketed or expressed their solidarity with the doctors. And, of course, the resources employed were not the economic weapons used in the private sector but the political resources of public service unionism.

Spotlight on the Nurses

In the settlement agreement that ended the doctors' strike, city officials agreed to fill all vacant RN positions at the large city hospital. Because of mandates inserted into the city charter in the mid-1970s, recruiting new nurses proved to be extremely difficult. Because nurses were categorized by the city charter as part of the "miscellaneous" city workforce, their pay was set by a rigid formula, ensuring that it remained a step behind prevailing wages. [21]

Nurses' pay surfaced as a major issue late in 1980. In January 1981, with 15 percent of the nurses' positions vacant at the hospital, health department officials decided to recruit nurses at the fifth rather than the first step in the city's five-step salary schedule. This 20 percent increase in starting pay was of no benefit to senior nurses, however; although it helped recruitment efforts, it exacerbated morale problems and failed to solve the problem of retention.

Pay was not the nurses' only grievance. As in the Santa Clara Valley's private sector hospitals, stress and burnout were central to the nurses' work experience. Increased patient loads due to restructuring and cutbacks in health care since the late 1970s had intensified the conflicts between nurses' personal and professional values, the needs and pains of their patients, and the conditions of hospital work and care. Because of the vacant positions, nurses were constantly threatened (both by their professional responsibility to patients and by management authority) with having to work extra hours, sometimes as long as two eight-hour shifts back-to-back.

Burnout, according to nurses who have worked in both sectors, was as bad or worse in the public sector as in the private. One older nurse, standing at an elevator in San Francisco General Hospital, compared her two experiences: "I've worked public, and I've worked private. And you know it gets pretty bad out there, but it's nothing compared to this. [In the private sector,] they take care of you better, and at least you don't have to deal with all of this." As she said her last words, she gestured down a hallway lined with poor people—the overflow from the emergency room.

Given the stress, it is not surprising that many city nurses, like the private sector nurses in the valley, chose to work part time. The city equivalent of the valley's registry system was per diem status, for which the nurses performed part-time, flexibly scheduled work and were paid an added amount in lieu of the city's hefty pension contribution. As in the private sector, this arrangement offered higher hourly pay and more autonomy and time off—or, in the nurses'

[21]See n16. Given the monopsonistic character of the RN labor market, the city officials may well have found it impossible to fill the positions even if they been able to offer fully prevailing wages (see chapter 5).

parlance, "mental health time." In response to the comment by the nurse in the elevator, a younger nurse replied:

> I don't know, I agree it's harder, but that's what I went into nursing
> for; these are the people I want to take care of. It sure does make you
> crazy though. That's why I stay on per diem. Once in a while I just have
> to get away and take care of me, lie on a beach for a week, just forget all
> about it.

Also in the early 1980s, San Francisco General Hospital experienced major management problems: turnover was high among its top leadership; the hospital was scrutinized by regulatory agencies for deficiencies in recordkeeping; it faced large lawsuits alleging malpractice, related to the short-staffing; and was the target of campaigns by health care activists on the same grounds. In short, the facility was a political and administrative nuisance for top city officials. By early 1981, those with responsibility for personnel and budget matters in the health department and the mayor's office finally decided that additional wages would somehow have to be made available for the nurses.

Through the nurses' informal sources in the mayor's office, this information was passed on to well-connected union officials—who saw in the potential raise a way to gain crucial internal support. At this point, Nancy Elliott, a former organizer for the United Farm Workers and a Local 400 staffer, was removed from her position representing hospital nurses and replaced by Pat Jackson. Twomey's previous appointee to Local 400's top position, Vince Courtney, was obliged to resign from office; Jackson was another Twomey operative, whom Twomey had designated as Courtney's successor. Elliott, by contrast, was associated with the "labor-community coalition" response to the fiscal crisis and had been organizing nurses and other hospital workers around quality-of-patient-care as well as wage issues.

Confronting the Salary Standardization System

Before a special raise for nurses could be put into effect, city officials and their allies among union officials first had to solve a technical problem. Since the mid-1970s, city workers' pay had been set by seemingly rigid salary formulas, closely tied to the logic of job classification and salary standardization. The problem was how to increase the nurses' pay without violating charter provisions. Normally, this would have been done with an internal adjustment, justified by some argument that the nurses should receive a higher raise than the benchmark class (for further discussion of this system, see the appendix). Unfortunately, the RNs *were* the benchmark classification. As the

charter now stood, no internal realignment favoring the nurses was techni-
cally possible. Nor would it have helped to designate a new benchmark class:
in the larger group of nursing jobs, there was no alternative classification that,
subjected to a salary survey, would produce data to justify giving the registered
nurses a significant wage increase.

The nurses' problem, then, was not management's unwillingness to grant a
higher raise—though it certainly appeared this way to the nurses themselves.
Rather, both union leaders and city officials were constrained by the rules
governing compensation and the nurses' position in the salary standardization
structure. Although the mayor's office and health department officials wanted
to grant a substantial raise, they were vetoed by the civil service commission
and the independently elected city attorney. When the final salary survey for
miscellaneous city workers was complete in March 1981, the result for the
nurses was a dismal 4.9 percent. Union representatives had succeeded in
winning a 2 percent additional "retention" adjustment (designated as a daily
"meal allowance," to get around salary-setting rules), bringing the total
to 6.9 percent.

Bending the Rules

On March 21, a membership meeting was scheduled to ratify the salary
package for Local 400's jurisdiction.[22] Unable to move the nurses' raise
beyond 6.9 percent, the union leadership recommended they accept that
rate. On the afternoon before the meeting, however, the nurses at General Hospital (which employed 288 of the city's 444 RNs) took matters into
their own hands. One hundred registered nurses gathered in the cafeteria at
General Hospital, voted to reject the salary package, and decided to strike if
necessary.

There was, of course, no comparable worth process under way in San
Francisco. But the publication of salary increases for different benchmark
groups had led, as usual, to ad hoc comparisons. For the city nurses, the "straw
that broke the camel's back" was a classic comparable worth issue: city
plumbers, whose loss of special craft pay provisions had sparked the craft-
workers' strike of 1975, still made $2.17 more per hour than the registered
nurses. Building trade craft workers' pay was now governed by the same salary
formula as miscellaneous city employees. The craft workers' political clout
still paid off, however, when civil service officials reinterpreted salary survey

[22]Although the salary formulas precluded real bargaining, city unions maintained a semblance of
collective bargaining by holding "ratification meetings"; the union's main influence on these
packages was accomplished by lobbying for internal adjustments.

procedures for construction trades workers to produce a 21.5 percent wage hike for plumbers (Jackson Rannels, "Board Approved $40 Million Pay Boost for City Workers," *San Francisco Chronicle*, March 24, 1981).[23]

In this case, as in the previous cases, a systematic investigation may have also revealed a racial dimension to the issue of pay equity. For example, the wages of the RNs, the overwhelming majority of whom were white, were more than 40 percent higher than the wages of the licensed vocational nurses, most of whom were black. Among the private sector nurses in the Santa Clara Valley, this issue was obscured (even though LVNs were hired to perform some RNs' duties during the strike) because participants focused not on wage relations within the differentiated internal organization of the hospital but on the RN labor market—sharply defined by formal licensure regulations as separate from the LVN labor market. In the city of San Jose, by comparison, racial disparities affecting "outsourced" custodians were obscured because the techniques of internal wage comparisons emphasized by the comparable worth agenda in that setting ignored the disparate racial impact of contracting out. In San Francisco, racial disparities were obscured because RNs and LVNs were placed for salary standardization purposes into different benchmark groups, and so wage comparisons among nurses were avoided.[24] In all three cases, formal bureaucratic boundaries coincided with racial differences, diverting attention from them and making them seem natural.

The San Francisco nurses' new union representative was Pat Jackson, who had brokered Feinstein's new relationship with SEIU and had been selected by the international union to assume leadership of the local. With Jackson's guidance, the nurses voted to prepare for a strike but to cancel it if "significant progress" could be made on getting a higher pay increase.

The administrator of General Hospital immediately made a proposal in response to the strike vote, which the nurses' negotiating committee embraced: the hospital nurses would be reclassified as "acute care nurses" and paid 8 percent above "regular" RNs, who would remain the benchmark class. The result would be 14 percent raise hikes for most hospital nurses and up to 25.5 percent raises for some. The rationale for the proposed reclassification was that nursing in an acute care facility such as General Hospital required higher levels of skill than nursing in other settings, such as the city's community clinics and its convalescent hospital.

[23]I was present at this meeting and participated in the other events described here.
[24]There was one exception: black LVNs performed *the same* duties as the higher-paid, mostly white female RNs and male emergency medical technicians in the medical clinic in San Francisco's county jail. In 1981, the LVNs—led by Naomi Bowden—mobilized for equal pay, asserting racial discrimination, and won a 43 percent wage increase.

There was, however, a flaw in the proposal: the salary formula for the benchmark class was already based on acute care hospital work. This undermined the formal justification for having a higher-paid "acute-care" class of nurses. So the city's civil service and legal staff vetoed the proposal; it violated, they argued, the principles of salary standardization. Of course, the representatives of nonhospital-based nurses, who would be excluded from the raise, opposed it as well.[25] As a result, the proposal was not formally offered to the union, and the nurses' strike preparations intensified.

Now a coalition of some of the most powerful players in city politics, along with hundreds of mobilizing nurses, confronted the powers of bureaucratic legalism. The final week of March was tumultuous, as hundreds of hospital nurses descended on City Hall for mass picketing. Given the perceived public interest in increased RN staffing and preventing a strike, it was not surprising that no public officials supported the civil service commission's and city attorney's position. Media attention centered on the threatened strike and on the threat it posed to patient care. Nurses at other locations besides General Hospital organized to strike as well and implored the hospital nurses—who formed the bulk of the bargaining unit—not to accept a formula that excluded some nurses.

Word leaked out that the money for the "acute-care nurse" scheme, still under discussion, would come from the budget of the convalescent hospital and, in the face of a growing movement of nurses at that site, health department officials amended their proposal to include the 137 nurses at that site as well. Similar protests by nurses in the medical clinic at the jail and the central emergency clinic added another nineteen positions to the new class. The new classification would now be called "institutional nurse," and now only forty-seven nurses in neighborhood public health centers and community health clinics would be excluded from the deal.[26]

As the nurses' strike deadline approached, the political force behind the proposal overcame its technical flaws. The civil service commission and city attorney agreed to pretend that the new classification would be legal, and the offer was now formally extended to the nurses through their union.

[25]Significantly, given the internal union politics described earlier, Elliott now represented the nurses at the convalescent hospital and I now represented the nurses at the community clinics, jail, and neighborhood health clinics.

[26]The proposal also included a charter amendment, which was supported by both the union and City Hall and adopted in an election and implemented a year later, to remove all nurses from the miscellaneous city workers category—with its perpetually lagging wage rate—and establish instead a formula that would mandate that nurses' wages and benefits be equivalent to those given to the highest-paid nurses in the region. This would make the "institutional nurse" category unnecessary, and the classification would be abolished.

The city's offer was presented for a vote before the union membership on the eve of the strike deadline. The community clinic nurses present pleaded with the hospital RNs to extend the strike deadline and return to negotiations until all the city's registered nurses were included in the settlement. In presenting the proposal, however, Jackson assured that it would be accepted. First, she explained that according to "the rules of negotiations," the nurses were required either to accept the proposal or to reject it and strike immediately; waiting for further negotiations would be considered "bad faith." Second, she said that the union leadership now had reliable information that if the nurses did strike, San Francisco General, the major source of care for the city's low-income residents, would be closed down. Third, she said that, under the city's charter, nurses who struck would be fired, and if they were rehired after the strike, they would lose all seniority. Fourth, and finally, she emphasized that the nurses should make up their own minds about how to vote and assured them that whatever they decided, the union would back them all the way. Not surprisingly, the settlement was ratified.[27]

Jackson's first and second points were simply false, and her third point departed sharply from the position the union had maintained on the legality of strikes since the passage seven years earlier of legislation prohibiting them. Jackson may well have been correct, however, in her judgment that this was the best settlement the nurses could achieve.

Ambivalence, Anxiety, and the Burden of Care

Groups mobilized to strike commonly have an effervescent quality; the energy of the nurses in San Francisco, however, seemed to have an extra edge. There was an emotional undercurrent in this group that I was unable to grasp or analyze at the time. Only later, after reflecting on the nurses' strike in the Santa Clara Valley, did I analyze the contradictory gender dynamics discussed in chapter 5. In that case, the reader will recall, the nurses identified with *all* nurses. They displayed an extraordinary degree of solidarity and optimism, followed by demoralization and depression, combined with intense hero-worship and later blame directed at their charismatic leader. I associated these dynamics with intense ambivalence over the tension between their assertion of autonomy and their commitment to care. In San Francisco, too, an emotional intensity, anxiety, and anger were evident at their strike meetings and in the prestrike period. This emotionalism grew as the deadline for the strike approached.

[27]For another account of this settlement, see *CPER* 49:22.

In contrast to the nurses of the Santa Clara Valley's private sector, the San Francisco nurses' hostility was directed *against other nurses* in other settings. Thus, nurses from the satellite clinics and the convalescent hospital were framed as invaders or as parasites. Specifically, the nurses at the convalescent hospital, most of whom were Filipino, were viewed as foreigners who were too timid to strike by themselves, and the nurses in the community clinics were perceived as outsiders who wanted to take advantage of "our strike." The political cleavages in the union may have reinforced these attitudes, although they were expressed by nurses with no involvement in those conflicts. This pattern is also consistent, however, with arguments, made in previous chapters, for the existence of a connection between occupational solidarity and the labor market orientation of private sector workers, in contrast to the "political-bureaucratic particularism" of the public workforce.

As in the ill-fated strike by private sector nurses a year later in San Jose, contradictory themes ran though the discourse put forth by the nurses in San Francisco. Although these women were preparing to strike for themselves, their rationale for the strike was expressed in a concern for their patients: the impossibility of providing adequate care when staffing levels were restricted because of the inadequate pay. At the same time, of course, these nurses were proposing to walk away from their patients to strike. As the deadline approached, this possibility became more likely. Perhaps for this reason, much prestrike activity focused on the "emergency services committee," which would have assessed staffing levels and authorized a pool of nurses to cross picket lines and work if medically necessary.

Like earlier mobilizations by health care employees in San Francisco, the nurses focused on public service issues. Their anxiety about the threat their strike might present to their patients was reinforced by rumors sweeping through General Hospital that the city was planning to close down the hospital altogether. When Jackson confirmed this (false) rumor at the meeting at which the settlement was ratified, acceptance of the divisive proposal suddenly became necessary to protect health services for the poor.

This emphasis on meeting the patients' needs and on staving off the threat to close the hospital reflects, of course, a now-familiar theme: that movements by public workers emphasize their role in meeting public needs. Like the women of San Jose, the nurses in San Francisco linked their defense of their own jobs and wages to services they struggled to provide; in short, they asserted the worth of their work in political as well as economic terms.

For nurses, however, this link evokes a tension rooted in the gendered character of nursing work: between the desire to assert autonomy and the commitment to care. Given that the nurses were torn between these needs, it is not surprising that they experienced anxiety and deeply ambiguous and emotional responses to their circumstances. Nor is it surprising that this anxiety found expression in outward anger; better to direct anger outward, after all, than guilt inward.

Comparison of the San Jose and the San Francisco nurses' movements suggests that sectoral location may have had as decisive an influence on the manner in which the dilemmas associated with the burden of care were perceived and addressed as it had on the more general character and course of these movements. While the nurses in San Jose immersed themselves in "the glory of a bond" as they reached out to nurses across the labor market, the nurses in San Francisco looked no farther than the nurses in their immediate organization. Further, while the issues of burnout and stress were channeled in the private sector strike into a demand for a market-clearing wage rate, in San Francisco they converged with the workers' identification with the mission of their publicly supported agency and with efforts to sustain and strengthen its resources.

Case Comparisons: Contrary Patterns of Development

It is useful, at this point, to review the patterns of similarity and difference among this and the previous cases. This account illustrates a point evident in the case of San Jose, which may well be obvious to many readers: public workers' movements depend directly for success on their ability to mobilize political resources. Also, despite many differences in the character of the two cities, labor relations in San Francisco and San Jose underwent strikingly similar periods of transition. The tensions and conflicts that bedeviled labor relations in San Francisco were precisely those that defined the course of developments in San Jose. In both cases, these developments were closely associated with the fortunes of the local growth coalition and its adversaries and with the unions' relationships to these shifting political alignments. In both cases, as the craft workers fell from a position of special favor, miscellaneous workers and human service workers in female-gendered jobs began to adopt a more adversarial model of unionism. In both cases, the latter allied themselves with neighborhood-based groups challenging the city's pro-growth agenda.

These parallel trends continued in those pivotal years around 1980. In both cities, groups of miscellaneous city workers approached the circles of power as upstarts but eventually entered those circles as allies in the face of the external threats associated with Reaganism. Perversely, in the era of Reaganism, human service union leaders in both cities enjoyed unprecedented union security and fiscal solvency.

The nurses' campaign in San Francisco was evidently successful. The nurses secured a completely irregular and probably illegal modification in their salary formula, granting most nurses (though not all) a substantial pay increase. Like the comparable worth plan in San Jose, the settlement in San Francisco was secured as a result of political mobilization, without having to resort to a traditional strike at all. In San Jose, the July 1981 strike had been necessary to secure an across-the-board increase that the public works employees would accept. On the one hand, if a comparable group had held similar power on the San Francisco nurses' bargaining team, the nurses might have had to go out on strike as well. On the other hand, if female-dominated occupational groups in San Jose had been in their own bargaining unit, as the city nurses were, their July strike might have been avoided.

The success of the nurses' campaign in San Francisco, like that of the city workers in San Jose, contrasts sharply with the demoralizing defeat of the private sector nurses in the Santa Clara Valley less than a year later. As in San Jose, the central problem for the negotiators in San Francisco was *not* how to overcome market constraints on wages but how to overcome political-administrative constraints. In both cases, the women's demands focused on salary comparisons with other occupational groups, and in both cases their achievements required tortuous but at least superficially rational modifications in the formal-legal mechanisms of salary standardization that carry such weight in public sector pay-setting. In each case, powerful political coalitions were needed to gain the leverage necessary to reinterpret bureaucratic personnel procedures. Further, both public sector campaigns were followed by the adoption of new union security or "agency shop" measures, while the private sector movement led to a virtual collapse of union strength, including in one hospital the decertification of the union.

Unlike the city workers in San Jose, the nurses in San Francisco never formed coalitions with other city workers.[28] In both cities, however, the women's relationship with other city workers was a central theme in their pay grievances: in San Francisco, a central problem as city and union officials sought to separate hospital nurses' pay from that of other nurses and miscellaneous workers; in both cities, a central political problem within the union itself.

Again, as in the city of San Jose and in sharp contrast to the situation in the private sector, conditions of austerity promoted labor-management coalitions in San Francisco, bringing union officials representing formerly marginalized parts of the workforce inside the governing political regime. In San Francisco,

---

[28]That failure was perhaps the core weakness of the San Francisco city workforce. Groups of city workers rarely succeeded in building coalitions founded on organic solidarity or mutual support.

this new labor-management coalition was formed before the nurses organized to strike; in San Jose, it occurred afterward. In both cities, though, mobilizations against the funding cuts were pivotal events in the formation of the new labor-management coalitions.

In both cities, public workers' movements surfaced as much outside as within collective bargaining institutions, in defense of public jobs and services. In San Francisco's larger, more complex political environment, two coalitions were formed, operating on different levels within the union and the city agency. One emphasized labor-community alliances at a grassroots level and challenged management to reform the city bureaucracy; the other relied on labor union officials' new entry into the city's governing political elite, demobilizing at the grassroots level. The latter coalition prevailed.

In the aftermath of this pivotal period, changes occurred in Local 400 more dramatic than but directly comparable to those observed in Local 101. Recalcitrant staff were purged, an agency shop provision was adopted with the support of the union's new ally in the mayor's office, and after continued internal turmoil, Local 400 was merged into Local 390, centered in Alameda County across the San Francisco Bay. In San Francisco as in San Jose, in other words, the new alliance with management strengthened the union bureaucracy by aligning it with the centers of political power in the city while diminishing the participation of its members.

In the private sector, both the custodians and nurses also asserted, in their own ways, the worth of their own work in terms that went beyond wages: "respect" and later "justice" for the janitors, "comparable worth" for the nurses. Neither struggled, however, to defend or expand the services they provided. In both cases, despite appeals to respect, justice, and comparable worth, their demands followed the deep tracks of bargaining unionism. By the mid-1980s, each group, though located at opposite ends of the working class, was overcome by the force of the labor market.

During the years of crisis that began in the mid-1970s, the custodians were devastated by increasing competition in product and labor markets. The nurses, in an industry facing comparable economic pressures and evidently deceived by the apparent shortage of labor in this monopsonistic labor market, were similarly unable to overcome the trend toward cost containment in the health care industry. In both instances, adversarial relations reached an unprecedented level of intensity during the 1980s—even as their public sector counterparts were entering into new coalitions with public officials.

In the following years, both the private sector nurses' union and the custodians' union continued to face conditions of crisis. While the Santa Clara Valley's private sector nurses sank into demoralization, however, the custodians revolted. Successfully ousting two sets of failed union leaders, they refused to tolerate their union's weakness. At the same time, in the Santa Clara Valley as elsewhere in the United States, some private sector unionists were driven—like some public sector unionists in the previous decade—to reexamine inherited models of unionism. Among the results of this reassessment, still under way, was the Justice for Janitors campaign, which reversed membership losses and revitalized the custodians' union in the valley and elsewhere.

Contrary patterns of development, then, emerged in the two sectors. After a period of crisis, activism, and organizational renewal in the public sector and relative calm and seeming stability and strength in the private, there was a reversal of sorts. While the weight of institutional stability shifted to the public sector, the center of crisis, change, and innovation moved, for the moment, to the private.

A Thought Experiment

Could events in San Francisco have taken a different turn? Given the structural forces at work in the 1980s, the answer may be no: the alternative tack of public service unionism may not have been viable, regardless of the vagaries of individuals' and groups' behavior. It is useful, though, to conduct an imaginary experiment on the San Francisco case.

Suppose that San Francisco's major public sector union had not consummated its alliance with Dianne Feinstein. Suppose it had somehow overcome the legacy of its past domination by supervisory and administrative employees, and suppose that rather than a new labor-management coalition, it had relied on coalitions with the city's vibrant progressive communities, the city's minority communities, the gay community, and various public service constituencies? Suppose it had continued to encourage its members to challenge "mismanagement" and to tax the corporations? With the active involvement of the city workforce, might policy agendas have surfaced capable of pointing the progressive coalition beyond defensive responses to urban development and beyond defensive responses to the fiscal crisis?

If Local 790 had been a stronger force for mobilizing and linking together the various parts of the progressive coalition, might the coalition that elected Art Agnos have been strong enough to limit his rapprochement with the business community, his embrace of the pro-growth agenda, and his subsequent abandonment by his supporters? Might the informal relationships so crucial to effective coalition governance have been deeper, more multiplex, and sustainable?

These are, of course, counterfactual hypotheses. On the one hand, it is likely that such a union would not have fared as well during the Feinstein years; in particular, without the active support of city management, the union might not have secured agency shop provisions; also, officials might have pushed for more efforts at privatization. On the other hand, forced to sustain a higher level of mobilization, the local might also have had a higher level of voluntary membership and more political resources to bring into election battles over city workers' wages, rights, and benefits and into larger political contests equally consequential for the policy agendas on which city workers' jobs and status depend.

The decisive difference might have occurred with the election of Mayor Art Agnos in 1988. As described in rich detail by DeLeon (1992), the Agnos years were marked by the ascendance of a progressive political force in the city—its slow-growth, neighborhood-based, middle-class radicals. Both Agnos and these activists failed, however, to sustain a broader coalition, or a viable governing regime. Rather, the triumph of the slow-growth agenda was accompanied by what DeLeon calls "antiregime," characterized by disorganization and paralyzing conflict. Lacking both the governing agenda and the internal cohesion needed to sustain itself, the antiregime proved to be an invitation to counterrevolution, which came with the election of conservative police chief Frank Jordan in 1991.

To be sure, the failure of Agnos's regime may have been due in good measure to his personal style of power politics. At the same time, as DeLeon observes, the progressives never consolidated policy agendas that went beyond the defense of neighborhoods. Given its potential capacity for mobilization, public service advocacy, and avenues for coalition-building with groups in the city's communities, this is a gap that Local 790 might have filled.

Of course, this path was not taken in San Francisco, or in San Jose. Nor was it taken in another pattern-setting place for public sector labor relations, New York City (Bellush and Bellush 1984; Maier 1987; Shefter 1985). On the one hand, given the powerful impact of the Reagan realignment in local government politics and labor relations, this path may not have been a realistic alternative. On the other hand, public sector unions did survive and far more energetic organizations did emerge during the 1980s in more embattled political environments than San Jose and San Francisco, such as Los Angeles County, which elected a conservative majority to its board of supervisors in 1980 (McNichol 1990); in Dade County, Florida, where business interests mounted a concerted effort to privatize the metropolitan transit system in 1986 (Banks and Grenier 1987); and in Philadelphia, where the city's first African-American mayor sought to privatize work performed by that city's black-led blue-collar AFSCME members in 1987 (Cohen and Dooley 1990). Without its new labor-management coalition, San Francisco's miscellaneous city workforce might have faced similar adversity in the 1980s, and it is impossible to judge how city workers' interests would have been affected.

This "what if?" exercise does underscore, however, the dampening influence of the political and fiscal trends of the Reagan era and the manner in which public sector unionists responded to them. It also suggests, without making any promises, public service unionism's as-yet-unrealized contribution to new urban political coalitions in local government.

8 Conclusions and Implications

Two astute observers of fiscal politics arrived at very different assessments of the surge in public worker militancy in the early 1970s and of the relationship of these movements to "the public interest." Frances Fox Piven, who focused on the predominantly white teachers and social workers of New York City, argued that

> the keenest struggle is with residents of central-city ghettos (who in any case now form a substantial segment of the "general public" in most big cities). . . . For their part, growing numbers of the black poor view police, firemen, teachers, public-welfare workers and other city employees as their oppressors (1972:146).

At the same time, in the final chapter to *The Fiscal Crisis of the State*, James O'Connor concluded that

> the main factor in the politicization of state workers is the developing relationship between state workers and state dependents. . . . Further alliances between teachers, students, and office and maintenance personnel, between welfare workers and welfare recipients, between public health workers and people who use public health and medical facilities, and between transport workers and the public served by public transit are possible and likely (1973:250 – 51).

Similarly, in this study, we found public workers in San Francisco and San Jose on both sides of a great divide in urban politics—as participants in the growth coalition, on the one hand, and as allies of neighborhood movements and advocates for human services, on the other.

How does one explain these divergences? The answer, if the arguments of this book are sound, is that the specificity of public workers' movements lie more in their form than in their substantive historical content. Public workers' movements are likely to be found on each side of every great social conflict.[1] But whether progressive or reactionary, fragmented or unified, inside or outside a public agency's inner circle of power, public workers' movements operate on the peculiar terrain of public organization. On this basis, it is possible to make some broad generalizations about their demands and their weapons—the form of their claims and their recipes for power.

In the first part of this chapter, I summarize these generalizations and the historical argument through which they are related to the cases considered here. I then discuss some implications of these conclusions. The argument made here has implications for social theory and empirical research as well as practical implications for public workers themselves; I discuss each in turn.[2]

Enacting the Public Agenda

Public workers are constrained to frame their claims and to adapt their strategic behavior to fit the formal bureaucratic institutional logic and political power relations of public organization. The character of their coalitions, the form of their demands, their arsenal of resources, and ultimately their successes and failures depend on the political-bureaucratic context in which mobilization occurs. Two features of this context mold these movements: first, the *political universe* within which the coalitions that govern public organization are formed and their "collective interests" defined; second, the *formal bureaucratic organization* of work and life within this jurisdiction.

Shaped in this context, public workers' movements differ from those that operate within the terms of private sector employment relations. Rather than terms for the sale of labor power, for example, demands in the public sector are framed as public policy. They are asserted as legitimate and administrable: as claiming to meet public needs, as appealing to scientific and univeralistic justifications, as adhering to the logic of bureaucratic administration. By the same token, while private sector workers mobilize within labor markets— building a culture of solidarity and a coalition within a relatively homogeneous

---

[1]Consider, for example, the June revolt of 1848 in Paris—for Marx, "the tremendous insurrection in which the first great battle was joined between the two classes that split modern society" (1964:56). This insurrection was launched by a movement of public workers in the National Workshops (an institution comparable to the Works Progress Administration [WPA] of the 1930s or the CETA program in the United States of the 1970s). The Mobile Guard—yet another group of public workers—rallied to suppress that insurrection (Traugott 1985).
[2]Also see the appendix, on gender issues and public personnel administration.

set of participants—public workers mobilize within the political universe of a public bureaucracy—building more tenuous coalitions among different interests *across* the political-bureaucratic division of labor. And again, while power in the private sector depends on labor market position and on resources that buttress that position, power in the public sector depends on public workers' position in the universe of political power in public organizations and on resources that buttress *that* position. Figure 8.1 provides a comparison of these goals and resources in the public and private sectors.

This scheme refers to pure types of market-oriented and politically regulated workplaces, and not to hybrid forms whose sectoral status is both ambiguous and contestable. The diagonal arrow refers to this contingency and also suggests that the public order serves—when neither politicized nor in crisis—as parameter or institutional context for market-oriented behavior (Powell 1991). It suggests choices and changes over time, not only for participants but also for political authority, which can either reinforce market-like bargaining or directly intervene in labor relations. This sheds new light on David Snyder's argument that while economic factors can (or could in the 1970s) explain postwar U.S. strike trends, political-organizational factors shaped strike activity both in the institutionally unstable 1930s through World War II (Snyder 1977) and in countries with politicized labor relations (1975), such as postwar France and Italy. The argument here suggests that Snyder's two cases refer to two different political unionisms. In the former case, political mobilization reframes the terms of market-oriented unionism; in the latter, on the other hand, politics directly manage labor relations.[3] The former case is comparable to the restructured labor relations environment of the 1980s in the U.S. private sector; the latter to the U.S. public sector.

This contrast points, however, to fundamentally different grounds for the emergence of adversarial relations in the two sectors. Public workers are spared the pervasive tensions over power, motivation, and the rate of exploitation that drive the politics of production in the private sector, although they may, depending on their political status, labor under fiscal constraint. In the public sector, adversarial (and collaborative) relations are driven, at least in part, by the changing political coalitions and policy agendas—rooted both in public organization and in nonstate institutions—that orient public employees' work and govern their workplaces. As these always tension-ridden alignments shift, particular groups of public workers are empowered or disempowered and are drawn into the broader conflicts that define the political

[3]This further suggests that political incumbency by a pro-labor party will have contrary effects on union recourse to economic action, depending on the model of labor relations in effect.

Figure 8.1. Goals and Resources of Labor Movements in the U.S. Public and Private Sectors

	Sector	
	Private	Public
Strategic terrain	Labor market	Single agency
Goals or demands		
Form	Commodity	Public need
Mode of allocation	Private exchange	Political administration
Resources or weapons		
Normal conditions	Market position	Organizational resources
Crisis conditions	Organizational resources Voice	Voice

Note: Diagonal arrow suggests the possible "statification" or socialization of the private sector.

life of the agency. These groups are not only affected by these currents of conflict and change but *participants*—in part through their own social movements.

Different groups of public workers thus find themselves unavoidably implicated in the policy agendas that orient their work and sustain their funding. They are thus linked to "extra-state," societally based political blocs, and their movements are necessarily involved in the endless effort to define "the public interest." They are not merely "interested" in these agendas, however; they enact them. In their training and work experiences, in their day-to-day interactions with clients and with one another, in their dependence on budgetary decisions and in their participation in the shared "definition of the situation" embedded in all this activity, they are the organizational embodiment of these agendas. So, although they assert their own interests, rooted in and shaped by their position in the public workplace, they are also shaped by and dependent on these policy agendas as active or passive participants in the shifting coalitions that seek to sustain or change these policies and, ultimately, to govern local communities. These connections explain the profound relevance, for the cases discussed in this book, of social theory that centers on issues such as gender and family relations and also the private economy. In short, to explain the status and fate of a particular group of public workers in a particular public organization at a particular time, one must locate not only the workforce but the agency in its historical and societal context.

This brings us to questions about developments in local government in the postwar era—the rise and crisis of the local growth machine and the rise and crisis of the local arm of the welfare state.[4] Although the historical analysis offered here draws heavily on recent work by scholars who emphasize the interplay of growth politics and neighborhood movements—in the Marxist formula, tensions between exchange value and use value; in the (more Weberian) neo-Marxist formula, between accumulation and legitimation—it focuses as well on related changes in gender relations in families and in public life.

So, rather than talking about public workers' movements per se, this book has focused on a specific surge of militancy. These mobilizations included a militant assertion of the worth of women's work, associated with neighborhood needs, and defensive mobilizations by previously privileged parts of the public workforce, associated with pro-growth coalitions. Because the workforce that served as the focus of our central case study produced an early and effective mobilization for comparable worth, we were able to trace the relationship between this particular demand—its origins, its form, and the course and fate of the movement associated with it—and broader changes in urban social organization, political life, and public organization.

Starting in the late 1970s, however, the new political reality of Republican ascendance and public sector austerity transformed the terrain of public sector labor relations. All parts of local government bore the brunt of a new effort, organized on a national scale, to shift the burden of federal fiscal crisis down through the states to the local level and to contain the expenditures as well as the political influence of interests rooted in local government. Under these conditions, the newly strengthened public sector unions assumed the role of key coalition-builders in defense of public services in local government.

But neither the public nor private sector labor movements described here were straightforward responses to structural conditions. Rather, each was decisively shaped by learning processes. Workers and their adversaries drew upon earlier scripts and experiences in other settings, with mixed results.

---

[4]In another set of cities, this would bring us as well to a more direct discussion of racial formation and racial succession in urban life and politics.

They also fashioned new strategies in response to their own sometimes painful experiences and to changing opportunities. These changes, and our responses, have produced a still-unfinished learning process.

Generalizing to Other Cases

The public sector cases I have studied are by no means "typical." The workers' experiences are not necessarily similar to those of workers in all cities and counties in California—much less workers in agencies such as schools and special districts or in other states in the United States or in other levels of government.[5]

States *are* distinct political, legal, economic, and fiscal environments for labor relations in the public sector, and state-by-state variations are obscured when data are combined in national trends. And California *is*, of course, the largest and most populous state in the United States. Also, certain important national trends related to this study appeared first in California.

In an important sense, though, no case is typical. Thus, we can only generalize from these cases at the level of theory—through the conceptual tools used to grasp their histories, rather than through those histories themselves. Because these cases are unique, the tools developed here are not likely to be applicable—except in this general sense—to many other cases. During the 1980s, for example, the new labor-management coalitions described here were not an option in local agencies that came under the sway of conservative politicians. In those cases, we might expect to find an ironic combination: weaker progressive influence in the broader political arena but more sustained social movement activity among public workers into the 1980s, including a more consistent emphasis on labor-community coalitions—the choice not taken, as we saw in the last chapter, in San Francisco. As a result of this uneven development, public sector unions in these more conservative communities might be better prepared to play a constructive role in progressive urban coalitions. Perversely, the workforces of cities likely to be most responsive to the progressive promise of public service unionism might be least prepared to do so.

One limitation of this analysis is that the significance of race has perhaps been understated. African-Americans have played a pivotal role in recent

[5]Based on my experiences organizing and representing school district employees throughout the Santa Clara Valley and later in San Francisco, it appears that alliances between administrators and real estate interests dominated local school districts during their early period of expansion and that in time candidates supported by teachers' unions, parent-teacher associations, and neighborhood groups challenged these real estate and construction interests on school boards. On postal workers, see Wright 1993.

urban (and national) politics, with wrenching and sometimes traumatic effects (Omi and Winant 1986; Reed 1988; Browning, Marshall, and Tabb 1990). According to the argument here, this racialization of urban regimes should be reflected in—and in turn affected by—the politics of public work: in the structure and composition of public organizations; in relations within the workforce and its unions; in relations among managers, workers, and clients; and in the timing, character, and course of public workers' movements. As with the gender-related political transition that occurred in San Jose, racial dynamics should presumably overlay—perhaps intensify, perhaps compli- cate—other contradictions in urban public life.

These racial fault lines are suggested, though not fully revealed, in the case of San Jose: in the marginalization of the mostly Mexican-American custo- dians, in their critical role as allies of the mostly white women of the city in their contest with the men in public works, and in the subsequent privatization of their work. Although I have also directed attention to the racial dynamics as they appeared in the public workers' movements in San Francisco and (briefly) Santa Clara County, for various reasons racial dynamics had not (or not yet, or no longer in the period studied) emerged as central axes of conflict and collective action in those cities.[6]

Very different stories could be told of other cities, especially in the North- east. In many instances, historical processes of ethnic succession were fol- lowed, in the 1960s and thereafter, by a far more polarizing racialization of local politics, subsuming various ethnic groups into "black" and "white" and other collective identities. Combined with the earlier growth of public work- forces, with different patterns of public worker organization, and with the historical strength of ethnically rooted political party structures, this process produced in some cities still more racialized worker-client relations and deeper tensions between public workers' organizations and minority communities than in those studied here. In those cities, these dynamics may well have limited the options of public workers' movements during the 1960s and 1970s, reducing their propensity to form labor-community coalitions and encourag- ing greater recourse to labor-management coalitions in a balkanized Demo- cratic party structure.

Similarly, the historical strength of civil service systems, public employee associations, and private sector unionism in California contrasts sharply with conditions in the emerging "new South" in the same period. Though low-wage black city workers were on the cutting edge of the civil rights movement across

[6]But see Gapasin's 1994 account (described on p. 112) of an important and deeply racialized surge of public service unionism among Santa Clara County transit workers.

the region, the strong antiunion climate limited the political force of labor-community coalitions in southern cities. As in the more unionized Northeast, the pivotal problem appears to have been the relative weakness of nonwhite civil service employees (Heshizer 1993). The fate of Atlanta's first African-American political regime is an important case in point. There, Maynard Jackson abandoned the city's black maintenance workers—who had provided crucial support in his election—when they struck in 1976, signaling his embrace of the city's white business elite.[7]

The differences between the California cases and the histories of these other cities are not absolute; San Francisco is in some respects more similar to the older cities of the Northeast than it is to Sunbelt cities such as San Jose. Even Piven (1972) qualified her description of civil service militancy as mainly a mobilization by white bureaucrats against black ghetto dwellers by noting that in New York City AFSCME District Council 37—the miscellaneous workers' union representing these lower-wage, disproportionately minority workers—refused to side with the teachers' union in its battle against community control.

In fact, if the main difference between the California cases and these other settings is the existence of racially based blockages to labor-community coalitions, then examining events in the cities studied here may help illuminate the possibilities open to public workers' movements that can successfully bridge the racial divide. This comparison may permit a glimpse into the future—through the California experience—and thereby reveal possibilities that can fully crystallize as African-American and other nonwhite workers move into majority status and more leadership roles within the public workforce.[8]

The more limited scope of this study, which resulted from a deemphasis on racial dynamics, is probably for the best, however. The need to draw together and develop work on urban political sociology, public sector industrial relations, and the gendered welfare state inflicts more than enough complexity on this argument. An adequate study of what Michael Omi and Howard Winant (1986) might term "racial formation in urban public organization" must await another scholar or a later date.

---

[7]Clarence Stone (1989) minimizes this turning point in his account; but see Austin Scott, "Sanitation Workers' Strike Loaded with Ironies," *Washington Post,* 17 April 1977. A variation on this theme appeared in the conflict in the 1980s between Philadelphia's first African-American mayor, Wilson Goode, and the black-led blue-collar workers of AFSCME, who had enthusiastically supported his 1983 election (Cohen and Dooley 1990).

[8]The recent consolidation—after a protracted and painful process of racial and generational transition in union leadership—of a brand of public service unionism in Local 1199, composed of New York health care workers, suggests that these possibilities are very real indeed (Hudson and Caress 1991). For another case in point, see Johnston 1984, an account of labor-community dynamics in a successful school strike in Oakland, California.

Theoretical Challenges

Perhaps the most challenging problem in studying the public workers' movement is that different aspects of the field are best illuminated by a range of different research traditions—most of which neglect one another, neglect the public workplace, and neglect its labor movement. When a group of female public workers mobilize in the midst of urban fiscal and political crisis—to raise their pay and status, to expand the scope of administrative justice, and to defend the public services they produce—do we turn to the tools of industrial, political, occupational, or urban sociology? Which tools are best for analyzing this phenomenon? Do we rely on feminist theory, class or stratification theory, state theory, organization theory, or social movement theory?

If our interest lies with scholarly work in one or another of these fields rather than the public workers' movement itself, the answer is easy. But if our interest is in public organization and its labor movement, we have less reason for accepting disciplinary blinders. When we seek to explain a concrete historical episode in all its messy multidimensionality, much of the theoretical payoff comes from the disclosure of gaps and silences in and among different streams of work.

For some industrial relations scholars and for economists, the central point in the argument made here—that the public and private sectors are qualitatively different contexts for labor relations—is nothing new. In other traditions, that observation has a cutting edge: those that have minimized the sectoral difference (e.g., organization theory), ignored the public workplace (e.g., state theory, labor process theory), or overlooked the public workers' movement (e.g., social movement research, comparable worth scholars). At the same time, the argument made here asks industrial relations scholars to digest work in these other seemingly alien traditions. Whether or not this effort is worth it depends, first, on whether it reveals processes that remain obscure, and, second, on whether it explains processes that remain unexplained.

Both the study and the practice of labor relations neglect the larger context at their own risk. The larger context for the theory and practice of public sector labor relations is, of course, political life, public organization, or the state taken as a whole. This is not a minor difference from the private sector context, no matter how politicized that other world of work might be. Nor is it sufficient to bring in one or another fragment of political theory to account for the peculiarities of labor movements in this context. Rather, we need a theory of the state—more specifically, in a democratic polity, a theory of public organization—that includes the world of public work and the social movements of those who toil there.[9] Only on that basis can we theorize social movements within and against those peculiar relations of production.

This problem bedevils political science and public administration theory, organizational sociology, and state theory. Recent developments in each of these traditions challenge dominant views of public organization in American social science: the rediscovery of institutions in American political science (March and Olsen 1989); the cognitivist neo-institutionalism in organizational analysis (Powell and DiMaggio 1991, and especially Alford and Friedland 1991); also state theory's trajectory toward the recognition of an autonomous logic of political organization (Offe 1975; Block 1987; Jessop 1990), which does not negate its interpenetration with capitalist social relations.[10] Each of these trends promises to move beyond the conventional reduction of the state to a power relation and therefore promises to clarify the character of public organization.[11]

In chapter 1, I briefly introduced the theory of public organization underlying the argument developed here. There, I described the modern state as a "monopoly over public needs" and described *public* organization as political organization that bases its legitimacy on a claim to define public needs with the consent of the governed. Without pursuing this further, I suggest that contained within this formula is the whole ensemble of institutions associated with the modern state: national identity, citizenship and exclusion, administrative justice, monopoly over legitimate violence, and the public workforce and the society on which it works.

The "public need"—politically defined and administrable—is the statist counterpart to the commodity: the "unit act," so to speak, of an entire way of life. Public workers are not the only actors who emerge and mobilize within and against this terrain. A variety of democratic movements, defined by this turf even when they define themselves against it, appear in the administered spaces of collective life and common interest that emerge as society wraps itself

[9]Michael Lipsky's (1980) study of street-level bureaucracy is an essential starting point. That study of the public labor process is remarkably parallel to Harry Braverman's classic (1974) analysis of the capitalist labor process. For Braverman, Marx's capitalist mode of production devours everything in its path; for Lipsky, Weber's bureaucracy does the same.

[10]Bob Jessop's (1982, 1985, 1990) sustained critique and development of Marxist state theory is the best resource in the latter tradition; interestingly, his most recent conclusions on "the state and other institutional orders" (1990:363 – 67) are strikingly similar to those of institutional sociologists such as Friedland and Alford (1991).

[11]Among organizational scholars, John Meyer and his colleagues (see, especially, Jepperson and Meyer 1991) describe this peculiar institutional logic in penetrating detail. When Friedland and Alford (1991:256) introduce collective action into this model, they arrive at the issue at stake in the conflicts described here (and in our efforts to analyze them). "Some of the most important struggles," they observe, "are over . . . by which institutional logic different activities should be regulated and to which categories of persons they should apply."

in public organization. If the state workplace does shape the demands and resources of such social movements, then social movement theory and state theory should come together to clarify the character and significance of these movements.

Empirical Agendas

Because the sectoral difference has important consequences for the character and course of labor movements in the two sectors, empirical research should routinely control for this difference. Then our grasp of the differences and the effects should improve over time. Further research might fruitfully be organized, in fact, around cross-sectoral comparison—not just to test and extend the conclusions drawn here but to clarify dimensions of difference not accessible through these case comparisons. This strategy would serve not only industrial relations research, and not only the study of social movements in and around the two workplaces, but also research on occupations and organizations more generally.

The same axis of comparison demands closer examination from the standpoint of basic theories of class and social stratification. The public-private sector distinction could provide a critical test of Weberian theory, which defines class position by the market opportunities associated with a given occupation, versus Marxist theory, which emphasizes the social relations of production. From the first perspective, public and private sector workers occupy the same class position; from the second, they are located within qualitatively different class structures.[12] The critical question for such a study would be the effects of class structure, not on attitudes or voting behavior, but on episodes of collective action and patterns of historical change.

All these issues are closely related to a problem squarely at the center of industrial relations research: explaining variations in collective action by different groups of workers and their organizations. The arguments developed here are particularly relevant to work on historical trends in strike activity and to research on union power. Although this book examines these issues in the context of case histories, many scholars would be more likely to rely on

[12]Class analysis has focused on other fault lines—manual versus nonmanual labor (Poulantzas 1975; Giddens 1981), supervisors versus nonsupervisors (Dahrendorf 1959; Carchedi 1977), credentialed versus uncredentialed workers (Parkin 1979), productive versus "political" labor (Collins 1979), professionals and managers versus workers (Ehrenreich and Ehrenreich 1977), and so on. Marxist scholars typically assimilate the public workforce either into the petty bourgeoisie or the working class of capitalism (Poulantzas 1975) even while describing state managers as a distinct class (e.g., Block 1987). Over the past decade, Erik Olin Wright (1983, 1985) has abandoned his influential theory of "contradictory class locations" (1979) in favor of a view similar in some respects to the one suggested here. See also the final chapter of Burawoy 1985.

aggregate data. Unfortunately, the analysis of U.S. strike trends has been limited by the cessation of most data collection in 1981. For the same reason, and because public worker militancy surfaced little more than a decade earlier, studies of public sector strikes have been limited to cross-sectional comparisons, which are of limited use for describing and analyzing change over time and for evaluating causal and historical arguments.[13]

Further, in the absence of detailed information on strike issues and outcomes, scholars interested in union power have been unable to examine conflict directly but have had to depend on indirect evidence, such as wage rates and contract provisions. The *CPER* data described on page 6 above may enable researchers to overcome some of these limitations, at least for one large state. They permitted me, for example, to perform some analyses of all of California's public sector strikes from 1962 through 1990. Although the results of those studies were inconclusive on the questions considered here, their limitations reflect some of the problems that remain.

In one study, I used multivariate regression techniques for time-series analysis to evaluate various combinations of variables that might be associated with trends in strike activity for the period 1962 – 90. Because correlations existed among important independent variables, however, it was impossible, using this method of analysis, to draw decisive conclusions about the value of one model over another.[14]

In another study, I focused on union power, drawing on the detailed information in the *CPER* database on strike issues and outcomes to examine characteristics of identifiable "union victories." For some strikes, it was possible to judge when the strikers emphasized union and worker rights and staffing and service levels in addition to economic demands and when alliances were formed among different occupational groups or different employee organizations. According to the argument made here, these strategic choices, among others, should be associated with union victory. These choices were associated

---

[13]See, however, Nelson, Stone, and Swint 1981, which examines public sector trends through 1973.
[14]Included were a variety of economic and institutional variables emphasized by other scholars, along with a pair of lagged variables based on the argument developed here. According to that argument, the strikes were a short-term consequence of the turn toward adversarial relations in local government and were curtailed in part after the experience left unionists groping for other strategies; also, the turn toward (and later away from) adversarial relations was a political response to an era of growth (and, later, an era of austerity). I used a lagged measure of annual union growth as a measure of the turn toward and then away from adversarial relations among the state's employee organizations and a lagged measure of employment growth as a measure of the fiscal climate. Fiscal trends proved to be good predictors of the turn toward adversarial relations; union growth, however, predicted changes in the cost of living ($r = .76$) and in the unemployment rate ($r = .54$), as well as strike frequency ($r = .73$). Because of this covariance, it is difficult to adjudicate between models of public sector militance that rely on familiar economic variables (Partridge 1991) or others that rely on the argument developed here.

with a higher rate of strike success, but with the exception of staffing and service-level demands, none of these apparent effects was statistically significant. As it stands, the sample is too small and/or the measure of success too imprecise to draw strong conclusions.

Organizing Prospects

When I began this study, I expected to document and explain success in the public workplace while unions in the private sector slid further into failure and decline. I did not anticipate that the center of activity and innovation would shift, by the late 1980s, from the public sector to the private. Despite its defeat, the nurses' comparable worth strike of 1982, for example, demonstrated deep grievances and the potential for powerful collective action in this largely nonunion workforce and the responsiveness of these workers to campaigns that articulate their identities and interests as nurses and as women. The Justice for Janitors campaign displayed similar potential for the custodians of the valley.

The Justice for Janitors campaign honed strategic innovations whose implications extend beyond the building maintenance industry and SEIU. In fact, the campaign appears to offer an effective strategy for counteracting the widespread trend toward outsourcing in the public and private sectors (Howley 1990). This strategy diverts efforts from unequal contests that pit a group of workers against a single employer and rather focuses on the larger networks of ownership and contractual relations that surround the new "lean and mean" corporation (Harrison 1994).

As I write, SEIU and other international unions are preparing organizing campaigns that seek to take Justice for Janitors – style tactics into other parts of the workforce similarly affected by the trend toward outsourcing service and manufacturing work. They are sure to encounter stiff resistance from the large and well-financed cadre of antiunion operatives who have honed their own skills in generally successful efforts to protect and expand nonunion environments in the 1980s. It is likely, then, that the second half of the 1990s will witness confrontations between potent and sophisticated new methods for organizing—and for counterorganizing—in the age of restructured labor relations.

In the public sector as well, outsourced employment may become the target of a broad new trend in union organizing. According to the argument developed in chapter 4, the recent wave of union growth in the public sector, in the 1960s and 1970s, reflected to a great (though unmeasured) degree the adoption of adversarial or unionate attitudes by existing employee organizations in an already organized public workplace, after the politics of growth destabilized labor relations in local government. As limits to growth restabilized employee relations, these sources of union growth have diminished if not disappeared.[15] More promising in the short run, however, are new responses to the widespread privatization of public services.

Public and private sector unions display a familiar difference in their responses to privatization. Private sector unions frequently respond to outsourcing and other competitive pressures by seeking to organize the competing employer's workforce. Public sector unions rarely if ever respond in similar ways. Rather, public sector unions respond to privatization by forming political mobilizations, armed with arguments against the quality of privatized work, the exploitation of public sector workers, the hidden costs of privatization, or the improvements in public sector productivity that are possible with better management (Bilik 1990; Magid 1990). In 1993, however, the SEIU's public employee unions decided to move beyond such essentially defensive strategies and to devote the attention of the public sector organizing department of the international union entirely to organizing privatized public service workers.[16]

Like the custodians at NASA described earlier, privatized workforces are only quasi-private, since they depend, like other public employees, on public policy to sustain their funding, define their missions, and, indirectly, set their wages and conditions of employment. Although organizing efforts targeting these workers are bound to be influenced by the well-known JfJ campaigns in the private sector, nonprofit community service agencies, home health care aides, school bus drivers, food service workers, and so on are also ideally positioned to build the politically potent labor-community coalitions that gave public workers' movements their strongest punch in the 1960s and 1970s.[17]

On the one hand, because disregard of the larger labor market context is so deeply ingrained in public sector union behavior, it will not be easy to channel public sector union activity into such organizing efforts. On the other hand, because neglect of public service issues is so deeply ingrained in private sector

[15]More of this affiliation-based union growth may occur if large independent associations such as the National Education Association, the Fraternal Order of Police, or the California School Employees' Association affiliate with the AFL-CIO. Moreover, the fifteen states that still lack public sector collective bargaining legislation may provide a burst of union growth at some future date.
[16]According to Nancy Mills, SEIU's director of public sector organizing, efforts to develop model campaigns are under way among school bus drivers in Hartford, Connecticut; mental health workers in Massachusetts; and home health aides in the Santa Clara Valley (interview, March 17, 1994).
[17]See also Wright's (1993) comparison of postal unions' responses to privatization, which contrasts the more market-focused U.S. strategies to the Canadian emphasis on labor-community coalitions. In terms very similar to those used here, he terms this "public interest trade unionism."

union behavior, private sector unions are unlikely to tap the community organizing potential of these quasi-private "cut-outs" for public work. Also, given the growth of nonprofit urban community-based organizations and their performance of much privatized public work, such campaigns are likely to be highly politicized. As in public organizations, the most successful campaigns are likely to be labor-community campaigns that emphasize community needs and the level and quality of services as well as workers' wages and working conditions.

Nonprofit "community-based unionism" would define itself as a resource and advocate for community-based organizations, brokering an alliance with the local labor movement. It would promote policy agendas for community development or urban social reform related to the work of the agency, worker involvement for program improvement, and—wherever possible—nonadversarial relations with managers and close working alliances with boards of directors. Because it could challenge funding sources in ways that agency administrators cannot, it would reintroduce a degree of autonomy lost by community organizations as they became dependent on the flow of grants from public and foundation sources.

Far and away the most important target on the cusp of the private and public sectors is the massive health care industry, with its restive, progressive, and largely unorganized workforce.[18] More significant even than the custodians or the contracted-out public workers in SEIU, for example, are employees of the nursing home industry—SEIU's major organizing target in the 1990s. Here, as in the public sector, organizing success is likely to depend on political conflict and change—stimulated, perhaps, by the impact of climbing health care costs and policies designed to contain them. Union success is liable to depend (as in the case of comparable worth among the women of the city) on organizers' ability to link workers' occupational interests with ascendant new policy agendas.[19]

As public regulation and funding for the health care industry becomes more visible through President Bill Clinton's health care reform initiative, the industry is likely to be increasingly influenced by both public and private

[18]U.S. employment in health services grew three times faster than the average from 1979 to 1992, increasing from 5 million to 8.5 million workers (Franklin 1993). Sar A. Levitan and Frank Gallo (1989) reported that the number of nurses covered by ANA contracts increased nearly tenfold between 1966 and 1988; they estimated that about 20 percent of all registered nurses were covered under contracts in 1989, although they did not consider how many of these might have been public employees.

[19]Not only employment and pay but also gendered interests in autonomy and care may be met, for example, by cost-containment strategies such as greater RN involvement in decision-making, decentralization of health facilities, and the expansion of public health nursing and nurse practitioner employment. The interests of non-RN health care employees can be aligned with RNs through identical strategies, including the expansion of physician assistant employment.

sector models of social movement unionism. The regeneration of New York's troubled Local 1199 in the late 1980s, for example, relied heavily on its grasping public sector levers of power; by the end of the 1980s, the local was functioning, in some respects, as a local government union.[20]

Health care workers and contracted-out public employees of all kinds, then, may form the next two waves of the public workers' movement. They may draw their models of unionism from either the public or private sector, depending on local experience and the influence of national networks of organizers. Like the local government workforces described in this book, however, they have the potential to grasp the levers of political power and may well find themselves forced to do so.

An Unfinished Learning Process

What will the future bring for the public workers' movement in local government? There is no good reason to expect an end to the abrupt and consequential change that has characterized the postwar period in urban life and politics. With the onset of the second fiscal crisis of the state around 1990, and the subsequent election of a Democratic administration to the White House, the political opportunity structure of the movement has changed again.

In the earlier years studied here, the course of the public workers' movement depended in part on invariant features of public organization, in part on the unique historical conditions faced by public sector workers and their employers, and in part on the learning processes of the participants. Thus, the combination of explanations offered here is inherently unstable and certainly limited in its relevance to future trends. Under the new conditions of today, public workers are likely to become political lightning rods once again— although the results of their actions are bound to differ from those a decade ago.[21] Neither fiscal trends nor external political developments will translate directly into a new pattern of labor relations in local government. Once again, local political alignments and the learning process of participants will be decisive factors.

If the ascendance of Republicans in federal government helped drive the labor-management coalitions of the 1980s, then the presence of a Democratic administration in Washington may set in motion a new chain of events in local

[20]According to Gerald Hudson and Barbara Caress's insider account (1991) of the local's reconstruction in the late 1980s, 1199 may provide models for organizing privatized public service workers, on the one hand, and for public service unionism in private sector hospitals, on the other. [21]See, for example, Martin Shefter's chilling but plausible scenario for a "neo-reformist" assault on nonwhite clients and "nonproductive" (i.e., nonuniformed) city employees (1985:211–16).

government. We may well witness circumstances in some ways similar to those of the late 1970s, when some local officials managed austerity by orchestrating conflict with public sector unions. These $17,000 streetsweeper agendas, which had been deferred in the defensive coalitions of the 1980s, are likely to assert themselves again with greater force in the 1990s.

Participants in local government labor relations once again face the challenge of adapting to changing conditions. Once again, behaviors institutionalized under earlier conditions—in this case, the Reagan-Bush era—may not fit conditions today. Among the legacies of that era are defensiveness and reactiveness bordering on passivity among some local government union leaders. This style of leadership is a far cry from the assertive activism of two decades ago. Public workers' unions will not be well served by a stance that cleaves to and defends public organization at all costs. The most effective unions may be those that link their interests to the antibureaucratic politics of reform, before they become its target.

As in previous decades, the deciding factor for various blocs of public workers will be how they are implicated—as losers or as winners, as scapegoats or as coalition-builders—in the still-shifting patterns of urban political regime formation. The policy coalitions that remade American communities in the postwar era—the untrammeled growth agenda and, to a lesser extent, the social welfare agenda—are exhausted. In many cities, they were already exhausted before the Reagan-Bush era of defensive coalitions and urban demobilization. But we have yet to see what new governing regimes will take their place. Instead, local governments suffer from political uncertainty and instability as well as fiscal crisis.

Whatever form or forms the new governing coalitions take, we can be confident that not only pro-growth coalitions of some kind but also public workers and neighborhood organizations will be important participants. What kinds of pro-growth agendas will be promoted? What kinds of human development agendas? Which neighborhoods and which workers will be involved, and in what ways? These questions wait to be answered. In any case, we have yet to see expressed the full political potential of broad coalitions of neighborhood residents and the public workers who seek to serve them.

Because they survey the territory from the mountaintops, so to speak, people at the commanding heights of union organization, public administration, and social research enjoy an expansive view of public workers' movements and the public organizations and larger political arenas within which they operate. The view from the valley—in a particular workplace, at the grassroots level of union involvement—is far more limited. Policy and organization that from above might appear fluid or at least open to contest instead seem solid and intransigent. Events that might appear from above as things that people—managers, legislators, union organizers—*do*, seem to workers and their co-workers to *happen to* or to be *done to* them. Recent decades of turmoil, moreover, punctuated by attacks on the worth of public work, have caused many public workers to withdraw to a relatively passive, privatized, sometimes cynical way of life and work. Finally, the public workers' movement itself is surely crippled by its clouded self-identity and uncertain strategic orientation.

Nevertheless, for better and for worse, public workers have played an important part in the business of making and shaping the modern state. When we look back into the history of any public workforce, we find exceptional moments when public workers' movements emerged as exceptional forces with lasting effects. These are, moreover, unfinished histories; one way or another, public workers' movements still have a role to play. To the extent that these past moments become part of public workers' collective memory, they may better perceive both the risks and the richness of their possibilities. If this book encourages that process, it will have served its purpose.

Appendix: Salary Standardization and Comparable Worth

The public organizations discussed in this book rely on elaborate systems of personnel administration, which include a variety of techniques for job evaluation, position classification, salary standardization, the administration of competitive examinations, and the treatment of employees based on job performance. These techniques are not independent of one another: each depends on the others. The logic that binds all the components of the system together includes a formal notion of equal treatment and administrative due process, or, to use Philip Selznick's (1969) term, administrative justice. Selznick's arguments to the contrary, this system flowers fully only in the public sector.

Organizational sociologists use the term "internal labor markets" to describe systems that use such techniques to define jobs, assign people to them, reward and punish them for performance in them, and so on. These systems are not markets in any meaningful sense, of course, but bureaucracies; the term "internal labor market" is highly misleading. Because of their prominent role in the public sector cases discussed here, I briefly describe and discuss these techniques and the system they attempt to organize.

Also, the claim to comparable worth or pay equity has repeatedly surfaced in these cases. In my emphasis on sectoral differences and, in the public sector, on what I term the regime context, the analysis departs somewhat from other studies that focus on comparable worth. My focus here has not been comparable worth per se, and, as a result, questions related to the study of comparable worth have appeared only in passing. There are, however, deep connections between public sector personnel systems and the claim to comparable worth as it has emerged in recent decades. This appendix addresses these connections.

The Emergence of Administrative Justice

It is useful to remind ourselves that, although people in a given organization may refer to a set of rules when they make personnel decisions, their decisions may be influenced by other factors. Despite their apparent rigor, for example, salary standardization systems leave a great deal of room for discretionary maneuvering, and the virtuoso personnel specialist knows how to use techniques to produce results demanded by his or her boss.

Because these systems are legalistic, apparently impersonal, and somewhat technical, however, they are also highly *legitimate*. Thus, whatever else they may do, they are very useful in justifying results that might in fact be the product of political conflict, or the result of other inequalities, because they can—in both senses of the word—*rationalize* results. In short, administrative justice is in good part a way of settling political conflict while leaving substantive inequalities in place.

The effectiveness of these formal procedures in managing conflicting private interests—even while preserving inequality—is certainly one source of the expanding procedural rationality of everyday life in public organization.[1] Not only salary standardization but the civil service system and the whole array of formal rights associated with public organization can be seen, at least in part, as such a political response to conflicting interests. Historical research shows that the extension of formal-bureaucratic personnel systems was driven to a great degree by such political processes within large private firms (e.g., Baron, Dobbin, and Jennings 1986; Lelchook 1974; Laski 1919; Burawoy 1979 and 1985; Edwards 1979; Jacoby 1985).

Most research on comparable worth or pay equity has focused on the public workplace. Leading feminist students of gender inequality in wages and employment have been preoccupied by debates with economists; as a result, they have been led to treat public workplaces as firms. Like most organizational scholars other than those who study public organizations, these scholars assume there is no essential difference between the firm and the state. Similarly, like most scholars other than those who study public sector industrial relations, when these feminist scholars refer to labor movements they assume sectoral differences are irrelevant. Consequently, the public organization as context for the comparable worth movement has remained untheorized (Steinberg 1987; Evans and Nelson 1989; Acker 1989; Blum 1991; England 1992).

I have argued that the political force behind the claim to comparable worth in the public sector flows partly from its association with a broader mobilization of interests linked to gendered human services and neighborhood needs. The comparable worth movements that swept state and local governments in recent decades (Cook 1985, 1986), in this view, are part of a broader movement of

---

[1] See in contrast John Meyer (1988), who similarly locates this logic in the state but disregards political processes; also Charles Perrow (1986), for whom bureaucratic universalism stems only from the standard of efficiency (1986: 6 – 14).

workers in gendered public organization who are asserting the political worth of what neo-Marxists such as O'Connor (1973) and Castells (1978) have termed social consumption functions. Equally important, however, is the affinity between the claim to comparable worth as it has emerged in the public sector and the public sector's own distinctive political-bureaucratic personnel system.

Salary Standardization

The ideal-typical position classification and salary standardization system fits neatly into a larger system that includes formal procedures for examination, certification, and appointment of employees—based on performance-related standards, produced as a result of job classification studies, encoded in job classifications, and so on. I will not describe the formal techniques for comparing different jobs here, since they have been amply described elsewhere (e.g., Beatty and Beatty 1984; Remick 1984). It should be noted, however, that although comparable worth studies typically involve relatively rigorous and systematic classification studies,[2] classification systems in actual organizations have generally evolved in a far more ad hoc fashion.

Regardless of how the system evolved, each job must be assigned to a job classification, with defined minimum qualifications and a defined scope of job duties; related job classifications (or classification series) must be arranged in some order, defining possible career ladders and also standard pay differentials—perhaps 5 percent. Within a classification series, pay differences are based on some judgment about the relative differences in job requirements and responsibilities.

Within a job classification series, then, wage relations depend on comparisons with *different*—but in some way related and so comparable—jobs. This axis of comparison is sharply different, of course, from what Maxine Jenkins likes to call "the market standard"—setting wage relations by comparisons with wages for jobs with *similar* duties in the larger labor market.

Standardized techniques of classification and comparison can be used to set wages based on comparisons among different classifications within an organization, on the one hand, or among similar jobs in the external labor market, on the other. Yet these methods have been used—together—in both public and private organizations in the United States. How do private firms and public agencies reconcile these conflicting standards? By dividing the workforce into occupational—or benchmark—groups, typically composed of related classification series.

---

[2]The trappings of technique are particularly important in a comparable worth study if the results are to be used to justify controversial changes in the compensation structure.

The tension between these contrary standards—internal bureaucracy versus external market—has been resolved by employing salary standardization techniques only within the major classification groups or benchmarks.
For each such group, a single job classification is selected—the "benchmark classification"—for comparison, through a salary survey, with comparable jobs in the external labor market. As pay for the benchmark classification changes in the labor market, so does the pay for the entire benchmark
group.

Thus, while bureaucratic salary standardization procedures are deployed
to set relative pay *within* a benchmark, the market standard guides annual
judgments about the appropriate pay adjustment for each benchmark as
a whole and so determines wage relations *between* benchmarks. "That,"
as Stephen Mangum observes, "is the role of job evaluation in the private sector—to fill in the interstices of the internal labor market between
the generic benchmark jobs for which wages can be set by comparison with
the internal market" (1988:5). Instead of a single great apparatus of comparable jobs, the organization includes several or many independent clusters
of job classifications, each internally organized through bureaucratic standards and each linked through its benchmark classification to the labor
market. Through this system, the organization limits the extension of bureaucratic salary standardization techniques across different occupational groups
within the organization; and, of course, gender-related—and other—wage
differences may be imported and exported to and from the larger labor
market.

Firms mainly use this system to manage the relationship between compensation and the labor market. In public organizations, what is important,
however, is not that these techniques produce the most competitive cost
structure or labor market position but that they are *legitimate*. The market
standard—"prevailing wages"—is no less political a criteria for determining
wages than internal job analysis, and managers favor the market standard *and*
the bureaucratic standard for the same reason: they appear to operate in an
impersonal manner and so underwrite the legitimacy of wage relations. The
combination of market and bureaucratic standards, represented by the
benchmark system, draws on both these justifications for salary-setting while
still keeping labor costs more or less in line with the labor market.

The Secret Politics of Public Personnel Systems

There is far more discretion to the bureaucratic system than implied by
its elaborate procedures and scientific trappings. Decisions have to be

made, for example, about internal bureaucratic relationships: Does a given set of job assignments merit its own job classification? What are the necessary minimum qualifications for jobs in a given classification, and what skills might be learned on the job? Which jobs can serve as career ladders into desirable promotional opportunities? What is the appropriate salary differential between hierarchically ordered classifications, and what constitutes "salary compaction"? What weight or value should be assigned to different kinds of job duties, to establish their position in the classification structure?[3]

Discretion also extends to the supposedly market-driven parts of the system. To which benchmark group, for example, should a classification be assigned? Within each benchmark, which group shall be selected as the benchmark class—one that is "moving well" in pay in the outside world or one that is moving slowly? Which slice of the external labor market—which employers—should be included in the salary survey?

Though these issues are all framed as technical concerns—and are typically addressed by personnel technicians who are professionally committed to applying the rules impartially—the system clearly both permits and conceals a great degree of discretion. Those "in the loop" know that these issues are frequently decided through political processes. Once in place, however, a political "fix" becomes part of the status quo legitimized by its bureaucratic form.

I first recognized the secret political contours of public personnel systems while organizing lower-wage blue-collar workers' efforts to open avenues into higher-wage, higher-skill jobs in Santa Clara County. In the building trades, we found job classifications for "journeymen" and for second- and third-year apprentices, each requiring previous service in the lower-level positions. There was, however, no first-year apprentice classification; the result was a quiet system of social closure, since only those coming out of the apprenticeship program for workers in the private sector building trades were eligible for these jobs. Here again, then, the special relationship of unions linked to the pro-growth agenda left its mark on the personnel system.

The job classification and salary standardization system invites lobbying by groups of employees—and bargaining by broader employee organizations—to influence how the system is to work in practice. Labor-management conflict, when it emerges, is partly channeled into this system. The upshot, in the salary-setting system, is a prominent role for the "internal adjustment."

---

[3]Less explicit and usually unaddressed but implicit in these questions and at least as important for feminists and others are issues regarding the organization of the work itself. One truly radicalizing demand would be worker involvement in decision-making over the content as well as the compensation of jobs.

Internal Adjustments

For the purposes of collective bargaining, benchmarks are assigned to bargaining units.[4] In addition to annual raises for a given bargaining unit, and the benchmarks within it, an important category of pay decisions applies to specific job classifications. These raises—termed internal adjustments—result from lobbying, technical arguments, bargaining, and general political "fixing" on behalf of particular groups. For labor relations in public organizations, these internal adjustments are frequently as important as across-the-board annual wage adjustments.

In an internal adjustment, special wage adjustments are engineered for particular work groups by changing the wage relations *within* benchmark groups. Typically, a technical argument is constructed for changing the relative pay of classifications within the benchmark group so that workers in various classifications will receive the benchmark raise plus an internal adjustment. This system reflects, as in San Jose, the formal and technical channels along which public workers' efforts must be directed to pursue wage claims. It also suggests the pervasive orientation toward relative standing in the large, diverse, bureaucratically ordered public workplace, in contrast to the fixation on the labor market in the private sector. In San Jose, for example, CLAW activists began their organizing—before the drive for comparable worth—with a campaign for an upward internal adjustment to reduce "wage compaction." Similarly, workers in public works classifications secured a stream of "special adjustments" at the same time that workers in female-dominated classifications received their comparable worth adjustments. Political resources are typically as important—frequently more important—than technical arguments for these internal adjustments or "fixes." If the political resources are in place, as they were for the nurses in San Francisco, a valid argument—or an agreement to pretend that an argument is valid—can be assembled.

There are limits to the flexibility in wage determination, however: direct violation of clear legal strictures, making city officials vulnerable to criticism and / or a lawsuit by the chamber of commerce or other concerned citizens; flagrant violations of civil service principles that may be of genuine importance to some civil service professionals; and blatant favoritism among work groups, which could result in formal complaints from less favored employee groups. In other words, technical arguments, and appeals to administrative justice more generally, are themselves political resources—especially in public organizations.[5]

---

[4]Benchmarks are often split into supervisory and nonsupervisory units, but both groups are linked by the benchmark structure and their shared interest in the benchmark-wide raise.
[5]Jacobs and Steinberg also emphasize the power of "the legitimation of employee demands by

Comparable Worth as the Ultimate Internal Adjustment

Implicit in the comparable worth agenda[6] is a political judgment that historically established institutions for wage determination are not legitimate but rather conflict with norms of equality. This judgment rests on the peculiar power of formal equity claims in public organizations. This is one sense in which the claim to comparable worth is native to the public sector. Also, as discussed in chapter 4, there is a structural and historical connection between the comparable worth movement and broader processes in and around the public workplace—the gendered revolt of neighborhood groups against the growth machine, the expansion of gendered public work, and related changes in the character of political regimes and the composition of public organization—that created the context for the eruption of comparable worth movements as part of a broader mobilization of "devalued" parts of the public workforce. This is a second way in which the comparable worth agenda is native to the public sector.

Moreover, the comparable worth agenda as it has emerged in the public sector directly challenges a public agency's relationship to the labor market. What had been used to "fill the interstices" now proposes to abolish them and organize the whole field on its own terms. By advocating cross-benchmark job evaluation and salary standardization, the comparable worth agenda asserts the value of formal-bureaucratic standards of decision-making over market criteria—challenging the compromise between the two reflected in the benchmark system. Such a challenge—"the ultimate internal adjustment"—is a viable option in the public sector only because wage levels there are constrained by "what makes political sense" rather than by "what makes economic sense." This is a third way in which the comparable worth agenda has an affinity to the public sector, and an antipathy to the private.

The gender dimension to the claim to comparable worth focuses the attention of budget writers, job evaluators, and salary standardizers on gender-linked wage differences and provides an avenue for revising those standards in a "scientifically" legitimated manner. But the logic of comparable worth is not limited to the feminist impulse—however much its content may be rooted in and motivated by that rebellion against gendered inequality. Rather, in the

---

recourse to an argument that carries compelling face validity" (1990:461). I hope that the comparison offered here between the power of voice in the first two comparable worth strikes suffices to demonstrate the distinctive force of this weapon in the public as opposed to the private sector.

[6]I use the term "comparable worth" because it was used in the two movements studied here and because it remains *far* more familiar to men and women in the workforce, despite the preference for the term "pay equity" among advocates. The latter term is designed to underline the legitimacy of the claim in the public sphere, but the former term is more precise.

peculiar form it has assumed in the public workplace, this logic should be seen as an expression of that impulse within a particular context: *politically regulated wage labor*. The form of the claim that results reflects the affinity between the formal universality of the bureaucratic ethos and the demand for equality—as distinct, analytically at least, from the gendered character of the work.

Similar arguments associated with the same principles of job evaluation and salary standardization could be used, for example, to challenge salary differentials or other unequal treatment between white and nonwhite workforces. In the case studies of the first public and private sector strikes for comparable worth, I show, in fact, how such racial dimensions were present but submerged by the movements and their organizations asserting the claim to comparable worth. Organizational boundaries, easily racialized, always defining insiders and outsiders, participants and "nonentities," cast their shadow over non-white workers, and their potential claims escape notice.

Finally, the "comparable worth" of nonmanagerial and managerial labor might also be weighed using similar technical arguments; so far, that question too has remained out of the discourse of the labor movement. Whether the content of the claim is associated, in other words, with gendered, racialized, labor-management, or other inequalities, its form is peculiar to state-organized production.

In their analysis of the male-female wage gap in New York State employment, Jerry A. Jacobs and Ronnie J. Steinberg (1990) advance a "political model of wage determination" that is to a great extent consistent with the model supported here. Jacobs and Steinberg challenge the economists' "compensating differentials" argument, which centers on market behavior and argues that differences in wages compensate for the less pleasant aspects of predominately male jobs. Although Jacobs and Steinberg's data are drawn from a public workforce, they emphasize their relevance to private sector behavior and in effect minimize the significance of the public sector context. Their data are entirely consistent, however, with the interpretation offered here: that gender inequality in the public workforce not only in pay but also, for example, in policy, programs, work organization, and union power reflect gendered aspects of the political regimes that have historically governed and shaped public organizations. Although they assume that the relatively high wages of craft and construction workers in their samples stem from "decades of conflict over their wage contract," for example, these same workers have also historically enjoyed a particularly favored relationship with powerful construction and development lobbies and with their political allies among public officials in the state (460).

It is not necessary, for this argument, to claim that the relatively low wages of women in public employment are solely the result of the marginalized political position of those functions in which they have been concentrated. For positions that have private sector analogues, for example, public sector wages may be best understood as the result of the application of legitimate principles for salary setting that reproduce and reinforce gender inequality by tying wages to private sector rates (even though the public employer is, after all, frequently the single largest employer in the local market). It is also credible that all jobs that are held predominantly by females are devalued because of the ubiquity of gender domination; other factors, from the gendered organization of domestic work to gender differences in human capital, are credible as well. My interest, however, is in the demands and the resources of labor movements. By locating workers in their actual strategic context—the world of public organization—we can gain some insight into the factors that drive, orient, and empower their movements.

Certainly there is far more to the claim to comparable worth than the extension of bureaucratic rationality—including, of course, the feminist impulse. Perhaps most important, in asserting the demand for equality and the value of "women's work," the claim to comparable worth provides a powerful ideological resource for grassroots movements of women workers. On the other hand, when it follows the logic of public sector labor relations, the claim to comparable worth can also reproduce and legitimize the bureacratic and hierarchical division of labor (Blum 1987; Brenner 1987; Steinberg 1987). Similarly, when it follows the logic of private sector labor relations, the claim can also submerge more qualitative feminist grievances, serving as an economism of the feminist movement.

There is a place, to be sure, for both bureaucratic and economic standards of equality. But it may be more apt and useful to frame the comparable worth movement as part of a broader historical assertion of the worth of women's work. In the private sector, this means linking claims for higher wages with agendas for occupational restructuring and public accountability, both to increase women's autonomy and to revalue the work of care. In the public sector, it also means identifying the comparable worth movement with broader movements by the same workers, defending and asserting the political worth of "female-gendered" human services. In either case, success or failure depends on a grasp of the significance of the sectoral context.

References

Aaron, Benjamin, Joyce M. Najita, and James L. Stern, eds. 1988. *Public-Sector Bargaining*. 2d ed. Washington, D.C.: Bureau of National Affairs.

Abbott, Carl. 1981. *The New Urban America: Growth and Politics in Sunbelt Cities*. Chapel Hill: University of North Carolina Press.

Abramovitz, Mimi. 1988. *Regulating the Lives of Women: Social Welfare Policy from Colonial Times to the Present*. Boston: South End Press.

Acker, Joan. 1989. *Doing Comparable Worth: Gender, Class, and Pay Equity*. Philadelphia: Temple University Press.

Adams, Roy J. 1992. "The Role of the State in Industrial Relations." In *Research Frontiers in Industrial Relations and Human Resources*, edited by David Lewin, Olivia S. Mitchell, and Peter D. Sherer, 489–524. Madison, Wisc.: Industrial Relations Research Association.

AFL-CIO Comittee on the Evolution of Work. 1985. *The Changing Situation of Workers and Their Unions*. Washington, D.C.

Aiken, Linda H. 1981. "Nursing Priorities of the 1980s." *American Journal of Nursing* 81 (2): 324–30.

Aiken, Linda H., Robert J. Blendon, and David E. Rogers. 1981. "A New Perspective on the Shortage of Hospital Nurses." *American Journal of Nursing* 81 (Sept.): 1612–18.

Alford, Robert R., and Roger Friedland. 1985. *Powers of Theory: Capitalism, the State, and Democracy*. New York: Cambridge University Press.

Anderson, John C. 1979. "Bargaining Outcomes: An IR System Approach." *Industrial Relations* 18 (2): 127–43.

Asher, Martin, and Joel Popkin. 1984. "The Effects of Gender and Race Differentials on Public-Private Wage Comparisons: A Study of Postal Workers." *Industrial and Labor Relations Review* 38 (1): 16–25.

Balser, Diane. 1987. *Sisterhood and Solidarity: Feminism and Labor in Modern Times*. Boston: South End Press.

Banks, Andy. 1991. "The Power and the Promise of Community Unionism." *Labor Research Review* 10 (2): 17–32.

Banks, Andy, and Guillermo Grenier. 1987. "Apartheid in Miami: Transit Workers Challenge the System." *Labor Research Review* 6 (1): 47 – 62.

Baron, James N., Frank R. Dobbin, and P. Devereaux Jennings. 1986. "War and Peace: The Evolution of Modern Personnel Administration in U.S. Industry." *American Journal of Sociology* 92 (2): 250 – 83.

Beatty, Richard W., and James R. Beatty. 1984. "Some Problems with Contemporary Job Evaluation Systems." In *Comparable Worth and Wage Discrimination: Technical Possibilities and Political Realities*, edited by Helen Remick, 59 – 78. Philadelphia: Temple University Press.

Bellush, Jewel, and Bernard Bellush. 1984. *Union Power and New York: Victor Gotbaum and District Council 37*. New York: Praeger.

Benecki, Stanley. 1978. "Municipal Expenditure Levels and Collective Bargaining." *Industrial Relations* 17 (2): 216 – 30.

Bilik, Al. 1990. "Privatization: Selling America to the Lowest Bidder." *Labor Research Review* 10 (1): 1 – 14.

Blackwell, Elise. 1993. "A Commitment to Organizing: Justice for Janitors." *Beyond Borders* 1 (2): 16 – 19.

Block, Fred. 1987. *Revising State Theory: Essays in Politics and Postindustrialism*. Philadelphia: Temple University Press.

Blum, Linda M. 1987. "The Possibilities and Limits of the Comparable Worth Movement." *Gender and Society* 1 (4) 380 – 99.

———. 1991. *Between Feminism and Labor: The Significance of the Comparable Worth Movement*. Berkeley: University of California Press.

Boehm, Randolph H., and Dan C. Heldman. 1982. *Public Employees, Unions, and the Erosion of Civic Trust: A Study of San Francisco in the 1970s*. Frederick, Md.: University Publications of America.

Braverman, Harry. 1974. *Labor and Monopoly Capital: The Degradation of Work in the Twentieth Century*. New York: Monthly Review Press.

Brecher, Jeremy, and Tim Costello. 1990. *Building Bridges: The Emerging Grassroots Coalition of Labor and Community*. New York: Monthly Review Press.

Bright, Charles, and Susan Harding, eds. 1984. *Statemaking and Social Movements: Essays in History and Theory*. Ann Arbor: University of Michigan Press.

Brody, David. 1989. "Labor History, Industrial Relations and the Crisis of American Labor." *Industrial and Labor Relations Review* 43 (1): 7 – 18.

———. 1991. "Labor's Crisis in Historical Perspective." In *The State of the Unions*, edited by George Strauss, Daniel G. Gallagher, and Jack Fiorito, 277 – 312. Madison, Wisc.: Industrial Relations Research Association.

Bronfenbrenner, Kate, and Tom Juravich. 1994. "The Current State of Organizing in the Public Sector: Final Report." Report to AFL-CIO Public Employee Department and various international unions.

Browning, Rufus P., Dale Rogers Marshall, and David H. Tabb, eds. 1990. *Racial Politics in American Cities*. New York: Longman.

Burawoy, Michael. 1979. *Manufacturing Consent: Changes in the Labor Process under Monopoly Capitalism*. Chicago: University of Chicago Press.

———. 1985. *The Politics of Production: Factory Regimes under Capitalism and Socialism*. London: Verso.

———. 1991. "The Extended Case Method." In *Ethnography Unbound: Power and Resistance in the Modern Metropolis*, edited by Michael Burawoy et al., 271 – 90. Berkeley: University of California Press.

Bureau of National Affairs. 1986. *Retail/Services Labor Report*. Washington, D.C.

Burton, John F., Jr. 1982. "Public Sector Unionism: An Economic Perspective." *Government Union Review* 3 (2): 26 – 42.

Burton, John F., Jr., and Terry Thomason. 1988. "The Extent of Collective Bargaining in the Public Sector." In *Public Sector Bargaining*, 2d ed., edited by Benjamin Aaron, Joyce M. Najita, and James L. Stern, 1 – 51. Washington D.C.: Bureau of National Affairs.

California Department of Industrial Relations. 1981. *Collective Bargaining Agreements in the Public Sector, Selected Provisions*. Sacramento.

———. 1982. *Independent State and Local Public Employee Associations in California*. Sacramento.

———. 1985. *Collective Bargaining Agreements in the Public Sector, Selected Provisions*. Sacramento.

———. Annual. *Work Stoppages in California*. Sacramento.

Campbell, Shirley. 1977. *How to Conduct a Successful Strike: The SEIU Strike Manual*. Washington D.C.: Service Employees' International Union.

Carchedi, Guglielmo. 1977. *On the Economic Identification of Social Classes*. London: Routledge & Kegan Paul.

Carnoy, Martin. 1984. *The State and Political Theory*. Princeton, N.J.: Princeton University Press.

Castells, Manuel. 1978. *City, Class and Power*. New York: St. Martin's Press.

———. 1983. *The City and the Grassroots: A Cross-Cultural Theory of Urban Social Movements*. Berkeley: University of California Press.

Chaison, Gary N., and Joseph B. Rose. 1991. "The Macrodeterminants of Union Growth and Decline." In *The State of the Unions*, edited by George Strauss, Daniel G. Gallagher, and Jack Fiorito, 3 – 46. Madison, Wisc.: Industrial Relations Research Association.

City of San Jose. 1957. "San Jose Plans Its Future." Report in support of bonding initiative. San Jose.

Clawson, Dan. 1980. *Bureaucracy and the Labor Process: The Transformation of U.S. Industry, 1860.1920*. New York: Monthly Review Press.

Clegg, Stewart R. 1989. *Frameworks of Power*. Newbury Park, Calif.: Sage.

Cockburn, Cynthia. 1977. *The Local State: Management of Cities and People*. London: Pluto Press.

———. 1991. *In the Way of Women: Men's Resistance to Sex Equality in Organizations*. Ithaca, N.Y.: ILR Press.

Cohen, Ann, and James Dooley. 1990. "Privatizing Philly vs. AFSCME DC 33." *Labor Relations Review* 9 (1): 15 – 24.

Cohen, Sanford. 1979. "Does Public Employee Unionism Diminish Democracy?" *Industrial and Labor Relations Review* 32 (2): 189 – 95.

Collins, P. Hill. 1990. "The Meaning of Motherhood in Black Culture." In *The Black Family: Essays and Studies*, edited by Robert Staples. Belmont, Calif.: Wadsworth.

Collins, Randall. 1979. *The Credential Society: An Historical Sociology of Education and Stratification*. New York: Academic Press.

Commons, John R. 1905. "Trade Agreements." In *Trade Unionism and Labor Union-ism*. Boston: Ginn.

——. 1909. "American Shoemakers, 1648 – 1895: A Sketch of Industrial Evolution." *Quarterly Journal of Economics* 24 (4): 39 – 98.

Cook, Alice. 1985. *Comparable Worth: A Case Book of Experiences in States and Localities*. Manoa: University of Hawaii, Industrial Relations Center.

——. 1986. *Comparable Worth: A Case Book of Experiences in States and Localities. Supplement*. Manoa: University of Hawaii, Industrial Relations Center.

Cornfield, Daniel B. 1987. "Decline and Diversification: Causes and Consequences for Organizational Governance." *Sociology of Organizations* 5: 187 – 216.

——. 1989. "Union Decline and the Political Demands of Organized Labor." *Work and Occupations* 16 (3): 292 – 322.

——. 1991. "The U.S. Labor Movement: Its Development and Impact on Social Inequality and Politics." *Annual Review of Sociology* 17: 27 – 49.

——. 1993. "Decline or Revitalization? Changes in the U.S. Labor Movement." Paper presented at the Eighty-eighth Meeting of the American Sociological Association, Miami, Aug.

Crouch, Winston Winford. 1978. *Organized Civil Servants: Public Employer-Employee Relations in California*. Berkeley: University of California Press.

Cyert, Richard M., and James G. March. 1963. *A Behavioral Theory of the Firm*. Englewood Cliffs, N.J.: Prentice-Hall.

Dahrendorf, Ralf. 1959. *Class and Class Conflict in Industrial Society*. Stanford, Calif.: Stanford University Press.

DeLeon, Richard Edward. 1992. *Left-Coast City: Progressive Politics in San Francisco, 1975.1991*. Lawrence: University of Kansas Press.

Derber, Milton, and Martin Wagner. 1979. "Public Sector Bargaining and Budget Making under Fiscal Adversity." *Industrial and Labor Relations Review* 33 (1): 18 – 23.

DiMaggio, Paul J., and Walter W. Powell. 1983. "The Iron Cage Revisited: Institutional Isomorphism and Collective Rationality in Organizational Fields." *American Sociological Review* 48: (2): 147 – 60.

Dinnerstein, Dorothy. 1976. *The Mermaid and the Minotaur: Sexual Arrangements and Human Malaise*. New York: Harper and Row.

Donovan, Ronald. 1990. *Administering the Taylor Law: Public Employee Relations in New York*. Ithaca, N.Y.: ILR Press.

Downs, Anthony. 1967. *Inside Bureaucracy: An Economic Theory of Democracy*. Boston: Little, Brown.

Durkheim, Émile. 1964. *The Division of Labor in Society*. New York: Free Press.

Eastwood, Granville. 1977. *Harold Laski*. London & Oxford: Mowbrays.

Edelman, Murray J. 1967. *The Symbolic Uses of Politics*. Urbana: University of Illinois Press.

Edwards, Richard. 1979. *Contested Terrain: The Transformation of the Workplace in the Twentieth Century*. New York: Basic Books.

Ehrenreich, Barbara, and John Ehrenreich. 1977. "The Professional-Managerial Class." *Radical America* 11 (2): 7 – 32.

England, Paula. 1992. *Comparable Worth: Theories and Evidence*. New York: Aldine de Gruyter.

Erikson, Kai. 1976. *Everything in Its Path: Destruction of Community in the Buffalo Creek Flood*. New York: Simon and Schuster.

Evans, Peter B., Dietrich Rueschemeyer, and Theda Skocpol, eds. 1985. *Bringing the State Back In*. New York: Cambridge University Press.

Evans, Sarah M., and Barbara J. Nelson. 1989. *Wage Justice: Comparable Worth and the Paradox of Technocratic Reform*. Chicago: University of Chicago Press.

Fainstein, Norman I., and Susan S. Fainstein. 1974. *Urban Social Movements: The Search for Power by Minority Groups in American Cities*. Englewood Cliffs, N.J.: Prentice-Hall.

Fantasia, Rick. 1988. *Cultures of Solidarity: Consciousness, Action, and Contemporary American Workers*. Berkeley: University of California Press.

Farnquist, Robert L, David R. Armstrong, and Russell R. Strausbaugh. 1983. "Pandora's Worth: The San Jose Experience." *Public Personnel Management Journal* 12 (4): 358 – 68.

Fava, Sylvia. 1980. "Women's Place in the New Suburbia." In *New Space for Women*, edited by Gerda R. Wekerle, Rebecca Peterson, and David Morley. Boulder, Colo.: Westview Press.

Feagin, Joe. 1988. *Free Enterprise City: Houston in Political and Economic Perspective*. New Brunswick, N.J.: Rutgers University Press.

Feldberg, Roslyn. 1992. "Comparable Worth and Nurses in the USA." In *Equal Value/Comparable Worth in the UK and the USA*, edited by Peggy Kahn and Elizabeth Meehan, 181 – 241. London: Macmillan.

Feree, Myra Marx. 1992. "The Political Context of Rationality: Rational Choice Theory and Resource Mobilization." In *Frontiers in Social Movement Theory*, edited by Aldon D. Morris and Carol McClurg Mueller, 29 – 52. New Haven, Conn.: Yale University Press.

Feree, Myra Marx, and Frederick D. Miller. 1985. "Mobilization and Meaning: Toward an Integration of Social Psychological and Resource Mobilization Perspectives on Social Movements." *Sociological Inquiry* 55 (1): 38 – 51.

Ferguson, Kathy E. 1984. *The Feminist Case against Bureaucracy*. Philadelphia: Temple University Press.

Flammang, Janet A. 1985. "Female Officials in the Feminist Capital: The Case of Santa Clara County." *Western Political Quarterly* 38 (1): 94 – 118.

———. 1986. "Effective Implementation: The Case of Comparable Worth in San Jose." *Policy Studies Review* 5 (4): 815 – 37.

Fox, Kenneth, et al., eds. 1982. *Crisis in the Public Sector: A Reader*. New York: Monthly Review Press.

Franklin, James C. 1993. "The American Workforce, 1992 – 2005: Industrial Output and Employment." *Monthly Labor Review* 116 (11): 41 – 57.

Franzosi, Roberto. 1989. "One Hundred Years of Strike Statistics: Methodological and Theoretical Issues in Quantitative Strike Research." *Industrial and Labor Relations Review* 42 (3): 348 – 62.

Franzway, Suzanne, Dianne Court, and R. W. Connell. 1989. *Staking a Claim: Feminism, Bureaucracy and the State*. Boston: Allen & Unwin.

Freeman, Jo. 1973. "The Origins of the Women's Liberation Movement." *American Journal of Sociology* 78 (4): 792 – 811.

Freeman, Richard B. 1986. "Unionism Comes to the Public Sector." *Journal of Economic Literature* 24 (1): 41 – 86.

———. 1988. "Contraction and Expansion: The Divergence of Public and Private Sector Unionism in the United States." *Journal of Economic Perspectives* 2 (2): 63 – 88.

Freeman, Richard B., and Casey Ichniowski, eds. 1988. *When Public Sector Workers Unionize*. Chicago: University of Chicago Press.

Freeman, Richard B., Casey Ichniowski, and Jeffrey Zax. 1988. "Collective Organization of Labor in the Public Sector." In *When Public Sector Workers Unionize*, edited by Richard B. Freeman and Casey Ichniowski, 365 – 98. Chicago: University of Chicago Press.

Freeman, Richard B., and J. Leonard. 1985. "Union Maids: Unions and the Female Workforce." NBER Working Paper no. 1652. Cambridge: National Bureau of Economic Research.

Freeman, Richard B., and James Medoff. 1984. *What Do Unions Do?* New York: Basic Books.

Freeman, Richard B., and Robert G. Valletta. 1988. "The Effects of Public Sector Labor Laws on Labor Market Institutions and Outcomes." In *When Public Sector Workers Unionize*, edited by Richard B. Freeman and Casey Ichniowski, 81 – 106. Chicago: University of Chicago Press.

Friedland, Roger, and Robert R. Alford. 1991. "Bringing Society Back In: Symbols, Practices and Institutional Contradictions." In *The New Institutionalism in Organizational Analysis*, edited by Walter W. Powell and Paul J. DiMaggio, 232 – 66. Chicago: University of Chicago Press.

Friedland, Roger, Frances Fox Piven, and Robert R. Alford. 1977. "Political Conflict, Urban Structure, and the Fiscal Crisis." In *Comparing Public Policies: New Concepts and Methods*, edited by Douglas Ashford, 197 – 225. Beverly Hills, Calif.: Sage.

Game, Ann, and Rosemary Pringle. 1983. *Gender at Work*. Sydney: Allen & Unwin.

Gamson, William A. 1985. "Goffman's Legacy to Political Sociology." *Theory and Society* 14 (5): 605 – 22.

———. 1988. "Political Discourse and Collective Action." *International Research in Social Movements, Conflict and Change* (1): 219 – 44.

Gans, Herbert J. 1967. *The Levittowners: Ways of Life and Politics in a New Suburban Community*. New York: Pantheon Books.

Gapasin, Fernando. 1994. *Union Organization and Changing Demographics: A Study about Activism*. Ph.D. diss., University of California at Santa Barbara.

Giddens, Anthony. 1981. *The Class Structure of the Advanced Societies*. Rev. ed. New York: Harper & Row.

Gilligan, Carol. 1982. *In a Different Voice: Psychological Theory and Women's Development*. Cambridge: Harvard University Press.

Gitlow, Abraham L. 1970. "Public Employee Unionism in the United States: Growth and Outlook." *Labor Law Journal*, Dec., 766 – 70.

Goffman, Erving. 1974. *Frame Analysis: An Essay on the Organization of Experience*. Cambridge: Harvard University Press.

Goldin, Greg. 1989. "Arriba! The New Surge in Latino Union Organizing." *Union* 6: 25 – 28.

Gordon, David M., Richard Edwards, and Michael Reich. 1982. *Segmented Work, Divided Workers: The Historical Transformation of Labor in the United States*. New York: Cambridge University Press.

Gordon, Linda, ed. 1990. *Women, the State, and Welfare*. Madison: University of Wisconsin Press.

———. 1991. *Black and White Visions of Welfare: Women's Welfare Activism, 1890.1945*. Madison: University of Wisconsin, Institute for Research on Poverty.

Gramsci, Antonio. 1971. *Selections from the Prison Notebooks of Antonio Gramsci*. New York: International Publishers.

Gray, David E. 1989. "Militancy, Unionism, and Gender Ideology: A Study of Hospital Nurses." *Work and Occupations* 16 (2): 137 – 52.

Greer, Scott. 1962. *The Emerging City: Myth and Reality*. New York. Free Press.

Gunderson, Morley. 1980. "Public Sector Compensation in Canada and the U.S." *Industrial Relations* 19 (3): 257 – 71.

Harmon, Michael, and Richard Mayer. 1986. *Organization Theory for Public Administration*. Boston: Little, Brown.

Harrison, Bennett. 1994. *Lean and Mean: The Changing Landscape of Power in the Age of Flexibility*. New York: Basic Books.

Hartmann, Heidi I. 1985. "Research Needs in Comparable Worth." In *Proceedings of the Thirty-Seventh Annual Meeting of the Industrial Relations Research Association*, edited by Barbara Dennis, 173 – 82. Madison, Wisc.: Industrial Relations Research Association.

Harvey, David. 1973. *Social Justice and the City*. Baltimore: Johns Hopkins University Press.

Heckscher, Charles. 1988. *The New Unionism: Employee Involvement in the Changing Corporation*. New York: Basic Books.

Hegel, G.W.F. 1967. *Philosophy of Right*. London: Oxford University Press.

Hernes, Helga Maria. 1987. "Women and the Welfare State: The Transition from Private to Public Dependence." In *Women and the Welfare State*, edited by Anne Showstack Sassoon, 72 – 92. London: Unwin Hyman.

Heshizer, Brian. 1993. "The Memphis Sanitation Workers' Strike of 1968." *Journal of Collective Negotiations* 22 (2): 99 – 118.

Hibbs, Douglas, Jr. 1976. "Industrial Conflict in Advanced Industrial Societies." *American Political Science Review* 39 (3): 1033 – 58.

Hiles, David R. H. 1992. "Health Services: The Real Jobs Machine." *Monthly Labor Review* 115 (11): 3 – 16.

Hirschman, Albert O. 1970. *Exit, Voice, and Loyalty: Responses to Decline in Firms, Organizations, and States*. Cambridge: Harvard University Press.

Hodson, Randy. 1978. "Labor in the Monopoly, Competitive, and State Sectors of Production." In *Politics and Society* 8 (3 – 4): 429 – 79.

Horan, Cynthia. 1991. "Beyond Governing Coalitions: Analyzing Urban Regimes in the 1990s." *Journal of Urban Affairs* 13 (2): 119 – 36.

Horton, Raymond D. 1986. "Fiscal Stress and Labor Power." In *Proceedings of the Thirty-Eighth Annual Meeting of the Industrial Relations Research Association*, edited by Barbara Dennis, 304 – 15. Madison, Wisc.: Industrial Relations Research Association.

Horton, Raymond D., David Lewin, and James W. Kuhn. 1976. "Some Impacts of Collective Bargaining on Local Government: A Diversity Thesis." *Administration and Society* 7 (4): 497 – 516.

Howley, John. 1990. "Justice for Janitors: The Challenge of Organizing Contract Services." *Labor Research Review* 15 (1): 61 – 72.

Hudson, Gerald, and Barbara Caress. 1991. "New York's 1199 in 1989: Rebuilding a Troubled Union." *Labor Research Review* 10 (1): 69 – 80.

Hurd, Richard W. 1973. "Equilibrium Vacancies in a Labor Market Dominated by Non-Profit Firms: The Shortage of Nurses." *Review of Economics and Statistics* 55 (2): 234 – 40.

Jacobs, Jerry A., and Ronnie J. Steinberg. 1990. "Compensating Differentials and the Male-Female Wage Gap: Evidence from the New York State Comparable Worth Study." *Social Forces* 69 (2): 439 – 68.

Jacoby, Sanford M. 1985. *Employing Bureaucracy: Managers, Unions and the Transformation of Work in American Industry, 1900.1945.* New York: Columbia University Press.

Jenkins, J. Craig. 1987. "Interpreting the Stormy 1960s: Three Theories in Search of a Political Age." In *Research in Political Sociology 3*, edited by Richard Braungart and Margaret M. Braungart, 269 – 303. Greenwich, Conn.: JAI Press.

Jenkins, Maxine, and members of Affirmative Action Committee. 1978. "Women Working." Position paper. San Jose: AFSCME Local 101.

Jepperson, Ronald L., and John W. Meyer. 1991. "The Public Order and the Construction of Formal Organizations." In *The New Institutionalism in Organizational Analysis*, edited by Walter W. Powell and Paul J. DiMaggio, 204 – 31. Chicago: University of Chicago Press.

Jessop, Bob. 1982. *The Capitalist State: Marxist Theories and Methods.* New York: New York University Press.

———. 1985. *Nicos Poulantzas: Marxist Theory and Political Strategy.* New York: St. Martin's Press.

———. 1990. *State Theory: Putting the Capitalist State in Its Place.* Cambridge, Eng.: Polity Press.

Johansen, Elaine. 1984. *Comparable Worth: The Myth and the Movement.* Boulder, Colo.: Westview Press.

Johnston, Paul. 1978. "The Promise of Public Service Unionism." *Monthly Labor Review* 30 (9): 3 – 27.

———. 1980. "Democracy, Public Work and Labor Strategy." *Kapitalistate* 8: 27 – 42.

———. 1984. "Parents and Teachers Unite: Oakland Rallies around School Strike." *Dollars and Sense* 3: 14 – 16.

Karper, Mark. 1990. "The Growth and Development of the Public Sector Labor Movement." In *Advances in Industrial and Labor Relations*, suppl. 1, edited by Sethi Amarjit, Norman Metzger, and Stuart J. Dimmock, 37 – 66. Greenwich, Conn.: JAI Press.

Kassalow, Everett M. 1969. "Trade Unionism Goes Public." *Public Interest* 14 (1): 118 – 30.

Katz, Harry. 1984. *The Impact of Public Employee Unionism on City Budgeting and Employee Remuneration: A Case Study of San Francisco.* New York: Garland.

Katzenstein, Mary Fainsod. 1990. "Feminisim within American Institutions: Unobtrusive Mobilization in the 1980s." *Signs: A Journal of Women in Culture and Society* 16 (1): 27 – 54.

Kaufman, Bruce E. 1982. "The Determinants of Strikes in the United States, 1900 – 1977." *Industrial and Labor Relations Review* 35 (4): 473 – 90.

———. 1992. "Research on Strike Models and Outcomes in the 1980s: Accomplishments and Shortcomings." In *Research Frontiers in Industrial Relations and Human Resources*, edited by David Lewin, Olivia S. Mitchell, and Peter D. Sherer, 77 – 130. Madison, Wisc.: Industrial Relations Research Association.

———. 1993. *The Origins and Evolution of the Field of Industrial Relations in the United States*. Ithaca, N.Y.: ILR Press.

Kautzer, Kathleen. 1992. " 'We Can't Eat Prestige': The Yale University Workers' Campaign for Comparable Worth." In *Equal Value/Comparable Worth in the UK and the USA*, edited by Peggy Kahn and Elizabeth Meehan, 137 – 65. London: Macmillan.

Kazin, Michael. 1987. *Barons of Labor: The San Francisco Building Trades and Union Power in the Progressive Era*. Urbana: University of Illinois Press.

Kelly, Rita Mae. 1991. *The Gendered Economy: Work, Careers and Success*. Newbury Park, Calif.: Sage.

Kerr, Clark, et al. 1960. *Industrialism and Industrial Man: The Problems of Labor and Management in Economic Growth*. Cambridge: Harvard University Press.

King, Roger. 1986. *The State in Modern Society: New Directions in Political Sociology*. Chatham, N.J.: Chatham House.

Klandermans, Bert. 1984. "Mobilization and Participation: Social-Psychological Expansions of Resource-Mobilization Theory." *American Sociological Review* 49 (4): 563 – 600.

Klein, Melanie. 1957. *Envy and Gratitude: A Study of Unconscious Sources*. London: Tavistock.

Kochan, Thomas A. 1974. "A Theory of Multilateral Collective Bargaining in City Governments." *Industrial Relations Review* 27 (4): 525 – 42.

Kochan, Thomas A., Harry C. Katz, and Robert McKersie. 1986. *The Transformation of American Industrial Relations*. New York: Basic Books; Ithaca, N.Y.: ILR Press, 1994.

Kochan, Thomas A., and Kirsten R. Wever. 1991. "American Unions and the Future of Worker Representation." In *The State of the Unions*, edited by George Strauss, Daniel Gallagher, and Jack Fiorito, 363 – 86. Madison, Wisc.: Industrial Relations Research Association.

Kochan, Thomas A., and Hoyt N. Wheeler. 1975. "Municipal Collective Bargaining: A Model and Analysis of Bargaining Outcomes." *Industrial and Labor Relations Review* 29 (1): 46 – 66.

Korpi, Walter. 1978. *The Working Class in Welfare Capitalism: Work, Unions, and Politics in Sweden*. London: Routledge & Kegan Paul.

Korpi, Walter, and Michael Shalev. 1980. "Strikes, Power, Politics in the Western Nations, 1900 – 1976." In *Political Power and Social Theory*, vol. 1, edited by Maurice Zeitlin, 301 – 34. Greenwich, Conn.: JAI Press.

Kramer, Leo. 1962. *Labor's Paradox: The American Federation of State, County, and Municipal Employees, AFL-CIO*. New York: Wiley.

Kurth, Michael. 1983. "Public Employee Unions as Political Firms." In *Research in Labor Economics*, suppl. 2, 101 – 25. Greenwich, Conn.: JAI Press.

Lane, Jan-Erik. 1993. *The Public Sector: Concepts, Models and Approaches*. Newbury Park, Calif.: Sage.

Laski, Harold J. 1919. *Authority in the Modern State*. New Haven, Conn.: Yale University Press.

Lelchook, James. 1974. "Study of State Civil Service Associations." *California Public Employee Relations Journal* 22.

Lentz, Bernard F. 1983. "Discussion." In *Research in Labor Economics*, suppl. 2, 149 – 53. Greenwich, Conn.: JAI Press.

Lerner, Stephen. 1991. "Let's Get Moving: Labor's Survival Depends on Organizing Industry-Wide for Justice and Power." *Labor Research Review* 10 (2): 1 – 16.

Levi, Margaret. 1977. *Bureaucratic Insurgency: The Case of Police Unions*. Lexington, Mass.: Lexington Books.

Levine, Marvin J. 1990. "Subcontracting and the 'Privatization' of Work: Public and Private Sector Developments." *Journal of Collective Negotiations* 19 (4): 275 – 82.

Levitan, Sar A., and Frank Gallo. 1989. "Can Employee Associations Negotiate New Growth?" *Monthly Labor Review* 112 (7): 5 – 14.

Lewin, David. 1983. "The Effects of Civil Service Systems and Unionism on Pay Outcomes in the Public Sector." In *Advances in Industrial and Labor Relations*, edited by David B. Lipsky, 1:131 – 61. Greenwich, Conn.: JAI Press.

———. 1986. "Public Employee Unionism in the 1980s." In *Unions in Transition: Entering the Second Century*, edited by Seymour Martin Lipset, 241 – 65. San Francisco: ICS Press.

Lewin, David, et al., eds. 1988. *Public Sector Labor Relations: Analysis and Readings*. Lexington, Mass.: Lexington Books.

Link, Charles R., and John Landon. 1975. "Monopsony and Union Power in the Market for Nurses." *Southern Economic Journal* 41 (4): 649 – 59.

Lipset, Seymour Martin, ed. 1986. *Unions in Transition: Entering the Second Century*. San Francisco: ICS Press.

Lipsky, Michael. 1980. *Street-Level Bureaucracy: Dilemmas of the Individual in Public Services*. New York: Russell Sage Foundation.

Little, Arthur D., Inc. 1964. "Potential Urban Growth: South Santa Clara County." Report to Board of Supervisors, Santa Clara County, Calif.

Logan, John R., and Harvey Molotch. 1987. *Urban Fortunes: The Political Economy of Place*. Berkeley: University of California Press.

Lowery-Palmer, Alma. 1982. "The Cultural Basis of Political Behavior in Two Groups: Nurses and Political Activists." In *Socialization, Sexism and Stereotyping*, edited by Janet Muff, 189 – 202. St. Louis: Mosby.

McAdam, Doug. 1992. *Political Process and the Development of Black Insurgency, 1930.1970*. Chicago: University of Chicago Press.

McCall, George J., and J. L. Simmons. 1969. *Issues in Participant Observation: A Text and Reader*. Reading, Mass.: Addison-Wesley.

McCarthy, John D., and Mayer N. Zald. 1977. "Resource Mobilization and Social Movements: A Partial Theory." *American Journal of Sociology* 82 (6): 1212 – 41.

McCourt, Kathleen. 1977. *Working Class Women and Grass Roots Politics*. Bloomington: Indiana University Press.

MacKinnon, Catharine A. 1989. *Toward a Feminist Theory of the State*. Cambridge: Harvard University Press.

McLennan, K., and M. Moskow. 1968. "Multilateral Bargaining in the Public Sector." In *Proceedings of the Twenty-First Annual Meeting of the Industrial Relations Research Association*, edited by Gerald Somers, 34 – 41. Madison, Wisc.: Industrial Relations Research Association.

McNichol, Liz. 1990. "Fighting on Many Fronts." *Labor Research Review* 9 (1): 37 – 44.

Magid, Marcia. 1990. "Cottage Cheese or Chicken? An AFSCME Fight for Public Food Service." *Labor Research Review* 9 (1): 53 – 60.

Maier, Mark. 1987. *City Unions: Managing Discontent in New York City*. New Brunswick, N.J.: Rutgers University Press.

Malveaux, Julianne. 1992. "Comparable Worth and Its Impact on Black Women." In *Equal Value/Comparable Worth in the UK and the USA*, edited by Peggy Kahn and Elizabeth Meehan, 82 – 94. London: Macmillan.

Mangum, Stephen L. 1988. "Comparable Worth and Pay Setting in the Public and Private Sectors." *Journal of Collective Negotiations* 17 (1): 1 – 12.

March, James G., and Johan P. Olsen. 1989. *Rediscovering Institutions: The Organizational Basis of Politics*. New York: Free Press.

Marmo, Michael. 1983. "Multilateral Bargaining in the Public Sector: A New Perspective." In *Proceedings of the Thirty-Fifth Annual Meeting of the Industrial Relations Research Association*, edited by Barbara Dennis, 49 – 59. Madison, Wisc.: Industrial Relations Research Association.

———. 1984. "Public Employee Collective Bargaining: A Mass-Mediated Process." *Journal of Collective Negotiations* 13 (4): 291 – 312.

Marx, Karl. 1963. *The Eighteenth Brumaire of Louis Bonaparte*. New York: International Publishers.

———. 1964. *The Class Struggles in France: 1848.1850*. New York: International Publishers.

Matthews, Glenna. 1977. "A California Middletown: The Social History of San Jose in the Depression." Ph.D. diss., Stanford University.

Melosh, Barbara. 1982. *"The Physician's Hand": Work Culture and Conflict in American Nursing*. Philadelphia: Temple University Press.

Meyer, John W. 1988. "Society without Culture: A Nineteenth-Century Legacy." In *Rethinking the Nineteenth Century: Contradictions and Movements*, edited by F. O. Ramirez, 193 – 202. Westport, Conn.: Greenwood Press.

Meyer, John W., and Brian Rowan. 1977. "Institutionalized Organizations: Formal Structure as Myth and Ceremony." *American Journal of Sociology* 83 (2): 340 – 63.

Milkman, Ruth. 1985. "Women Workers, Feminism, and the Labor Movement since the 1960's." In *Women, Work and Protest: A Century of Women's Labor History*, edited by Ruth Milkman, 300 – 22. Boston: Routledge & Kegan Paul.

———. 1987. *Gender at Work: The Dynamics of Job Segregation by Sex during World War II*. Urbana: University of Illinois Press.

Miller, S. M. 1969. "The Participant Observer and 'Over-Rapport'." In *Issues in Participant Observation: A Text and Reader*, edited by George J. McCall and J. L. Simmons, 87 – 89. Reading, Mass.: Addison-Wesley.

Mitchell, Daniel J. B. 1986. "Concession Bargaining in the Public Sector: A Lesser Force." *Public Personnel Management* 15 (1): 23 – 40.

———. 1988. "Collective Bargaining and Compensation in the Public Sector." In *Public-Sector Bargaining*, 2d ed., edited by Benjamin Aaron, Joyce M. Najita, and James L. Stern, 124 – 59. Washington, D.C.: Bureau of National Affairs.

Mollenkopf, John Hull. 1983. *The Contested City*. Princeton, N.J.: Princeton University Press.

———. 1992. *Phoenix in the Ashes: The Rise and Fall of the Koch Coalition in New York City Politics*. Princeton, N.J.: Princeton University Press.

Moody, Kim. 1988. *An Injury to All: The Decline of American Unionism*. New York: Verso.

Morris, Aldon D. 1992. "Political Consciousness and Collective Action," in *Frontiers in Social Movement Theory,* edited by Aldon D. Morris and Carol McClurg Mueller, 351 – 73. New Haven, Conn.: Yale University Press.

Mueller, Carol McClurg. 1992. "Building Social Movement Theory." In *Frontiers in Social Movement Theory*, edited by Aldon D. Morris and Carol McClurg Mueller, 3 – 28. New Haven, Conn.: Yale University Press.

Naples, Michele. 1987. "An Analysis of Defensive Strikes." *Industrial Relations* 26 (1): 96 – 105.

Naples, Nancy A. 1992. "Activist Mothering: Cross-Generational Continuity in the Community Work of Women from Low-Income Urban Neighborhoods." *Gender and Society* 6 (3): 441 – 63.

Nelson, William B., Gerard W. Stone, Jr., and J. Michael Swint. 1981. "An Economic Analysis of Public Sector Collective Bargaining and Strike Activity." *Journal of Labor Research* 2 (1): 77 – 98.

Nisbet, Robert A. 1976. "Public Employee Unions and the Decline of Public Trust." In *Public Employee Unions: A Study of the Crisis in Public Sector Labor Relations*, edited by A. Lawrence Chickering, 13 – 43. San Francisco: Institute for Contemporary Studies.

Niskanen, William A. 1971. *Bureaucracy and Representative Government*. Chicago: Aldine-Atherton.

O'Connor, James. 1973. *The Fiscal Crisis of the State*. New York: St. Martin's Press.

———. 1984. *Accumulation Crisis*. New York: Basil Blackwell.

O'Donnell, Guillermo. 1986. "On the Fruitful Convergences of Hirschman's *Exit, Voice and Loyalty* and *Shifting Involvements*: Reflections from the Recent Argentine Experience." In *Development, Democracy and the Art of Trespassing: Essays in Honor of Albert O. Hirschman*, edited by Alejandro Foxley, Michael McPherson, and Guillermo O'Donnell, 249 – 68. Notre Dame, Ind.: University of Notre Dame Press.

Offe, Claus. 1984. *Contradictions of the Welfare State*. Cambridge: MIT Press.

———. 1985. *Disorganized Capitalism: Contemporary Transformation of Work and Politics*. Cambridge: MIT Press.

Olson, Mancur. 1965. *The Logic of Collective Action: Public Goods and the Theory of Groups*. Cambridge: Harvard University Press.

Omi, Michael, and Howard Winant. 1986. *Racial Formation in the United States from the 1960s to the 1980s*. New York: Routledge & Kegan Paul.

Oppenheimer, Martin. 1985. *White Collar Politics*. New York: Monthly Review Press.

Pahl, Raymond. 1975. *Whose City?* Harmondsworth, Eng.: Penguin.

Panitch, Leo. 1976. *Social Democracy and Industrial Militancy: The Labour Party, the Trade Unions and Incomes Policy, 1945.1974.* Cambridge, Eng.: Cambridge University Press.

Parkin, Frank. 1979. *Marxism and Class Theory: A Bourqeois Critique.* London: Tavistock.

Partridge, Dane M. 1991. "A Time Series Analysis of Public Sector Strike Activity." *Journal of Collective Negotiations* 20 (1): 3 – 21.

Pateman, Carole. 1988. "The Patriarchal Welfare State." In *Democracy and the Welfare State,* edited by Amy Gutmann, 231 – 60. Princeton, N.J.: Princeton University Press.

Pearce, Diana. 1990. "Welfare Is Not *for* Women: Why the War on Poverty Cannot Conquer the Feminization of Poverty." In *Women, the State and Welfare,* edited by Linda Gordon, 265 – 79. Madison: University of Wisconsin Press.

Perrone, Luca. 1984. "Positional Power, Strikes, and Wages." *American Sociological Review* 43 (3): 412 – 26.

Perrow, Charles. 1979. "The Sixties Observed." In *The Dynamics of Social Movements: Resource Mobilization, Social Control, and Tactics,* edited by Mayer Zald and John McCarthy, 192 – 211. Cambridge: Winthrop.

———. 1986. *Complex Organizations: A Critical Essay.* Third edition. New York: Random House.

Piven, Frances Fox. 1972. "Militant Civil Servants in New York City." In *Blacks in Bureaucracy: Readings in the Problems and Politics of Change,* edited by Virginia N. Ermer and John H. Strange, 145 – 54. New York: Crowell.

———. 1986. "Women and the State: Ideology, Power, and Welfare." In *For Crying Out Loud: Women and Poverty in the United States,* edited by Rochelle Lefkowitz and Ann Withorn, 339 – 40. New York: Pilgrim Press.

———. 1990. "Ideology and the State: Women, Power and the Welfare State." In *Women, the State and Welfare,* edited by Linda Gordon, 250 – 64. Madison: University of Wisconsin Press.

Piven, Frances Fox, and Richard Cloward. 1987. "The Contemporary Relief Debate." In *The Mean Season: The Attack on the Welfare State,* edited by Fred Block et al., 45 – 108. New York: Pantheon Books.

———. 1988. "Popular Power and the Welfare State." In *Remaking the Welfare State: Retrenchment and Social Policy in America and Europe,* edited by Michael K. Brown. Philadelphia: Temple University Press.

Polanyi, Karl. 1957. *The Great Transformation.* Boston: Beacon Press.

Poulantzas, Nicos A. 1975. *Classes in Contemporary Capitalism.* London: New Left Books.

Powell, Walter W. 1991. "Expanding the Scope of Institutional Analysis," in *The New Institutionalism in Organizational Analysis,* edited by Walter W. Powell and Paul J. DiMaggio, 62 – 87. Chicago and London: University of Chicago Press.

Price, Robert, and George S. Bain. 1989. "The Comparative Analysis of Union Growth." In *Recent Trends in Industrial Relations Studies and Theory, Proceedings of the Eighth Annual Congress of the International Industrial Relations Association,* 99 – 110. Brussels: International Industrial Relations Association.

Rainey, Hal G. 1992. "On the Uniqueness of Public Bureaucracies." In *The State of Public Bureaucracy*, edited by Larry B. Hill, 111 – 40. Armonk, N.Y.: M. E. Sharpe.

Reed, Adolph. 1988. "The Black Urban Regime: Structural Origins and Constraints." In *Power, Community and the City*, edited by Michael P. Smith, 138 – 89. New Brunswick, N.J.: Transaction Books.

———. 1994. "Sources of Demobilization in the New Black Political Regime: Incorporation, Ideological Capitulation and Radical Failure in the Post-Segregation Era." Paper presented at the Institute for Social Policy Studies seminar on inner-city poverty.

Reinhardt, Richard. 1965. "Joe Ridder's San Jose." *San Francisco Magazine*, Nov., 48 – 70.

Remick, Helen. 1984. "Dilemmas of Implementation." In *Comparable Worth and Wage Discrimination: Technical Possibilities and Political Realities*, edited by Helen Remick, 90 – 98. Philadelphia: Temple University Press.

Riccucci, Norma. 1990. *Women, Minorities and Unions in the Public Sector*. New York: Greenwood Press.

Saegert, Susan. 1981. "Masculine Cities and Feminine Suburbs: Polarized Ideas, Contradictory Realities." In *Women and the American City*, edited by Catharine R. Stimpson et al., 93 – 108. Chicago: University of Chicago Press.

Saltzman, Gregory. 1985. "Bargaining Laws as a Cause and a Consequence of the Growth of Teacher Unionism." *Industrial and Labor Relations Review* 38 (3): 335 – 51.

Sassoon, Anne Showstack, ed. 1987. *Women and the State: The Shifting Boundaries of Public and Private*. London: Hutchinson Education.

Saunders, Peter. 1981. *Social Theory and the Urban Question*. London: Hutchinson.

Schmitter, Philippe, and Gerhard Lehmbruch, eds. 1982. *Patterns of Corporatist Policymaking*. Beverly Hills, Calif.: Russell Sage Foundation.

Schutt, Russell. 1986. *Organization in a Changing Environment: Unionization of Welfare Employees*. Albany: State University of New York Press.

Selznick, Philip. 1969. *Law, Society and Industrial Justice*. New York: Russell Sage Foundation.

Sethi, Amarjit, Norman Metzger, and Stuart J. Dimmock, eds. 1990. *Advances in Industrial and Labor Relations*, suppl. 1. Greenwich, Conn.: JAI Press.

Shalev, Michael. 1978. "Lies, Damn Lies and Strike Statistics." In *the Resurgence of Class Conflict in Western Europe*, edited by Colin Crouch and Alessandro Pizzorno, 1:1 – 20. New York: Holmes and Meier.

Shefter, Martin. 1985. *Political Crisis/Fiscal Crisis: The Collapse and Revival of New York City*. New York: Basic Books.

Shorter, Edward L., and Charles Tilly. 1974. *Strikes in France, 1830 to 1968*. New York: Cambridge University Press.

Shostak, Arthur. 1991. *Robust Unionism: Innovations in the Labor Movement*. Ithaca, N.Y.: ILR Press.

Skocpol, Theda. 1979. *States and Social Revolutions: A Comparative Analysis of France, Russia and China*. Cambridge, Eng.: Cambridge University Press.

———. 1985. "Bringing the State Back In: Strategies of Analysis in Current Research." In *Bringing the State Back In*, edited by Peter B. Evans, Dietrich Rueschemeyer, and Theda Skocpol, 3 – 43. New York: Cambridge University Press.

Sleemie, Fehmida, John D. Borum, and Edward J. Wasilewski, Jr. 1991. "Wage and Compensation Changes in Settlements, 1991," *Monthly Labor Review* 114 (1): 1 – 8.

Smith, Adam. 1937. *An Inquiry in the Nature and Causes of the Wealth of Nations*. New York: Modern Library.

Smith, Michael P. 1988. *City, State and Market: The Political Economy of Urban Society*. Cambridge: Basil Blackwell.

Smith, Russell L. 1985. "Public Employee Unions and Politics in American Cities." *Journal of Collective Negotiations* 14 (1): 1 – 12.

Smith, Sharon P. 1983. "Are State and Local Government Workers Overpaid?" In *The Economics of Municipal Labor Markets*, edited by Werner Z. Hirsch and Anthony M. Rufolo, 59 – 89. Los Angeles: University of California, Institute of Industrial Relations.

Snyder, David. 1975. "Institutional Setting and Industrial Conflict: Comparative Analyses of France, Italy and the United States." *American Sociological Review* 40 (3): 259 – 78.

———. 1977. "Early North American Strikes: A Reinterpretation." *Industrial and Labor Relations Review* 30 (3): 325 – 41.

Spain, Daphne. 1988. "The Effects of Changing Household Composition on Neighborhood Satisfaction." *Urban Affairs Quarterly* 21 (3): 581 – 600.

Spero, Sterling D., and John M. Capozola. 1973. *The Urban Community and Its Unionized Bureaucracies: Pressure Politics in Local Government Labor Relations*. New York: Dunellen.

Spizman, Lawrence M. 1980. "Unions, Government Services, and Public Employees." *Public Finance Quarterly* 8 (4): 427 – 42.

Stacey, Judith. 1990. *Brave New Families: Stories of Domestic Upheaval in Late Twentieth Century America*. New York: Basic Books.

Stanford Environmental Law Society. 1971. *San Jose: Sprawling City*. Stanford, Calif.: Stanford University.

Steinberg, Ronnie J. 1982. *Wages and Hours: Labor and Reform in Twentieth-Century America*. New Brunswick, N.J.: Rutgers University Press.

———. 1987. "Radical Challenges in a Liberal World: The Mixed Success of Comparable Worth." *Gender and Society* 1 (4): 466 – 75.

Stieber, Jack. 1973. *Public Employee Unionism: Structure, Growth, Policy*. Washington D.C.: Brookings Institution.

Stone, Clarence. 1989. *Regime Politics: Governing Atlanta, 1946.1988*. Lawrence: University of Kansas Press.

Stone, Clarence, and Heywood T. Sanders, eds. 1987. *The Politics of Urban Development*. Lawrence: University of Kansas Press.

Stratton, Richard W. 1985. "Monopoly, Monopsony and Union Strength and Local Market Wage Differentials." *Journal of Economics and Sociology* 44 (2): 305 – 18.

Summers, Robert S. 1976. *Collective Bargaining and Benefit Conferral: A Jurisprudential Critique*. Ithaca: Cornell University, New York School of Industrial and Labor Relations, Institute of Public Employment.

Suttles, Gerald D. 1990. *The Man-Made City: The Land Use Confidence Game in Chicago*. Chicago: University of Chicago Press.

Swidler, Ann. 1986. "Culture in Action: Symbols and Strategies." *American Sociological Review* 51 (2): 273 – 86.

Swimmer, Gene. 1982. "The Impact of Proposition 13 on Public Employee Relations: The Case of Los Angeles." *Journal of Collective Negotiations* 11 (1): 13 – 22.

Thomas, George M., et al. 1987. *Institutional Structure: Constituting State, Society and the Individual*. Newbury Park, Calif.: Sage.

Tilly, Charles. 1978. *From Mobilization to Revolution*. Reading, Mass.: Addison-Wesley.

———. 1988. "Solidary Logics." *Theory and Society* 17: 451 – 58.

———. 1992. "How to Detect, Describe and Explain Repertoires of Contention." Working Paper no. 150. New York: New School for Social Research.

Touraine, Alain. 1981. *The Voice and the Eye: An Analysis of Social Movements*. New York: Cambridge University Press.

———. 1986. "Unionism as a Social Movement." In *Unions in Transition: Entering the Second Century*, edited by Seymour Martin Lipset, 151 – 75. San Francisco: ICS Press.

Traugott, Mark. 1985. *Armies of the Poor: Determinants of Working-Class Participation in the Parisian Insurrection of June 1848*. Princeton, N.J.: Princeton University Press.

Trejo, Stephen J. 1991. "Public Sector Unions and Municipal Employment." *Industrial and Labor Relations Review* 45 (1): 174 – 80.

Trounstine, Philip J., and Christensen, Terry. 1982. *Movers and Shakers: The Study of Community Power*. New York: St. Martin's Press.

Troy, Leo. 1984. "The Convergence of Public and Private Industrial Relations Systems in the United States." *Government Union Review* 5 (3): 37 – 52.

———. 1986. "The Rise and Fall of American Trade Unionism: The Labor Movement from FDR to RR." In *Unions in Transition: Entering the Second Century*, edited by Seymour Martin Lipset, 75 – 111. San Francisco: ICS Press.

U.S. Department of Commerce. Bureau of the Census. *City Employment*. Annual. Washington, D.C.: Government Printing Office.

———. 1984. *Current Population Survey*. Washington, D.C.: Government Printing Office.

U.S. Department of Labor. Bureau of Labor Statistics. 1994. *Union Members in 1993*. Washington, D.C.

Valletta, Robert G. 1989. "The Impact of Unionism on Municipal Expenditures and Revenues." *Industrial and Labor Relations Review* 42 (3): 430 – 42.

Victor, Richard B. 1977. "The Effects of Municipal Unionism on Wages and Employment." Ph.D. diss., University of Michigan.

Vosloo, Willem B. 1966. *Collective Bargaining in the United States Federal Civil Service*. Chicago: Public Personnel Association.

Waddington, David. 1986. "The Ansells Brewery Dispute: A Social-Cognitive Approach to the Study of Strikes." *Journal of Occupational Psychology* 59 (9): 231 – 46.

Walsh, David J. 1994. *On Different Planes: An Organizational Analysis of Cooperation and Conflict among Airline Unions*. Ithaca, N.Y.: ILR Press.

Waste, Robert J. 1989. *The Ecology of City Policymaking*. New York: Oxford University Press.

Wellington, Harry H., and Ralph K. Winter, Jr. 1971. *The Unions and the Cities*. Washington, D.C.: Brookings Institution.

Wekerle, Gerda. 1980. "Women in the Urban Environment." In *Women and the American City*, edited by Catharine R. Stimpson et al., 185 – 211. Chicago: University of Chicago Press.

Wekerle, Gerda, Rebecca Peterson, and David Morley, eds. 1980. *New Space for Women*. Boulder, Colo.: Westview Press.

Western, Bruce. 1993. "Postwar Unionization in Eighteen Advanced Capitalist Countries." *American Sociological Review* (58) 2: 266 – 82.

Whyte, William H. 1956. *The Organization Man*. New York: Simon and Schuster.

Wines, William A., Robert D. Ley, and Jack Fiorito. 1986. "Gender-Related Wage Differentials for Public School Teachers under Objective Survey Grids: Some Lessons on Comparable Worth." *Journal of Collective Negotiations in the Public Sector* 15 (1): 61 – 68.

Wolfe, Alan. 1982. *America's Impasse: The Rise and Fall of the Politics of Growth*. New York: Pantheon Books.

Wright, Erik Olin. 1979. *Class Structure and Income Determination*. New York: Academic Press.

———. 1983. "Capitalism's Futures." *Socialist Review* 13 (2): 77 – 126.

———. 1985. *Classes*. London: Verso.

Wright, Michael D. 1993. "Privatization, the State, and Public Interest Trade Unionism: A Comparison of Canadian and American Postal Services." Dissertation, Stanford University School of Law.

Zax, Jeffrey, and Casey Ichniowski. 1988. "The Effects of Public Sector Unionism on Pay, Employment, Department Budgets, and Municipal Expenditures." In *When Public Sector Workers Unionize*, edited by Richard B. Freeman and Casey Ichniowski, 323 – 64.

———. 1990. "Bargaining Laws and Unionization in the Local Public Sector." *Industrial and Labor Relations Review* 43 (4): 447 – 62.

Author Index

Subject Index

About the Author

Paul Johnston worked as a union organizer for ten years before attending college, and received a Ph.D. in sociology at the University of California at Berkeley in 1989. Since 1989, he has been an assistant professor of sociology at Yale University, where he is writing books on local government and public organizations.